"I've had many pleasant associations with Mr. Downs (formerly Head of the Amerika Haus in Berlin) when I was in Berlin. He has enterprise and a capacity to get things done."

> **Dr. James B. Conant**, (former President of Harvard University for 20 years and former U.S. Ambassador to West Germany)

"This has more quality stuff on WW2 than any book I have seen in a long time."

> **Lt. Col. Frank O. Vavrin**, Chief of Chaplains 173rd Airborne Division

"It was not until Hunton Downs showed me the evidence he had amassed that I became convinced that the Glenn Miller mystery had at last been solved."

> **Peter Michalski** (former London Bureau Chief of Germany's vast Springer Publications empire)

"... he is a remarkably keen investigator and knows how to keep a secret. Of all the stories breezed about Glenn Miller in the past half-century, Downs's documentation as presented in his book, would be the only possible scenario..."

> **Mark White** (Program Director AFN Berlin 1952-1988)

D0813661

THE
GLENN MILLER
CONSPIRACY

THE GLENN MILLER CONSPIRACY

For information contact:

Global Book Publishers
269 S. Beverly Drive, Suite 1442, Beverly Hills, CA 90212.
www.bookpubintl.com

THE GLENN MILLER CONSPIRACY
ISBN-13: 978-0-9779131-6-9

Library of Congress: 2007931116

Typography & Cover: Kirk Thomas, www.kirks-graphics.com

ACKNOWLEDGMENTS

The writer is indebted to the following institutions who gave generous access to previously withheld files and documents of personal, confidential or secret nature concerning the Glenn Miller tragedy.

AACS (Army Air Corps) Alumni Association of America

BENEKE-MILLER ARCHIVES, DeQuincy, LA, USA

BUREAU OF TOURISME, Versailles, France

CHARLES WHITING LIBRARY OF OTTO SKORZENY, York, England

DEUXIEME BUREAU (REGISTRE DE PARIS), France

HOTEL THISTLE (MT. ROYAL), London, England

RAF LIBRARY (Royal Air Force), Croydon, England

STAATARCHIVEN LIBRARY OF NAZI DOCUMENTS, Freiburg, Germany

THE PUBLIC RECORD OFFICE OF GREAT BRITAIN, London, England

THE IMPERIAL WAR MUSEUM of Great Britain, London, England

THE NATIONAL PUBLIC RECORD CENTER, St Louis, Mo, USA

THE DOCUMENT CENTER (CAPTURED NAZI FILES), Berlin, Germany

TOWNSHIP OF ST. GERMAINE EN LAYE, France

TOWNSHIP OF BEDFORD, Bedfordshire, England

TRIANON PALACE HOTEL, Versailles, France

UNIVERSITY OF TRIER LIBRARY OF JOSEF GOEBBELS, Trier, Germany

WILBUR WRIGHT LIBRARY OF GLENN MILLER, Southampton, England

Contents

Who was Glenn Miller vii

PROLOGUE
Why it Took Sixty Years xi

CHAPTER 1
Five Stars and an Oak Leaf 1

CHAPTER 2
'Scholarships' at Yale 23

CHAPTER 3
Wings of a Double Life 38

CHAPTER 4
Getting a Hand on Slippery Eclipse 66

CHAPTER 5
Nazi Files: Miller, Lampshades and "Kultur" 77

CHAPTER 6
Hitler's Last Gasp: A Three-pronged Double Cross . . 96

CHAPTER 7
Clearing a Besmirched Hero 115

CHAPTER 8
USA Comes To Bat: Guys Who Were There 140

CHAPTER 9
Into the House of Secrets 160

Index 189

Glossary 193

Bibliography 200

Documentation 209

Who was Glenn Miller?

A fair question today considering the several generations come-and-gone since the musical hero's strange disappearance in 1944, leading to one of the Mysteries of the Century.

This question back then would have been laughable, as if one had asked in the 1960s "Who are the Beatles?" Or commensurately in 1956; "Who is Elvis?" Glenn Miller was America's wartime icon of valor, talent and inspiration. He skyrocketed to near mythological proportions when he went missing at the start of the Battle of the Bulge. Official Britain and the U.S. didn't bother to wink conspiratorially or give the public a knowing nudge. They just served up a story, whistled and walked away—for over 60 years.

Glenn Miller led a dance band that was the "top of the pops." One could say he led the dance band field from the late 1930s – and on. ... and on. America danced way back then. On the sidewalk, at home. We didn't need a dance floor. Whew! Everything from jitterbug to sweet 'n slow, from spin-around frenzy, to "over my head...just like this!" And dance bands made it happen.

Glenn was the era's "superstar."

It took more than radios and record players to guarantee a dance epoch, freaked on Big Band swing. Radios in the home (and in cars!) needed stations to send out the catchy stuff. These ranged from 250-watt transmitter voices in lesser towns to powerful 50,000 watters from the big cities. I grew up listening to WLW Cincinatti, WOR Newark, CKLW Toronto, KDKA Pittsburgh—all clear as a bell— offering dance band remotes from local clubs at the end of a broadcasting day (a cheap way to fill the time). We kids listened to these late night freebies, compared notes, and bought records. But that wasn't the technological kicker that made Glenn Miller. The juke box was.

Those magic-lantern, color-winking bastions of sound cost a nickel a tune, and they took over entertainment at every coke bar, dance pad or Saturday night kiss-coven in the country. This is where Glenn Miller became mighty. Never known as an outstanding trombonist, Glenn had two things that made him and his band great. He was head of the class as an arranger. And as a disciplinarian, he made his musicians play like he felt it, not how it looked as notes.

For sure, he felt it one auspicious spring day in 1939 when the band, doing only average business, was booked at the Glen Island Casino. Joe Ripley of WOR brought on the band with the news that Glenn had a new tune he wanted folks across the land to hear. Glenn in his inimitably warm voice took up the words: "Everybody knows this tune. I hope you like the way we play it." There followed a folk tune which became Glenn Miller's first international hit. It went on to bust the record book, <u>Little Brown Jug</u>.

Little Brown Jug was the first of the many Miller-crafted arrangements that caught global attention. Still, it never matched Glenn's "Big Five" in sales. Each of the Big Five topped 11 million in sales. (2005) in a day when one million sales made headlines. In order, they were *Chatanooga Choo Choo, In the Mood, Moonlight Serenade, Sunrise Serenade* and *American Patrol.* Then, still above 11 million sales, and well into 12 as of last tabulations, *Little Brown Jug, Kalamazoo, Pennsylvania 6-5000, Tuxedo Junction, String of Pearls, St. Louis Blues March, At Last, Serenade in Blue* and *I Know Why.* If you know more than three of these numbers from way, way, way back, you stand to be called a Glenn Miller fan! And why not? The book in your hand means something special.

A huge number of these nickel music boxes existed across the land then (300,000). In a special research study conducted by Sid Robinson in 2005 with facilities offered by the *Dallas Morning News*, he determined that the simple juke box had much to do with Glenn's success. One could say, more than much. It had plenty to do with Glenn's fame and subsequent international acclaim. Now there was an accountable way to measure one individual tune. How many times was it played last week? Which tune made the most nickels? Glenn Miller tunes were listed on up to 12 of the 24 disc selections in the average large-sized juke box, the result of a hard cash principle based on the number of five-cent pieces at the side of each title. As a result, Glenn Miller was known to hold a place in his heart for *Juke Box Saturday Night.* The song, in effect, made him famous beyond others, one stanza of which tells the story; "Money we really don't need bad. We make out all right. Let the other guy feed that...Juke Box Saturday Night." A Miller-version of *Juke Box* lyrics preceded Glenn's goodbye to commercial radio and entrance to the military in 1942.

And thus Miller popularity, a personal story in each of his great hits, soared on to influence a fighting army, navy and air force. There's a story about *Elmer's Tune* which shows another side of the war hero's empathy, and is one of the rare cases where he let himself be talked out of his own feelings for a song. Glenn was asked if *Elmer's Tune* didn't belong among his list of all-time hits. He shook his head. "No, I never liked that song," he is reported to have replied. "Then, why do you continue to play it?" The interviewer asked. Glenn said, "Helen likes it. If she likes it, it must be good."

Helen was his wife.

Hunton Downs, October 11, 2008

PROLOGUE

Why it Took Sixty Years

The most frequent question I am asked is—why did you wait sixty years to write this book?

Basically, because the evidence came like diamonds out of a deep pit; the perfect metaphor, one could say: "Ugly and buried." Governments—US, UK, German and French— were unwilling to open up unpleasant subjects of war which could challenge old decisions and harm reputations. Unspoken waves of the hand—go waaay! confronted me and all researchers who sought to discover what really happened to Glenn Miller. The story of Major Glenn Miller's mysterious disappearance in December 1944 on the eve of the Battle of the Bulge just wouldn't go away. As the years piled up, Glenn's disappearance became for me one of the most daunting death mysteries ever to involve a historical personage.

I am looking at a statement now which I saw for the first time in 1974 (*Moonlight Serenader* now in continuing editions, Roland Taylor, Editor-in-Chief). The journal quotes

OSS and CIA executive Miles Copeland of sixteen years longevity in both agencies.

Investigating the OSS's highly-classified file on Glenn Miller, Copeland declared: "Miller was on his way to some kind of an engagement. He was taking a plane from some unknown point to an equally mysterious destination." That's all the man would say about it, or *perhaps* could say about it, but it certainly didn't match the "official story" of a fog-shrouded single-engine plane dropping in on a jam-packed RAF base, picking up a hitch-hiking Glenn Miller, then ending in icy December waters with no subsequent search, no radar report, no procedural accountability. Maybe I'd been in the Army too long. But the Army doesn't work like this.

Something bigger was afoot, something huge; something involving the Supreme Commander of SHAEF, General Dwight D. Eisenhower. Trumpeter Johnny Best, Glenn's pal in the commercial band, put it succinctly: "Glenn couldn't have dreamed of the fate two governments were to assign him."

Accountability? The final pieces of this long-lost story emerged only in 2005 and 2007.

The single engine plane's MACR (Missing Air Crew Report) should have solved everything. This official document was supposed to settle all questions as to whether Glenn Miller was aboard, where he was going, who else was on board, destinations interim, final, etc. It had to be filed no later than 24 hours after the incident by an adjutant of the home airfield, RAF base Abbots Ripton. This MACR was filed accurately and on time, but SHAEF Headquarters in Versailles, France took five days to make it disappear, then bury a false one at Maxwell Air Force Base in Alabama which lay undisturbed for 44 years.

Only after researcher Wilbur Wright appealed to former

President Ronald Reagan in 1989 was the simple, original MACR brought to light. It was discovered in the Glenn Miller Burial File, Washington, D.C. The MACR matched testimony that was provided half-a-century earlier by Colonel (then Captain) Harry Witt personally, the officer who was waiting for the lone flyer at Villacoublais, Versailles, France. The single-engine Norseman, Warrant Officer John Morgan at the helm, was posted, charted in operation, was in transit with no stops, declared delayed, then called missing.

Witt flew an immediate search, but was blocked by impenetrable fog along the Seine; he turned back, tried again the next day. No sighting. Just another lost plane, but one grabbed onto as a coffin for a celebrity the world has since wondered about. So *now* pilot John Morgan flew *alone*. No Glenn Miller aboard. Destination, Villacoublais, Versailles, France, not Bordeaux, Twinwood or any other landings as previously alleged. Colonel (then Captain) Harry Witt was waiting for his friend Morgan, (fully testified to on tape held by Sid Robinson brother-in-law of former Miller band star Tex Beneke). The 2005 taping was affirmed by email to half-a-dozen correspondents, and to me by phone and letter, what he did to try to save his friend back then on Dec. 15, 1944.

Just whose busy-body hands were at work? Don't forget the government had prepared a false MACR in case it was needed to prove "the Channel" dip. While I was sorting out famed researcher Wilbur Wright's papers (4000 documents) with full Estate permission (Wilbur had died in 1994), the Scotland Yard adjudication of the "false" MACR came through. This "Ansell Report" showed up the hidden fake for what it was. The adjutant's signature had been falsified. Glenn's name had been added to victims (adjudged by different spacing). Different typewriters had been used. The falsifiers had even gotten destinations wrong trying to fit in pre-conceived plans of what Supreme Headquarters claimed had taken place.

So what happened to Glenn Miller? Why is his fate only now so painfully revealed? I don't mind admitting I was a sleuth for the U.S. Army in the years following the war, concentrating on Berlin. Then afterward from the '60s through the '90s, I sleuthed for myself, getting ever hotter on Miller as government after government slowly acceded to my requests for a look-in on their war-time secret files. A rash of UK books by OSS post-war experts, coupled with more books published in the 1970s, confirmed my belief that the answer to Glenn's true fate was in Berlin.

The best of these helpful books were by Fest, Casey, Cockridge, Persico, Trevor-Roper, Shirer, and of course Peter Grose's fine profile of the top wartime U.S. spy in Switzerland, Allen Dulles, who maneuvered eight attempts on Hitler's life, and who managed a strong German under-ground in-and-around Berlin, even after the July 20th 1944 unsuccessful Hitler assassination attempt. These writers poked questions at why an extensively-planned "Operation Eclipse" didn't work to the Allies' advantage (ending the war by New Years 1945 with generals-on-both-sides cooperating and arresting Hitler). From these writers I picked up key words of intelligence useful for dropping into certain conversations with people who knew of Ike's secret plans for Glenn Miller in Berlin. More or less concurrently, I became a Voice of America correspondent for the besieged city for which the CIA had great influence.

Here are some of those key words: *Reichbanner* was a World War One organization of Social Democrats, pro-Allied, holding police and firemen's power throughout Brandenburg, even in the dangerous post July 20th days. *George Wood* was a pseudonym for Fritz Kolbe, leader of the German underground. *28 Unter den Linden* was a guaranteed safe house for underground conspirators, a hiding place for scouts and guides who could spread out in minutes to guide safe-drop Allied landings.

I visited the place. Despite bomb damage, it was a warren of passage-ways and trap doors descending deep below ground. I picked up the rumor that 28 was planned to be a safe house for Major Miller on his curious mission to Berlin. *Kummersdorf* was a magic word that I was told would open gates to the Nazis' secret true power—its rocketry embankment, V-1 and V-2, known in the West since 1930 as the *Verein fuer Raumschiffahrt*, or Organization for Space Ship Flights: or simply said—"*VfR*." I needed to find out what Glenn's fix into this mix was, why he was to be sent into enemy-held Berlin on special orders of the warring generals of both sides, and why he never arrived.

On Active Duty during the war, I worked with General David Sarnoff on bomb-run carrier wave communications for the Air Force. We were at AFHQ Algiers at the time. I had been privileged to hear what few Americans ever heard— that alluring "Chesterfield" voice of Glenn Miller speaking in German to *Wehrmacht* troops, assuring them of POW sanctity, divorcing them from any pledges to the *Fuehrer,* if they had made such, and promising peace with dignity in surrender, a peace close at hand—then Glenn played the music all troops wanted to hear, Glenn Miller's own.

Instinctively I must have realized that Glenn had made himself an enemy of the Reich by these broadcasts. It wasn't until 1951 when I received orders as a Reservist Major of Intelligence to review files held in the so-called *Document Center of the SS, SD, Amt.IV and Amt.VI* in Berlin—found under a grassy lawn in *Sektor Zehlendorf.* It was there I learned that our famed psychological-war broadcaster and music maker had been made a death target by *Irrefuehrung,* a Dirty Tricks organization—a special branch of Nazi double-dealing led by the infamous Walter Schellenberg and Otto Skorzeny.

Miller broadcasts had become a "problem of morale" for the *Wehrmacht*. Major Glenn Miller and his immediate boss British movie star-soldier David Niven were to pay for their raiding and radio propaganda activities by being named as *Kommandos*—a designation by Hitler's order of October 18, 1942 "invoking death in or out of uniform, in battle or in flight, on one side of battle lines or the other." No surcease.

As I read that dire prediction in the SS's own journal of destruction, I knew I was facing some sort of a destiny to follow through to the end, no matter what happened, to get to the Glenn Miller Truth—no matter the twists and turns, no matter how many threats I and others received: bodily threats, personally insulting threats, or whatever. If I could do it, I would. Strange, while I was reading and had made a copy of that chillingly prophetic *Erlass*, I thought of a public statement made by pilot extraordinaire Anthony Bartley, back at the time the Miller disappearance was news. Bartley declared, as reported in British Press, that he had warned Glenn not to go to Paris. "Too dangerous." What did Bartley know?

A one-time Ike pilot, husband of movie star Deborah Kerr, a dashing man-about-London and two-time winner of the Distinguished Flying Cross, Bartley must have known more than he was talking about. If he was in on the Glenn Miller operation, I was determined to chase him down, and did over the years. He consistently denied any special knowledge, but I suspected then, and know now, that he and his sidekick pilot Tony Pulitzer were the Bobcat pilots who flew Glenn Miller on his special mission to Krefeld, Germany to help conduct the business of ending the war in 1944. So far, I had hunches and whispers and cover-ups aplenty. Proof was needed.

Berlin gave me a lot to put together, but the RAF Museum at Croydon gave me more. Croydon came through in robust fashion with records of whatever flights had been flying on that eerie, forbidding night of December 16-17. That was the night so vividly described by Joan Heath when she drove Major Glenn Miller from Ike's presence at Versailles to Buc Field, saw him aboard a two-motor plane in the snow, saw him sitting in a square window and saw him waving her a kiss goodbye as the two-motor plane took off. Croydon cleaned out its traffic for me that night and came up with three urgent, priority-classified messages questioning, then confirming, an "Odin" flight wanting permission to enter the restricted zone of St. Omar, France—in the direction of enemy lines at Krefeld, Germany, Group B Headquarters under command of General Gerd von Rundstedt.

Here was tangible proof that a plane had been spotted—but what was *Odin*? There was only one source which might know more about Odin. And that was the new intelligence HQ at Cheltenham, Gloucestershire.

Since 1945, British spooks had disbanded their great Bletchley Park complex where geniuses gleaned intelligence from Nazi codes and could anticipate most tactical Hitler moves since North Africa—no-small factor in Allied eventual victory. Now, postwar, Bletchley Park was set up as a museum, clamped shut, moved brains and baggage to Cheltenham, Gloucestershire, including the world's first computer, Colossus, which had broken the codes and from which builders Alan Turing and Tommie Flowers were forever prohibited from profit-taking. A shame, too, for these brilliant men were told they had to keep the secret until they died. Others took the idea and the money.

But a move was essential for me. I had to slide into British Intelligence ground, and not make it look purposeful. I had some hints as to who was hiding Glenn Miller's part in the "secret" war. One was a national name, aligned to the defense industry, and he was in Cheltenham. I don't mean he or others were spies for the Nazis. They were carrying and hiding links of an operation that proved Glenn's official Odin mission, and that, to put it plainly, was not nice. I moved to Tetbury, a small village of Gloucestershire near GCHQ Cheltenham, where I had good neighbors, Prince Charles and Diana in their Highgrove estate, and a film producer, Stanley O'Toole, who owned a hotel. You could walk from one end of the village to the other in five minutes and that's just the kind of "retirement" I wanted to lounge under.

Yes, Cheltenham was British Intelligence in spades. And its front door was open to U.S. Air Force squadrons. When U.S. bombing fleets took off to 'Shock and Awe' Iraq, they took off from Cheltenham Air Field, roaring over continents to their duty. I had one advantage as an American closeted in an All-Brit community. A Brit could be called on the carpet for revealing security intelligence, willingly and knowledgeably, which prejudiced the good name and allegiance of any officer whose rights and reputation were so clouded by such actions. As an American civilian, I couldn't be touched. I could be kicked out of the country maybe—but not hauled into military court under British law. The guy with the papers I wanted to get lived under this constant threat, if I chose to press him, and I let it be known he was among several I was after. When he avoided me, I knew this was the guy.

It wasn't at HQ in Cheltenham that he gave up. I was in Southampton preparing my novel Murder in the Mood (1998) for publication when two sheets of dry old Nazi documentation were shoved under the Wright doorstep in Southampton—sans fingerprints. At last! Data that made sense of "Odin," properly tagged "Odin 7/13." Two signatures dominated these *OKW* messages which were Nazi transcripts back and forth from Berlin to Front Line Group B Hdqrs. authorizing "Odin 7/13" and lifting of the flak curtain guarding Krefeld, and other information concerning 7/13, the passenger on Odin. And who was 7/13?

Count up the alphabet to 7 and 13. You'll get G and M, and if that doesn't tell you who the passenger was, don't guess. These two documents represented highest Hitler authority. The one signed *Schellenberg* was easily enough attributable to Walter Schellenberg, kingpin of Dirty Tricks, but *A. Bergmann* wrinkled the brow. One of those keywords from E.H. Cookridge's <u>Spy of the Century—Gehlen</u> (1972)— tumbled through my mind. Frau Bergmann was the name Martin Bormann's wife had adopted when she was left on her own after the war. Also, the name was penned *Oberst*, meaning Highest or No Higher. I was in fair communication at the time with Joachim Fest, possibly the greatest of German writers on the Hitler epoch. His book, <u>Inside Hitler's Bunker</u> (2005) was made into that incredible movie, *The Downfall*, portraying Hitler's last days with a spectacular performance by Bruno Ganz as the dictator. Dr. Fest lived not far from where I did once in Bad Nauheim, close to Frankfurt. Could he help? Was *Bergmann* a pseudonym for Bormann? The name had more than superficial meaning, Fest told me. Bormann (mountainman) *imagined himself* a woodsman, a mountaineer in every sense of the word. He swallowed up properties in his own name all over the Reich, including Hitler's own *Berghof*. Thus, it was Hitler's administrator Bormann who gave the word to pass Glenn Miller to Berlin.

The film-making family of O'Toole had long wanted to do a movie on the Glenn Miller material I had gathered, utilizing other materials made available by Wilbur Wright, John Edwards, Henry Whiston, Charles Whiting and others. In fact, Stanley O'Toole himself had titled my book, *Murder in the Mood*. The book was a novel based largely on facts.

Wow! Word scampered through that GCHQ bastion of M's with implied intent that such would not be allowed. O'Toole immediately opened offices at Cheltenham Studios with an announcement that *Murder in the Mood* was to be made in the UK Security's own home ground of Cheltenham; and while only a novel, it would highlight who had been covering up all these years, and why!

A shipment of book materials was dispensed from the publisher in Southampton to O'Toole at the Studios in Cheltenham. It never arrived. That's when Daniel, one of the O'Toole boys shouted foul, and called on me to intervene. I made as much noise as I could by calling on Prince Charles, certainly a guarantor of Royal Mail sanctity, and the next thing I knew there was a full front page edition of the daily Gloucestershire Echo, with 72 point headlines quoting O'Toole: "SPIES FIDDLED WITH MY POST"—GLENN MILLER TALE IS TOO HOT FOR GCHQ.

Meanwhile, Prince Charles had gone to work in his tactful way, and while Shipment Number One was lost forever, Number Two got through safely to Cheltenham Studios and the integrating process of setting up and financing a movie began. Alas, film efforts fizzled, given casting problems and the myriad of details that can sink a film in pre-production.

I knew my time was short in Tetbury (if one death threat wasn't enough, three separate invitations to leave the country written by GCHQ individuals sort of gave me the idea to say *Auf Wiedersehen*). From 1998 onward, the September date of that front page, I concentrated on access to the secret archives of the Germans and French, with the results that made this present book of evidence possible.

In reporting for Voice of America during the 1960s from Berlin, and winning a coveted Edward R. Murrow citation for Excellence in Radio Journalism, I don't believe my sideline interest in Glenn Miller prejudiced in any way my accuracy or ability to get facts. The sense of news was inborn as it was for me in Vietnam, 1967, when my reportage of war throughout the country, hands-down, no b.s. was nominated for a Pulitzer by famed editor George C. Chaplin, a Harvard fellow and editor-in-chief of Hawaii's major morning newspaper The Honolulu Advertiser. It didn't win, but—possibly more important—it created national attention.

How I came to the attention of fabled Murrow is a story in itself. When the Wall went up, I was in the city and got a pre-dawn reportage out before even Bonn knew what was going on. This, thanks to American Forces Network's Mark White whose stringers alerted him. We managed to tour East Berlin while the cement blocks and rolls of wire were being trucked to the border lines, and before *Vopos* (East German People's Police) even took up their threatening positions. In the crisis, VOA sent in Vienna-born John Albert, a veteran reporter, to manage things. He sat me in a helicopter. We took off and squatted somewhere above Checkpoint Charlie. There were only the three of us: the pilot, John and me pretty much squashed together. Light was breaking. This was the second Day of the Wall. John said: "We're going to circle West Berlin following this new wall. I figure it'll take twenty one minutes at normal chopper speed. All the way around and back here. We may get shot at, we may never get back, but I want you to start talking… right now, into this mike— tell me everything you see in front of you that has taken place, or is now taking place, every incident, every escape, tunnels, flyovers, watchtower killings, leaps from buildings, joys, tears, the works, that you've experienced in your time here. I want your description of this Wall, its circumference, its dangers, its deaths, in twenty minutes, so our listeners, people in the world not here, can understand."

I don't remember what I said, but I talked. When it was over and we hung tight over Checkpoint Charlie for the second time, John said quietly: "Thanks, Hunt. Nobody else could have done that." I suspect John played that twenty-minute tape for Edward R. Murrow back in Washington. I don't know, but I pride that citation more than anything I have ever won.

Did we need the 21st Century to wrap up The Glenn Miller Conspiracy? We did, and now there were Americans in on the action. Guys who had worked for years tearing aside falsehoods of the Miller tragedy and I didn't even know about them or what they were doing. Now I do and you'll see what they—in their own investigations and diggings—and I accomplished to get to our final Truth. My book is by all of us. It couldn't have been written until now.

HUNTON DOWNS, Asheville, North Carolina

"In the long run, it is what we do not say that will destroy us."

- General George Patton
from his Autobiography
"War As I Knew It" (1947)

CHAPTER **1**

Five Stars and an Oak Leaf

Never before in history, I'm reasonably sure, have those two monarchs of the 20th Century been compared. General of the Armies Dwight D. Eisenhower and Major Alton Glenn Miller, acknowledged No.1 master of modern dance-band music.

Yet, they have much in common: they stemmed from the same soil-rich flatlands of Mid-America, served in the same army at the same time, and had common German derivatives for names: Eisenhower (iron-hewer) or ironmonger, Miller (from Mueller, a mill grinder). Antecedents of both crossed the Atlantic in the 19th Century. When they met (secretly) in 1944, Ike as he was familiarly called was 54; Glenn (he used his middle name preferably) was 40. History says they never knew each other, despite serving in the same headquarters (SHAEF – Supreme Headquarters Allied Expeditionary Force).

But what evidence has surfaced proves that the Supreme Commander of SHAEF in Europe was the last American to see Glenn Miller alive. Glenn, did not get lost over the English Channel or die from a jettisoned bomb by RAF British-made Lancasters, as alleged in communiqués by SHAEF and government officials. These allegations were never "officially" investigated. To bring military law to bear, legal officers of JAG (Judge Advocate General) have noted, could invite aspects of criminality into the case.

Certainly, proven facts were bare bones in the Miller disappearance (December 1944), if at all laid out. There was no official investigation of the tragedy either during the war, or afterward—up to today. Lt. Philip Lorber in the Frankfurt JAG Section of USAREUR (U.S. Army Europe) made an interesting comment to me in 1954 that if foul play were suspected in an officer's death, even in wartime, criminality of intent alone could involve court martial, up to and including high ranks.

In other words, if Miller's "officially stated" Twinwood Farm takeoff was proven a sworn impossibility, then suspected foul play might be involved and affect upon an "official" investigation. In the case of a field grade officer, higher grades could be involved. How best to avoid such a mess? Harshly stated, a cover up.

Lt. Lorber, a well-known Baltimore lawyer, was on Reserve duty. He also told me "it is not the act in itself, say murder, which might implicate higher-up officers but the cover-up, if such was proven. Say, if the Twinwood claim of Glenn Miller taking off into thin air was positively disproved, and there was withheld knowledge of another, far different set of death circumstance, all hell could break loose."

It must be said from the start, that criminality as a motive in the Glenn Miller mystery has never entered the picture. To my mind and to dozens of other truth-seekers, our aim is to credit the band leader for an act of great bravery in combat possibly deserving of a Congressional Medal of Honor. We only seek to gather evidence to let it speak for itself, wherever it leads. Blatant threats for us to stop, which we all experienced, only justified our keeping on the trail. I don't believe any of us thought of ourselves as detectives solving a crime. We were patriots, one and all, American, British and Canadian.

Following is the alleged incident on which over a half-century of falsification and often bitter argumentation is based. A telegram, dated December 22, 1944, announced the "disappearance," in a single-engine Norseman plane en-route from England to France, of the world-renowned musician and band leader Major Glenn Miller. Follow-up publicity *backdated* the incident to December 15, 1944.[9]

The plane presumably was lost in bad weather over the English Channel. This story was supplemented 40 years later by an equally unexpected tale, hooked onto the same Dec.15, '44 tragedy. The new tale claimed an unused 4,000-pound bomb was dropped from a Lancaster bomber at 6,000 feet, a jettison procedure, and that it hit the single engine craft carrying Glenn Miller a mile below. "From a height of 6,000 feet in cumulus clouds?" a lot of GI disbelievers shouted (and still do). There was just one witness to claim this was true, navigator Fred Shaw of South Africa, who took 40 years to make up his statement. It was bought lock, stock and barrel by officialdom. Why? That was another question to be investigated and solved.

The pilot of that particular Lancaster, Captain Gregory, reported that no such jettisoning had taken place, nor was he aware of the alleged tragedy below. Two other proclaimed witnesses in the plane's crew were by then deceased. "No briefing was recorded for that flight or that plane," Shaw stated. Thus, for this aborted mission of 100-plus bombers, at an estimated cost of about $20,000,000 in today's money—including all those wasted 4,000 pound bombs—there was no record? The official (Secret) RAF register of the flight gave a different story.[39]

There was no bomb drop on the way, destination: Siegen, Germany. No flight that date with Fred Shaw aboard. Officialdom kept a straight face. The story of Shaw's tale of the bomb helped cover up a sensitive element in the tragic Battle of the Bulge with its 80,090 U.S. casualties. This attempt to distort the truth suggested that Glenn Miller was somehow involved in a critical phase of that famous battle because his disappearance happened exactly as the battle was starting.

So what does this have to do with resplendent, affable General Ike, the boss at SHAEF, Supreme Headquarters of American Expeditionary Forces in Europe and his far junior-ranking Major of Music?

Quite a bit. At that critical juncture of war in Europe, "Glenn was on a mission for Ike," said famed movie actor Broderick Crawford, a sergeant then, and Glenn's pal in London and Paris. Brod, Oscar winner for *All the King's Men*, had been assigned by Eisenhower as chum and roughneck bodyguard to "stick close" to the singer-broadcaster in England and in France.[3] Crawford, a toughie in movie roles, was officially assigned to the Paris MPs, the unit which actually later discovered Glenn's body when he was dead or near death outside a brothel in disreputable Pigalle.

Of all people who should know what happened to Glenn Miller—and keep his yap shut—Brod was the guy. Yet, he felt overburdened with an enforced secret he was required to bear most of his life. This was the secret which prevented the musical world and the mystery-fascinated public from learning Glenn's fate. Brod shared this dilemma with two in Glenn's family, wife Helen and brother Herbert. Neither believed the official claim and with good reason. Long before I met the movie star, I interviewed Herbert in London after his BBC-TV appearance with jazz presenter Malcolm Laycock. This was in the early 1950s not long after the war. Trumpeter Herbert was downright angry, disbelieving that his own U.S. government would turn down the "family request" to see the Miller files. He was angry, too, for Glenn's wife Helen who, he said, "had traveled from cemetery to cemetery on the continent for traces of Glenn's body... to no avail." I interviewed Herbert again in 1974, the year when writers on the war came out with "exposé" books just after expiration of the Official Secrets Act's 30-year-keep-mouths-shut provision. Brother Herbert was still waiting for the "family" files to open up. But the lid was on, and the key thrown away.

Yet bits of evidence—which both U.S. and British Defense chiefs ignored; worse, denied—kept cropping up. Such as the falsification of official records at Maxwell Air Force Base listing as Provost Marshals on duty in Paris that December four names which didn't exist. Then a real zinger: Both US and UK officialdom refused to admit a computer downloaded message by a Frankfurt journalist.

Udo Ulfkotte, a highly respected *Frankfurter Allgemeine* reporter, looked at what his printer had printed.[19] It was a missent document, circa 1945, in which CIA Washington conceded what Nazi propagandist Josef Goebbels had proclaimed when Glenn Miller went missing—that he was found in a Paris brothel, dead of a heart attack. Nothing was said about the brothel being Nazi-owned since 1935. Or that Hitler had been a curio-visitor to the place in 1940. Or that Miller may have been kidnapped and tortured there. Or that a number of GI's had witnessed his body being taken from outside the notorious house by MPs. Ulfkotte's find, thanks to a an errant semi-conductor somewhere, revealed not only that Twinwood was a bald lie but that there was much more to be told about Glenn than had ever surfaced.

Udo Ulfkotte was writing a book on the German Secret Service, he told me when I telephoned him at the height of the brouhaha over Glenn. He said that worms or viruses got their wires crossed out of Washington. Udo concluded his widely-read article in German: *Naturlich lagern in den Tresoren der Geheimdienst unzaelige weitaus brisantere Erkenntnisse....* "Naturally, in the secret treasury there lie stored countless further shocking documents."[19]

Udo's not unwelcome gift of a story from the CIA was one of several rumors bruited about in the Paris of the 1970s— others claiming Miller had a business interest in the place, a lover among the girls, was killed by a jealous husband, etc. What Udo's story did was help substantiate the activities taken back in 1944 to provide cover-ups for Miller's death.

Authorities back then naturally felt that as Miller had been found outside the brothel, and word of this would spread, it was important to create a rationale for his having been found there that had nothing to do with the real reasons, Thus the stories were created.

Researcher John Edwards spoke to U.S. press (April 20, 1976) in a Frank Durham story[49] in which he offered proof that Miller was murdered in Paris. The sensational claim had a purport of fact. Edward's life was threatened. He gave up his search.

Then came the capper: Brod Crawford's confession. A sergeant in the Paris MPs, Brod confirmed to me later that Glenn's "mission for Ike went sour." This added to a CIA executive's written statement that Glenn had a job in the big Bulge battle.

Badgered by music fans demanding to know what

happened, Miles Copeland, a major player in the OSS and a founding father of the CIA, answered a storm of letters to *Moonlight Serenader*, a Glenn Miller fan magazine: "I spoke to the Intelligence men who had the job of sorting out what actually happened (to Glenn Miller) and I was no nearer the truth. Even the facts as they were given out seemed to shroud the affair deeper in mystery. Miller was on his way to some kind of engagement. He was taking a plane from some unknown point to an equally mysterious destination." According to Roly Taylor, editor of the Glenn Miller Society's magazine *Moonlight Seranader*, this quote appeared in the June 1974 issue in an article entitled "Miller, Man or Myth."

And then, to further stampede the feigned cover-up, a US major in the Reserves, while doing a report on the infamous Himmler papers discovered in postwar Berlin, found Miller's name scribbled next to a *Fuehrer Erlass* (secret decree) that called for immediate execution of a Kommando, "in enemy uniform or not, on German side of the lines or not." A Kommando included enemy psywar (psychological warfare) broadcasters, as well as operatives; that is, any person on a secret mission against the Nazi forces. Glenn's BBC broadcasts in German to the *Wehrmacht* were held "Most Secret" so as not to reveal his presence, time, or location to Nazi agents. You have the extracted Himmler notes later in this book to prove that Glenn was a target: the major officially reporting this information to Washington was Yours Truly.

All Nazi notes convey without a doubt that there were enemies at work in SHAEF, Supreme Headquarters Allied Expeditionary Forces. They had Eisenhower well-spied upon. They had his work routine at the Trianon Palace down pat, his villa, his limousine and car number—even down to its color (tan). So Ike, his job, et al were well-tabbed by the *Reichsicherheitshauptamt*. This tonsil-twister is the organization which in 1943 merged all of the Nazi horror organizations we read about, the SS, Gestapo, SD, Black Shirts, the Amts underneath, not to exclude the concentration camps familiarly called K-Zed. All were brought under this single command. This twister is easily broken down: *Reich* "country"—*sicherheits* (with s- possessive) "security"—*haupt* is "high"—*amt* is "office." Two colonels we shall meet later, Walter Schellenberg and Otto Skorzeny, took over this evil twister toward war's end. The slang word for it was *Irrefuehrung*: Dirty Tricks.

It's baffling, even bewildering, to consider that Glenn Miller, a musicians' musician, held such a vital role to effect "a mission for Ike" but the proof pops up everywhere—from documents, from Glenn's ability to speak German, from Ike's trust in him; and perhaps most importantly, from Churchill to Roosevelt and down the chains of command, not excluding Big Boss in Washington of both wars east and west, General George C. Marshall. Aside from the esteem and near idol-worship Glenn was held in, there was no doubt that the one person whose voice was so-well known by *Wehrmacht* soldiers and German people alike that it could be picked out of a crowd was Glenn—from his broadcasts in German. Who else would make a better go-between, general-to-general, or to commanders (all except Himmler's SS forces) or more importantly, to a national audience explaining subtle differences in peace and surrender understandings? That question was to arise more than once in a scheme by generals of both sides to finish the war and arrest Hitler, circa 1944.

Chum Brod Crawford tells in Chapter Eight about Glenn's "close-mouthedness" and fear that he might say something to reveal "the mission." About nights out in London and Paris—they went "trompin' the Champs" in Brod's own vernacular. On one occasion Bing Crosby joined them, hitting bars, carousing and "gett'n feeble." But no women!!! Crawford got angry at the insinuation that Glenn died in a whorehouse and Brod would know, being an MP in the thick of SHAEF's chaos when Glenn's body was taken to a hospital, then shipped secretly to Wright-Patterson Airfield at Dayton, Ohio, as some stateside documents indicate.

It has to be pointed out that in 1944, Glenn Miller's celebrity far out-distanced Eisenhower's. Two movies (*Sun Valley Serenade* and *Orchestra Wives*) had been released starring Glenn, increasing his rise to super-fame. Eisenhower was an army officer who'd been promoted to Lt. Col, sent to North Africa, then moved to England to supervise the eventual landings in France and the race to the German border. He was just becoming a household word, and politicians in Washington were beginning to consider him as a Presidential candidate for the future—when and if he won. To the million-plus dogfaces on the ground, Glenn was more important than distant Eisenhower. He was, in a personal way, "the" VIP of Europe. He was the warm-voiced co-smoker who brought them music from home with sweet memories of apple-tree kisses and Kalamazoo and Saturday nights at the jukebox.

A close friend of mine, ex-Sergeant Wayne F. (Raw) Hyde reminisces. A paradropper, he caught a burst of machine gun fire across his body and became known as the "most ventilated GI in the Bulge to pull through." About Glenn's morale music, Hyde recalled, "I don't think we would have made it when things got tough if we hadn't had that great voice and the music to always massage our shoulders with hope and the will to go on. We didn't know he had died until a lot later, after the Bulge. If we had, it might have been goodnight for a lot of us."

Trumpeter Johnny Best, a Miller star from the US

commercial band, tells how Glenn would end a night out. "In London, he fell asleep in his own bed while talking. It was in his suite at the Mt Royal hotel. He was in full uniform sometimes when he slept. Just zonked out. I had a room next door. I would go in sometimes in the morning to wake him up. He'd be still asleep, still in uniform. That's how beat he was from the tough band-and-broadcast schedule."

Major Glenn Miller never kept it secret that he wanted to see combat, and increase his fame which he sensed was on the way. "I want to see some combat before this thing is over," he is quoted as having declared again and again. Then disparaging over chances he would survive the conflict, he told friends at his Mt Royal Marble Arch hotel, "I may go down as a hero." These two statements, portending a shadow of combat to come, have been documented by famed musicians Billy May and Britain's band leader, Geraldo.

Probably the best proof of Major Miller's "Mission for Ike" lies in the storehouse of Miller material at the UK's Imperial War Museum on Lambeth Road in London. There is a chronology of letters penned from Vic Porter, a companion of Miss Joan Heath, a SHAEF driver with top security clearance who was pestered after the war about her remembrance of the night the fatal Battle of the Bulge began. "Most Secret—cleared" Joan told her friends about Glenn's disappearance. She drove him to his mission takeoff. "Shut up about that," she was told. Later, it became, "Shut up or else." She would have been liable to the Official Secrets Act (which expired in 1973). That meant two years in the jug, no questions asked, like a military tribunal.

But even after 1973, she was frightened. The incidents at SHAEF Headquarters that night, despite Joan's precise detailed memory, were made secret in the strictest classification—Bigot by the two governments, U.S. and UK.

Cover-up disinformation was targeted against Joan all of her life, even suggestions of insanity. This despite able support from her training ground associates at Bletchley Park, the famed Ultra code breakers, and her immediate boss, Ike's Deputy Marshal Tedder. Some of her testimony is reprinted in this book.

Years before, however, when the operation called "Eclipse" first gained credibility, Miller was proposed as a language go-between to act for the generals on both sides, many of whom were determined to end the war thought lost already.

Glenn was called to Paris by Eisenhower several times before that fatal day when he disappeared. In the Supremo's opulent office—a part of the glittering Trianon Palace—he was presumably asked if he would take a role in "ending the war early, with Hitler arrested and out of the way." Who wouldn't volunteer? He was given a GI driver to take him back to his transient quarters, the Raphael, a middle-grade officer's hotel. The driver was a British vet, Stewart Singer, who, in 1992, confirmed this by letter. Singer wrote to Flight Lieutenant Wilbur Wright, who had compiled considerable evidence on the real Glenn Miller tragedy and had published a book, Millergate (1990). Here is an excerpt from Singer's letter:

"On my first day off at Versailles (near the Trianon), leaving my office in the *Grand Ecurie*, driver Joe Angelico was waiting in his jeep. 'I can give you a ride into town,' he said, 'but I have to wait for a VIP.' Soon Captain Glenn Miller (later Major) arrived and we spent the rest of the day together sight-seeing, visiting the Eiffel Tower and the Champs Elysees. He was down to earth, a great individual, and told me, "After the war I must bring Helen over to Paris—she'd love it."

A private at the time, Singer's greatest thrill of the war

was this magical day. Later in July Glenn made major rank, so this was his first secret trip to Paris from London. Only two others have been charted, one in November, and the other, the fatal one, Glenn's secret flight to help end the war.

The silver-paper shine on American heroes is not to be crumpled. They are to be gods, not just extraordinary people. Ike is one. Glenn Miller is not. And that one factor has prompted my research efforts. Not to detract from the SHAEF Supremo—Ike was letting Operation Eclipse go as far as it would, hopefully to its mission end. There would have been credit had it worked, backtracking if it didn't. But nobody dreamed it would be a disaster, which it was, thanks to rotten intelligence. There were spies at SHAEF—Charles Whiting, the Ardennes expert has verified this, as did Omar Bradley postwar and also the Himmler papers from Berlin.

The Soviets held most of the aces in the spy deck of WWII. After the war it became clear that one American and one Brit had been reporting regularly to Stalin: FDR's confidant Alger Hiss and British Secret Service's Number Two, Kim Philby. The Nazis spied better than we. Historian of the war years Hugh Trevor-Roper (famous for his historical essays published by the University of Oxford Press, 1953) wrote in one essay: "Himmler went on Goebbels' air (1943), named every British SIS officer from 'C'—Stewart Menzies, the top man, all the way down." Ian Fleming, the James Bond author, was on the death list as was Patrick Dalzel-Job. Few recognize the latter as Fleming's inspiration for Bond.

Poor security, even with protective classifications caused 80,090 US soldiers to be killed, captured or carried off wounded before Hitler's Autumn Mist (*Herbst Nebel*) was turned back and the Battle of the Bulge was history. This escapes Americans today in large measure because no body bags came home. The GIs are buried....over there. France has eleven cemeteries for Americans; Belgium three; England and Italy two each, Luxembourg and Netherlands have one each. Total: more than 100,000, not counting North Africa. Twice as many as on the Vietnam Wall.

Supreme Headquarters personnel totaled 17,000 (General Bradley's estimate), virtually all living in Paris, not in Versailles. This royal abode was for Ike, his section chiefs, their tiny staffs, some intelligence personnel, guards, and GIs for routine work. Everybody knew everybody. There was a friendship binding this elect group as existed in few other combat camps of history—sparked by the affable Ike who looked after his team with the diligence of a father. No outsiders. No Press. Keep Out.

Needless to say, there are no plaques of honor to distinguish Glenn's role in the Trianon Palace; neither for Miss Heath. She lived at SHAEF through the course of the war, and drove an Eisenhower contingent of generals to Rheims, France for the official surrender of the Nazis. Miss Heath dictated her letters to good friend Vic Porter a half-century later. She feared two years in prison, still an operative punishment in Britain. Shortly before she died, Joan told Porter she had to clear her conscience before facing her Maker. And she did, with the series of letters plus a single confession, taken up in my investigation years later. Her letters linked friend Glenn Miller to her boss Dwight Eisenhower with details that today cannot be put aside. As recently as 2001, the British Meteorological Office confirmed her description of unexpected snow at Buc Field, France, where she drove Glenn to a two-engine plane destined for a secretly arranged flight through the Ruhr Flak zone to General Von Rundstedt's base at Fichtenhein near Krefeld. This was German High Command for the sprawling front of opposing armies extending diagonally across Europe. The date December 16, 1944 was close to midnight, two hours before the long guns of the SS Panzers opened fire.

If General Eisenhower okayed the hastily constructed Twinwood story after the wire signed "Early" was sent to him... and he did,[11] he must be fairly charged with naiveté. He should have known of the immense radar system blanketing the coasts of Britain which clocked without exception every flight coming and going. The Twinwood flight would have been monitored, easily affirmed or denied. It was not. As proof of the pudding, Glenn Miller's real flight from Buc Field to St. Omer to Krefeld was charted by radar and reported in a message.[1]

F. W. Winterbotham, second in Ultra Command at Bletchley Park, published <u>The Ultra Secret</u> (1974). His book confirmed radar's blanket of the coasts of Britain as far back as 1940. "Not even the Germans knew how far and how accurately our radar operated," he wrote. "Radar was the first key to our survival. Ultra was to be the second." Radar could have spotted the controversial Twinwood flight, had anybody bothered to inquire.

Everybody in the world now knows how Eisenhoweer, one-time lowly Field Grade officer, took only three years and three months to be elevated to Supreme Commander of all Allied Armies in Europe. Five stars. Some naiveté could perhaps be excused. Bluntly admitted, Ike got his shot at immortality because he won in Europe and he won in Washington. Still, the youth of today might ask, "Who is this guy Glenn Miller who deserves to be called Hero? You put him alongside General Dwight D. Eisenhower?"

Nearing the height of his own career, Glenn did a self-analysis, answering a questionnaire from Bluebird Records.[27] His comments read less burdensome when you recall his background and long ago forebears in Hesse, Germany.

Many came to America, settling in a group of colonies
called Amana (Song of Solomon) meaning "Remain True."
America's frontier in the 1850s needed both protection and
opportunity. Germanic ingenuity provided both. The land
was ripe for cultivation. The Mississippi ran nearby, and
farming seemed the most profitable occupation. For defense
against displaced Indians and the ever-gunning badmen of
the West, Amana was made into eight different colonies;
each, six miles apart from the other. Intermarriage thus had
variety plus German stability and the Biblical faith. Belief
was a personal connection to God. The "Amana" Glenn
was born into came a half-century later when the clan's
business and social codes had widened, east and west. The
eight Amanas spread their moralities with them. Speaking
German was maintained. One book per house was honored:
a Bible. A house had to be unpainted to be pure, nor could
it harbor revelries of music. The Muellers and the Burgers
settled in the area known as Clarinda, Iowa. As more and
more newcomers adopted American ways and names,
Glenn's mother, Mattie Lou Cavander, secretly ferreted in
a piano, and when she got away with that, one of the four
children was given a trombone. By this time, Glenn's father,
Lewis Elmer Miller, had a longing for the road and a better
life for his swarming family. He tried Tryon, Nebraska, then
Grant City, Missouri, and finally Fort Morgan, Colorado.
Glenn went to high school there, graduated despite little or
no interest in anything but music. Then he put in two years
at the University in Boulder, Colorado, where his presence
is now honored with a memorial—as well as in Clarinda, his
birthplace.

By the end of World War One, Glenn was into Dixieland,
financed college by playing in various bands before joining
Boyd Sentner's band. He caught on with the legendary Ben

Pollack where he met the brothers Dorsey, Tommy and Jimmy. He was arranging by then, having a knack for math and intricate counting. Mouthing on the horn was fairly good, not big time, but the legends liked his stuff and put up with his average "bone." Glenn carried this inferiority about his mediocre playing all his life, even into the magnificent AACS band days. Arranging was his forte plus discipline in playing. In Europe, he seldom if ever put horn to mouth.

In 1937 he tried his own band. It didn't work. By 1938, feeling he needed publicity and records, he signed on with Victor and Bluebird. Requisite to the deal was a Personnel Fact Sheet which delved into attitudes and aptitudes, far more detailed than any of the current box-office boomers-of-the-muse.

It's as interesting to note the questions answered without hesitation and those he skipped. Viz : The Bible; When Were You Married?[22] Glenn's contrariness and obstinacy is clear in a few answers, as if he were saying, "None of your damned business." Amazing, Glenn's ready admittance of weaknesses. This interview, follow-up recordings and publicity skyrocketed his fame. From 1938 on, Glenn Miller and his Orchestra could do no wrong. The GM signature on a tune ignited the youth of America and a goodly part of the rest of the world. (Notably: two of the countries most recognized today for Glenn Miller loyalty are Germany and Japan.)

Hero worship exploded along with the two inevitable movies.

With *Sun Valley Serenade* (1941) and *Orchestra Wives* (1942) he was chart-wise top of the pop world, prompting a joke which spread like a prairie fire. President Roosevelt favored an open-topped limousine for his guests, sitting comfortably in back where he could wave to street crowds. Two kids watched from the sidewalk. One asked, "Who's that in the back with Glenn?"

And his voice on the Chesterfield radio show, crisp, warm, unmistakably Glenn—just whetted their affection (and their habit). Glenn was a heavy smoker, the best ad for his cigarette sponsor.

Before 1938 his was "only one of the bands on radio"— prompting perhaps his white-lie over age in the questionnaire. Mod music to an adulating public was a young man's game. Glenn cut off 4 years. His birth document is March 1, 1904. Tommy Dorsey called him "Old Klondike!"

He hadn't studied languages. In my opinion his not listing German was likely because he didn't consider it a "language." He had in his near-autistic memory a collection of German phrases from grandparents which he wouldn't have considered worthy of a formal study offered in school. Though there is no doubt as to his ability to speak the language. Former German Chancellor Helmut Kohl was a war-time listener. In later years he spoke fondly of *In the Mood* which introduced him to his wife (Spiegel magazine). "It's now our song," he said.

There was no stiff "German-ness" in Glenn Miller's public stance… perhaps his dog-headedness and unbending will were Teutonic characteristics. If so, they were absorbed by his band, traits which served to give the group a matchless precision. Glenn's arranging and conducting were criticized by some jazz buffs as "too damned symphonic." Glenn: "Making a buck is what it's all about!" And was he ever making bucks!

On romance and marriage, Helen Burger was his college sweetheart in the sense of "being pinned." So busy was he in rising to the top, she felt neglected, and let it be known that their engagement was imperiled. The family-oriented Glenn, playing in New York, picked up the phone and ordered her to New York. They were married the next day.

The war was on and Glenn Miller (beyond draft age) wanted to do his bit. One night during a Chesterfield broadcast, in 1942, he introduced to his continent-wide audience one of his top hits, *Juke Box Saturday Night*. In the tune there are replicas of a Harry James trumpet. Number done, he introduced Harry James himself in person as the player, and told unbelieving listeners that Harry and his band were replacing him next week. "From now on, I am Captain Glenn Miller in the United States Army." The greatest band of the times was "disbanded."

The Air Corps was part of the Army, not the separate Air Force as it became near war's end. Ordered post-to-post by the Army, Glenn livened up oom-pah bands, did concerts for troops, but was unhappy. He wanted to be in the AAC (air). Dreaming of making a switch, he went to see a Pentagon friend. A few generals' letters did the trick. Little did he know what was in store, but something was itching in his mind and he couldn't quell it. He didn't want to go through this great conflict only waving a stick. He entrained for Washington, DC, and made himself known at the newly-formed Office of War Information. Biographer George T. Simon in his book, <u>Glenn Miller and his Orchestra</u> (1974) explains the motive: "He volunteered his services to the Office of War Information, proposing that his band make propaganda transcriptions beamed into foreign countries along with announcements in the local languages." Simon's book was the first public admittance of the programs Glenn created in the German language all during 1944. These were "The Secret Broadcasts," his psywar propaganda programs— later target for *Irrefuehrung*, the Dirty Tricks echelon of Hitler's fear-generating Black Shirts.

With Glenn's history fairly well espoused, there's less need to go into Ike's. Biographers aplenty enthuse. It's worthy to note, however, that "Ironman the First," the earliest immigrant Eisenhower, first touched foot in the New World, circa 1750. Ike could lay claim to this ancestry. Eisenhower translates as an "iron hewer."

The OWI (Office of War Information) was in Foggy Bottom, a section of Washington in a "temporary quarters" building, a leftover from World War One. Glenn was expected. He was a class VIP and everybody knew him. He was far more a VIP at that moment than General "Wild Bill" Donovan, FDR's pal and head of this new agency, now to be Glenn's boss. The curious thing about the OWI, a CIA employee later told me, was that the outer door was emblazoned by a sign—OWI. You walked in, closed the door. On the other side of the same door was far different lettering—OSS.

Office of Strategic Service was the agency which postwar (1946) became the CIA. General Donovan is said to have greeted Miller by saying, "Welcome to the real war, Captain Miller." Donovan was the boss of both agencies, an agreement okayed by FDR, approved by Congress. Thus in America, Glenn was a soldier making radio programs. Across the Atlantic, he belonged to the fighting front. That is to say: he was OWI in Washington but OSS in London and Paris. Some critics of Glenn Miller believe he was sent overseas "to entertain the Germans." I don't know what kind of war we're fighting when the object is to entertain the enemy. If we do it, it's to capture attentive ears and convince whoever is in front of those ears to do what we say. And that was Glenn's job as the Himmler notes (captured and archived in The Document Center, Berlin) gave evidence.

Getting the war over fast turned out to be the goal in Glenn's job that he was most in favor of. By 1944 he was full blast into it. Even two years before, German generals were complaining about the untenable struggle—Nazis against the Brits, the Yanks and the Russkies . And in 1943, Reich territory was shrinking. By 1944 only Hitler and his fanatics stood solidly against an armistice. In the secret process to come, recordings and instructions to utilize Glenn's voice and music to help win the war were laid down. The letters G and M became significant, the 7th and 13th letters of the alphabet. Not many months later they were to be part of a secret operation "Odin 7/13" in which Glenn Miller was to do more than his bit.

General Donovan's idea of influencing troops of the enemy by broadcasts was a proven asset in waging war—that is psychological warfare. Almost immediately when Glenn and his enlarging band were transferred to Yale campus at New Haven, his training began. To be effective in psywar, Glenn had to improve his German. His warm, appealing voice would have to be as effective in German as it was in English. Pig-Latin GI German wouldn't suffice. Instruction for at least a year was necessary. There are wiseacres today who claim that Glenn spoke broken German. Considering the pride, even arrogance, with which Germans view their own high language, it is doubtful if pig-German would have influenced *Reich Soldaten* to quit, or even to listen to Miller's music and messages. The thought of Glenn's playing "to entertain enemy troops" (sometimes said today) is so ridiculous as to go beyond stupidity.

Was Glenn fluent—or not? Having some fifteen years residence in Berlin, Munich, Frankfurt and Cologne, I can profess a more-than-adequate knowledge of *Hoch Deutsch*. I was educated for such assignments by the Foreign Service Institute in Washington. I tested Glenn's spoken German, from recordings. And so did my boss in North Africa and

Italy. Glenn's appeal in German was good enough, and my boss, General David Sarnoff, thought he was good enough, too. Sarnoff, born in Minsk, Russia, was conversant in languages. A fixture of the 20th century, Sarnoff invented the commercial "broadcast band" radio, and rising within the new industry of radio founded RCA and NBC.

Sarnoff, at 22, had a job with Marconi on top of the Wanamaker Building in New York City, scanning Morse codes. He picked up an SOS from a ship called the Titanic. He was the one who spread the alarm, cross-haired the spot in the ocean where the ship was going down, got the California on its way to pick up survivors. It was his most precious memory, more than founding two of America's great companies and in introducing color television at the 1939 World's Fair.

During World War Two, I was sent to a part of the world where I spoke no German. Never mind, I thought. When I heard Glenn broadcasting, I said to myself, "If he can speak it, I can." Some of you ex-GIs know that funny beginning in textbooks to learn German—"*Wo ist der Bahnhof?*"—(Where is the railroad station?) That phrase tickled me. Why was it used to start a language book? When I finally got to Germany after the war, I realized the irony in that phrase. Where is the Bahnhof? There wasn't any. All the stations had been blown to hell. (German humor—they prepared the textbooks.)

Few in WWII services on the Allied side bragged about knowing German. Worse for them was being of Germanic origin. Odd that two mighty personalities, on whom 80,090 lives were to hang in balance, were engaged in war against common ancestral folk on the German side of the Atlantic. It's a tribute to the characteristics of "being American" that nobody in those critical years of the Forties even thought of Ike and Glenn as being anything but red, white and blue.

Where are the GM recordings today? The BBC says they were melted to make more vinyl, there being a serious shortage. Some were pilfered as souvenirs, including one I heard up close in 1954, and Glenn's psywar messages in German were deleted from the current set of "lost" broadcasts on sale now. Still, GIs and AAC crew members have reported in recent months that they listened back in '44.... they didn't understand the German but the *Musik* was there and they didn't need the words.

What follows are chapters of painstaking, exciting, sometimes life-threatening research for The Truth. The results, mine aided by others to be sure, bring this shocking revelation of a heroic major out into the open after it's been trampled and kicked under the carpet for years. Why didn't anybody check General Eisenhower when he left Europe for America in 1945, penning these orders: "I am unalterably opposed to any story concerning the Ardennes Battle, or even of allowing any written explanation to go outside the War Department" (taken from a letter to Secretary of War, Robert Patterson, Washington, D.C. from Dwight D. Eisenhower, 18 December 1945, held at Eisenhower library Ablilene, Kansas).

It should have been known that eventually the Truth would out, even if the Internet's fabulous sky of information had not been anticipated then, and I am grateful to this boon of the 21st Century which has filled in much of the Miller Tragedy with facts—in particular, a little-known message from U.S. General Marshall to German General Walter Dornberger at the height of the war's 1944 crisis, an attempt to bring German atomic and rocket scientists to our side. It was a hair-brained idea to some, actually illegal. But it worked, and altered the outcome. And yes, it involved our hero.

CHAPTER 2

'Scholarships' at Yale

There's been enough written about Glenn Miller's "mystery" to choke the Channel he supposedly drowned in. And here we are, sixty-five years later, no better for acceptance than what information a few scribes have hoisted only to be almost immediately battered down. Officialdom is not supposed to be questioned. Are we under a dictatorship of believe-what-I say or believe-what-is-true?

My search for the hero I know Glenn to be has earned me no money– just the opposite, the same as colleagues from 1946 on who have spent thousands of dollars from their own pockets. It's not just the music which in a time of dire strife attained magical proportions—and lives on today. Nor the man who created it called GM. It's right versus wrong, a principle which millions of Americans fought for and not a few kissed the earth the last time for. We can mourn and hype and lay flowers for one soldier who "bought it" in Iraq or Afghanistan. But the Battle of the Bulge? What's that? How many were lost there? Just one buried here today seems more poignant than 80,090 buried overseas, a loss in which Major Glenn Miller was a battle all to himself. For his death he won, belatedly, a Bronze Star for <u>combat</u> published in a long "Restricted" list of Frenchmen. This kept the award from being generally known. Then, decades later came much ceremonious whoop-ti-do yet still no mention of the heroism we are now proving.

RESTRICTED: Feb. 1, 1945 (*Last in two-page list of awards*)—By direction of the President, under provisions of Army Regulations... the Bronze Star Medal is awarded, for meritorious service in connection with military operations, to Major Alton Glenn Miller (Army Serial No 0505273. Air Corps, United States Army—9 July 1944 to 15 December 1944).[47]

Every "official" document put together in 1944-46 declared Glenn's "last flight" as a "<u>passenger, non-combat</u>." But his battle and death was in combat, under command of General Eisenhower, A BRONZE STAR means BATTLE. Nothing less.

To Glenn at Yale... He was there with his band about a year. George T. Simon, who wrote the biagraphy <u>Glenn Miller and His Orchestra</u> (1980), was in the group as a drummer, so this one year is replete with droll stories of the Enlisted Men and Simon's efforts to dig up members of the commercial band and get them assigned to New Haven. Little is said about the officer, Captain Miller, who lived apart, kept his distance, became more West Pointish than expected of an ex-band-leader. Simon's work is the best chronology still available on the Yale hiatus.

The networks were full of Miller music; so were the juke boxes on Saturday night, and most other nights. Special programs emerged such as *I Sustain The Wings*, an OWI presentation. Network shows and secret recordings in New

York for the BBC were de rigueur for Glenn's schedule. The band enlisted radio and recording specialists, announcers, writers, composers. Glenn, the "exactist," was getting on with his German, and having enough scholarly genius to make melodies out of those mystifying, longish words. He had favorite expressions. Ed Polic, who did a two-volume work on Miller's life in America, an encyclopedia (published privately), maintains he dug out of Glenn's correspondence a number of favorites. But German wasn't simple. It was damned hard work.... I know. It's not like English. It's got those verbs at the end of sentences, declensions, three genders, capitalizing nouns.

At that 1943 moment-in-time, I had no awareness of Glenn Miller's whereabouts or what he was doing. Of course, I had his records and the few V-discs I could find packed in my gear for Teheran, Iran. This curious assignment was to build and sustain a network of transmitters extending from Kasvin, Iran on the Soviet border to Basra, Iraq, down and through the formidable 17,000 ft. plus Elburz chain of Himalayas. Ostensibly our powerful beams were to bring news and music to American and British troops taking supplies to the Russians. Our other secret mission was to let our radio beams guide Allied bombers from North Africa and Italy attacking the Ploesti Oil Fields in Rumania, Hitler's main source of fuel, then eastward safely to Soviet Georgia and Iran. The heavily loaded bombers were being eaten up by Nazi fighters before they could get back to Algiers and Bari, Italy. If they could turn sharply eastward after unloading, they would be in Soviet territory, safe all the way to Iran with a landing strip on the way to refuel. The USSR provided one in Georgia near Yalta, a strip at Tiflis (now Tblisis). Our B-24s and B-24 Consolidated could now

fly in reasonable security from Bari, Italy or Algiers to the
oil fields in Rumania, drop bombs and hide eastward over
Soviet lands, out of reach of Nazi fighters. This operation
drained so much fuel from Goering's *Luftwaffe* that there
was virtually none left at the end of the war. I never
learned the name of this operation. I don't think it had
one, but you can search B-24 Missions and read about it
on the internet.

I mention this misson as it was instrumental in my
assignment to General David Sarnoff, Eisenhower's Special
Deputy in PsyWar Communications. Sarnoff helped
organize a triangular beam process which guided the
bombers until they were "on target" and on beam. Then
Sarnoff got involved in PsyWar, which was my introduction
to the Miller project. With my radio background, I was to
be his Aide-de-camp for three months.

Sarnoff came to Teheran to take over a 50,000 watt
transmitter, a gift from Hitler to the Old Shah when Iran
was in the Nazi coalition. The transmitter had sat idle until
Sarnoff found a use for it. He figured that with virtually no
radio traffic "east of Suez," it could boom all the way to
Ploesti and let our pilots enjoy American radio entertainment
to Tiflis, thence to Teheran. The bombers route was Algiers
or Bari on the heel of Italy to Ploesti, then sharp east to
Tiflis, to Teheran, to Cairo, then back to Algiers/Bari and
go again. The 50,000 watter became part of the American
Expeditionary Network.

David O. Sarnoff's war duties were so highly classified
that he never got the kudos he deserved. This may stem
from his birth in Russia or the shock that, after a trusting
policy toward the Soviet Union, we found the USSR a Cold
War enemy. He was a magnificent man, one of the greatest
Americans I ever knew. I made a tape for the Princeton

Sarnoff Library, detailing his unmatched feats. "We had blank on his war until that," said Intendant Alex Amagoun.

To beg, borrow or steal power transmitters to join the 50,000 watt *Telefunken* at Teheran, we toured North Africa and the Middle East, We had proven that with our transmitters in Iraq/Iran villages and at various mountaintops we could provide clear-quality directional signals to our bombing pilots and get them safely back. Now we had to put the surrender heat on Germans in uniform. It was yet to be proven that shortwave transmitters from the Middle East and Africa could relay programs such as Glenn's *Musik fuer die Wehrmacht* clearly enough to drench the Third Reich—not only by shortwave but to be picked up by BBC, Radio Calais and early American Forces Network field broadcasters.

We originated programs as test runs, then as actual features on NBC in the U.S., and they came through. From halfway around the world, my family heard them. This was the first scheduled networking ever done globally, west to east with cueing instructions going both ways shortwave. Sarnoff's NBC and his personal intervention made this possible. One of the Nazi villains you will meet later in this book tried with a team to interrupt one of these NBC test programs; its purpose: assassination of a VIP on our side. But the men failed. They were after pro-Western Mohammad Reza Shah Pahlavi, the Shah of Iran for more than three decades, until 1979.

All hush-hush: the obtaining of power transmitters from governments we were allied to and some who weren't, and how we redirectionalized the beams. I heard Glenn's psywar programs in German dozens of times, receiving it, sending it—just great music and broadcasting with hard-hitting messages to surrender which he himself delivered with friendship and sincerity. This programming format of the Miller shows mixed music and talk in a semi-formal style the Germans like. Although recorded, they gave a pretense of being live and fresh.

Curious, I tried to find out how current tunes by the band got so fast to BBC in London while the band was at Yale, but had no luck until 2001. In WWII there were no telephone lines from New Haven to Europe of broadcast quality, and recordings during the war had a low shipping priority. But Glenn's boys in uniform got the jump on every other band in America, and in Britain as well, spilling over into the continent. How? The answer: secret recordings. Wallace R. Forman of St. Paul, MN showed me one reason why, even long before Eisenhower, Glenn Miller became a showpiece at Mme. Toussaud's Wax Museum in London.

As ex-GI Wallace R. Forman would recall, "I went on active duty 4/5/43 and after basic training in the combat engineers and some classification sites, I was sent to the College of the City of New York. We were billeted in an abandoned Jewish orphanage at 1260 Amsterdam Avenue (128th St.). It was a bore because the chicken s__t was piled high in basic training and got even higher when sent back to school. But duty in New York City offered a lot of pluses.

"Across from Grand Central Station, space was donated for the USO to open a ticket office for passing out free entertainment tickets for GIs. As long as our grades were OK, we could get a pass every weekend. We befriended some girls working there and one weekend they said they had something special, and gave us tickets for an old mangy, off-Broadway theatre and told us to be there a little before 6 p.m. on a Saturday night. We settled in and found before us a bunch of musicians tuning up on stage.

"It was Glenn Miller and his Air Force band. For a 19-year-old kid who a year before had been a snot-nosed high school senior playing in what was loosely represented as a 'swing band', this was pig heaven! They practiced until 6:30 p.m. and we paid rapt attention to the best swing musicians in the country, many of whom we knew by name and reputation.

"At 6:30 we were all shushed and some civilians rolled out a big console, about three feet square and four feet high. For the next half-hour we listened to them wire-recording the best music ever, to be flown to Europe for broadcast there. At the end of the recording session, we left and the band went back to New Haven. This kept up every Saturday night until February when I was transferred to the Air Corps at Truax Field in Wisconsin."

I immediately wrote to Foreman with a series of questions: Was Glenn Miller there? In which theatre was the recording? Was any German spoken? How do you know the recording was by wire? Did Johnny Desmond sing in German?

In a note dated Jan. 29, 2001, Wallace Forman answered:

"Johnny Desmond did not sing in German—to hear that I had to wait until I bought the 6-tape series from the Air Force Museum. There was no text recorded at these sessions. Prior to the recording portion, Glenn Miller came out and prepared to lead. I'd say he ignored the presence of an audience completely. I expected him to use a baton; he didn't, using only his hand [or hands] and hardly used them! As for wire recording, I had worked as projectionist in a theatre before the service and I knew what the disc-cutting recorders of the day looked like and this was not like them. The consoles were about three feet square and about four feet high. I could just see enough over the top of them to recognize they weren't disc-cutting recorders and the only other technological advance that came to mind was wire recording, about which I had read a little."

Johnny Desmond knew German and sang it well, one strike against his GI popularity, although a home-run for Germans listening to *Musik*. His career lagged after the war, surprising for a Miller alumnus, since his voice was on a par with warblers Como, Russell, Bennett. He was thumbs down for Lt. Don Haynes, however. Author Simon indicated in his Miller saga that Desmond had denied Haynes' claim that Glenn was up in Bedford living with the band. No, Glenn was billeted at the Mt. Royal Hotel in London, separate from the band. This truthful assertion, conceded now by everybody, put a lie to Haynes' Diary and the whole concept of the Twinwood theory.

At that stage of the war, wire was coming into use in England, just as tape was being developed in Germany (*Magnetafon*). I had experience with both. I brought a vest-pocket wire to New York for a joke. I had it well-hidden in my jacket pocket. The friendly custom guys were amazed when I pulled it out and played back our conversation to them.

The difference between wire and tape recording was obvious. Wire may be more compact, but how do you splice it when it breaks? Tape is re-usable, far better quality, and you can splice tape free of errors. Still, wire was more practical for field use than the awkward metal discs which had to be cut into tracks. As their coatings were fragile, they had to be melted down and recast for further cuts, which explains why few if any of the original Glenn Miller *Musik fuer die Wehrmacht* discs can be found today.

We can be grateful to ex-Billboard writer George T.

Simon, for details of the extraordinary hiatus at Yale. He was there as a soldier, a Private, and told with refreshing bluntness of Miller's constant absences, his increased separation from his band (officers and EM), of firings and the origin of one fabulous piece of Americana.

The *St. Louis Blues March* was premiered in the Yale Bowl and the cadets really strutted, according to Simon, whose job was to find, and get transferred, the best musicians in America. He tried for Tex Beneke, but the star of movie hits, *Chattanooga Choo Choo* and *Kalamazoo* had gone into the Navy. The Army had rejected him for flat feet, proving the joke that the Navy swears that flat feet stick better to a rolling deck. At any rate, Tex fought it out in Oklahoma, and suspected the Army of faking Miller's lost-in-the Channel-disappearance. "Like chop suey in an aft wind is what they got for proof," Tex said about the government's rhetoric—this from brother-in-law Sid Robinson.

Fortunately for we hundred or so vets into the 21st Century, Tex's brother-in-law Sid joined my team of investigators. He has accumulated such a vast library of Miller facts that I would have hesitated to present this book without his steadfast help. He and British historian Charles Whiting (51 books) and a now-deceased RAF pilot, Wilbur Wright <u>Millergate</u> (1990), need to be credited. We four disagreed on fine print of the equation but on the phoniness of the Channel dunk or a 4,000- pound bomb catching up with Glenn, we stood in accord. The proof is presented here, and the Glenn Miller Society of Britain—which still holds to Glenn's "disappearing" in channel waves—will have to sit up and take notice.

2nd Lt. Don Haynes, fresh from Officer Candidate School (OCS), came in as Administrative officer of the Yale detachment. He was Glenn's band manager of civilian days, a good-looking showbiz hustler, the sort of individual needed in the knock-down wrestle of competitive bands where one's word changed with the breath of an extra dollar.

Haynes was never named officially as witness to Glenn's disappearance. Yet, in his diary's claim, <u>he</u> was the <u>only</u> witness. This diary, upon which the government rested its case, has been proven so full of falsities, exaggerations and pure lies that even the GM Society has to blush when swearing by it. Haynes did write an original "diary" but somehow it got lost when it counted. Some Miller experts say he tore up the original because it mentioned girl friends and he didn't want his wife, Polly, a close friend of Helen Miller, to find out. This testimony, by experts who should know, is included here. So, we can assume with assurance that the diary which rests uneasily in the Library of Congress—basis for *The Glenn Miller Story* movie with James Stewart—is a fabrication. Did Haynes devise it from memory, scramble it together for a film plot, plain "sell it" to the Army and new Air Force to be believed by the world? For sure it has worked, until now.

I am not alone in my supposition of fakery. I personally have been in correspondence with Alan Cass, as has my colleague Sid Bobinson. We both know this to be his position of the "Don Haynes' band diary" which has never come to light. This following quote received publicity in 1953 when Glenn Miller executives in Boulder, CO were asked about the references upon which the movie, The Glenn Miller Story was based. The position stated by Cass who was also made known at the annual celebration of Miller's birthday at Clarinda, Iowa—reported by Robinson who attended. Here is the judgment of Alan Cass, Curator of the Glenn Miller Museum and Archives at the University at Boulder: "That alleged diary first surfaced in 1953 when *The Glenn Miller Story* was filmed. Haynes saw a chance to make a buck so he wrote that diary from memory and from notes. Haynes bragged that he kept a diary of the band's wartime history but no one ever saw that real diary, and it does not exist today."

From Dale Titler who, circa 1954, corresponded with me on the subject, and who has amassed enough facts for a Miller book. "The official version of the GM tale is NOT true. Haynes had his reasons. If you try to force-fit any other account to mesh with the Don Haynes Story, you will have trouble doing so."

Not least, my colleague Sid Robinson who has a huge collection of Miller correspondence on the disappearance: "Up to now, the general belief had GM departing 15 Dec. 44 from Twinwood Air Field (never to be seen again), but the statement of one person, Don Haynes, 2nd Lt., who claimed to have witnessed the departure, was never confirmed. We were told to take the word of this one man whose writing contains all sorts of errors and untruths. The time of departure is not precise and no one corroborated. It is evident to me that no authoritative investigation and/ or report was ever made in this case. Documents that did exist regarding departures, arrival times and ETAs were never collected or were allowed to get lost."

A lifelong student of law, Sid Robinson is a close friend of author Ed Polic of Milpitas, CA Glenn Miller Encyclopedia (published privately). According to Polic: "You are correct in stating that Don Haynes did not tell the truth, the whole truth and nothing but the truth and that he promoted himself and was self-serving. Neither of the two Don Haynes "diaries" that exist: (the "red" book at the Library of Congress, or the manuscript "Minus One") are original, and you can even find discrepancies between these two. I am also sure that he destroyed the original diaries for that period for personal reasons. Don was a womanizer and I have several photographs of him with his lady friend in Europe in 1945. Of course, Don had a wife in the USA." This from Polic, from a bimonthly information exchange between himself and Robinson conducted from July 1, 1999 to January 23, 2005.

Others who answered the call for memories of Glenn Miller at Yale are: Walter Portune, Kettering, OH; Bob Hunckley, Lexington, MA; Dick Proper, Dunkirk, NY; Joe Way, Painesville, OH; Miles K. Luke, Monroe, LA; John T. McEntee, Clearfield, UT; Harry Richardson, Glen Cove, NY; Seymour Abrams, Tucson, AZ. Their stories are meat for extra pages, but the mere mention of their names shows the nationwide appeal of Glenn Miller music, even half a century later, and our GIs' desire to learn what really happened.

Senior pilot Harry Witt of Austin, Texas was in the same unit as John Morgan who flew the "missing" plane: "Somebody big would have gotten hung if the truth had been told. I think that diary and the statements of so-called witnesses to that arrival and departure of a C-64 Norseman, purported to be flown by Morgan, form a post-event fabrication. Lt. Haynes' diary has many questions regarding its veracity. Nobody would have gotten Base Operations clearance much less authority to take off in that weather. To put it in perspective, that weather would be very marginal in today's world with its autopilot and beam/radar approaches, such as Dallas/Forth Worth and Chicago O'Hare. That landing and takeoff never occurred."

So why the phony facts to make the world believe a phony story? There was something to hide, something BIG and BOMBASTIC, something Don Haynes and a few top-level personages knew, something closely involving Major Glenn Miller which couldn't be made public. Was Haynes manipulated to keep secret a monstrous lie? Did he become a tool of civilian "Early" who had no military rank? (Steve Early was PR Chief for President Roosevelt.) Early was the signature on the wire advising Ike of Glenn's loss.[11]

Back at Yale, Lt. Don Haynes' assignment to the band brought order—and grumbling. He was too well known and disliked as "Madison Avenue" to make friends. Remember, most of these musicians knew him or (worse) knew his nasty, hard-assed reputation. But March 23, 1943 brought a whiff which would fill the sails of this Glenn Miller Yankee Clipper. Into Glenn's office marched a smartly buffed sergeant who saluted and crisped his identity: "Sergeant William B. Crawford, 39267223, reporting as requested, Sir." The two fell into each other's arms, protocol be damned. Glenn had requested him from Colonel Ed Kirby in Washington who had pulled a string or two. Thus, Academy Award winner, Broderick Crawford (*All the King's Men*) had landed where he wanted to be. Bear-chested, brash, a drinker and as straight as a T-square, Brod was one of the actor-announcer persons needed by Miller for his OWI bond-raising sallies and more. Brod was to stick to Glenn as close as a solid-gold watch chain to a Wall Street vest. As noted, he was to be keeper, bodyguard, chum, whatever—because Captain Miller was already a security item. Brod was to prove his loyalty all the way through the war, past tragedy, and down to the Eternal Flame under the Arc de Triomphe in Paris. There, finally, he surrendered his word to keep quiet and provided the key to what happened to Major Miller as I describe more fully in Chapter 8.

In New Haven, it was "Sir." In London, it was "Me and

Mill and Croz" (trio of Hollywood pals—Crawford, Glenn and Bing Crosby (who came on a USO tour). In Paris, it was "trompin" the Champs (bars along the Champs Elysees). Then... at the Flame, tears and an admission.

Finally, I can't excuse Don Haynes but I can understand him. War is based not only on principle or gain, but on deceit. Successful deceit wins, and no student of Clausewitz would deny it. Haynes was a product of the times. English took on a new vocabulary in World War Two. Close-to-the-vest held facts assumed new importance—Restricted, Confidential, Secret, Most Secret, Top Secret, Ultra Secret and Bigot. What was left unclassified became consequently "suspect." "We want them to believe that" is what it connoted. So loose lips were to be sealed. To be deceitful was, in a word: acceptable. Don Haynes could make up what he wanted; true or near true or I don't remember or to hell with it—just make it good! George T. Simon took his word: "I learned that he had kept a diary on him, of Glenn's and the group's overseas activities," was Simon's rather lame excuse in the one big book of Glenn Miller. I can't help but ask: "Where are all those other books about Glenn Miller that friends should have written? By people he knew and who knew him? Many of them published memoirs after the war...and not one word about Glenn, not even in Harry Butcher's extensive diary of SHAEF.

Mr. and Mrs. Miller, this newly-married couple, lived in Tenafly, New Jersey. They wanted a family. Both Glenn and Helen loved children. He had doubts until he had one, adopted Stevie, and then he fell over himself in adoration for the kid. They put in for adoption of another and got a girl, Jonnie Dee. Dad never got a chance to see her. This fact rouses emotion in me, as I never saw my own daughter, Kitty, until war's end, and lost her three weeks later.

That there were groups determined to champion Haynes' put-together fantasy as fact, there can be no doubt. Some researchers were threatened, including this writer as recently as 2000. That shivery episode comes up later.

We know from a good German source that the Miller music with Glenn's appeal found tens of thousands of willing ears.

It's surprising today to realize that there were so many hand-held radios back then, particularly in Nazi Germany of the 1930s and 1940s. These sets helped Hitler's rise to power, as it was the magnetism of his voice which propelled the NSDAP party out of obscurity. The rate of radios per population at that time exceeded that of Britain and the United States.

A 15-year-old German named Kohl was fiddling with his radio, picked up Glenn Miller music, and loved it. Young Kohl didn't get caught up in the final struggle, but was inspired to pursue politics. In 1994 toward the end of his career in government, then German Chancellor Helmut Kohl told an audience, reported in the massively-circularized *Das Bild*: "As a young boy (*Knabe*) I listened to the Glenn Miller broadcasts. Much later when I was at a dance looking for a pretty partner, I met my wife, Hannelore. *In the Mood* was playing. It's been our song ever since."

CHAPTER **3**

Wings of a Double Life

Captain Glenn Miller flew to London, his movement details kept secret although the band moved en masse by the liner Queen Elizabeth—"NY-8245" in military parlance. The sailing of the giant ship was secret as well, carrying many a thousand troops to battle. That prize would have been a rich target for Nazi submarines. Pal Brod went with the boys.

It was unusual for an under-field-grade officer to get the luxury of a trans-Atlantic flight, an indication of Glenn's VIP status and a hurry-up need for his psywar program to be recorded on the spot. He landed at Northolt, just outside London, called The King and Queen's Airfield; strictly VIP and not for the common carrier. Glenn's orders, July 1, 1944, indicated a destination of Bedford, a town north of London. The area was central to many secret activities, well guarded by fighters and bombers in three fields nearby. It was close to "Ultra," the highly-sensitive home for Bletchley Park Intelligence. David Niven of the Secret Intelligence

Service (SIS) "Phantoms," a British Lt. Colonel, met him at the London plane. He was to be Glenn's boss in the espionage game, as well as "supervising" the band. Stitched under vest was the premise that Glenn would not live in Bedford near the band but in London at the Mount Royal Hotel, Marble Arch (now Thistle Marble Arch). He would broadcast at BBC Bush House, a 20-minute walk down Oxford Street. The walk became a daily exercise for Glenn. Facilities were jerry-built at Bedford for the band members. Broadcast-quality lines were laid from an old pottery plant south to the BBC facilities in London.

The shows poured forth immediately with Glenn up-fronting some appearances to satisfy clamoring soldiers. Captain Robert Baker, one of the Ike-assigned pilots, noted in a letter: "With the band in the back and Glenn in the front with me, I was Glenn's air-taxi. My converted B-24 bomber called "Ain't it Awful" tickled hell out of Glenn."

The Miller music was a great boost, not only to our armies, ever widening in France, but to the long-buffeted British population, and of course the Germans. Close-mouthed Col. Niven had tabs on the undergrounds of Belgium, Holland and France. Diplomat Allen Dulles, our Chief in Switzerland for Intelligence and Counter-Intelligence, was running more than 200 agents undercover in and out of Germany, according to Peter Grose's amazing biography Gentleman Spy (1995). What passed for surveys in those days rated Glenn's programs *hoechstens* (highest).

Dulles' main business was getting rid of Hitler. He orchestrated eight attempts, any one of which could have worked, no fault of the Reich officer assigned: 1941 Col. Tresckow, 1943 Col. Brandt, 1943 Major Gersdorff, 1943 Captain Bussche, 1943 Capt.Bussche-2nd Attempt, 1943 Colonel von Stauffenberg, 1944 Captain von Kleist, 1944

Colonel Stauffenberg—2nd Attempt—July 20th, (Courtesy: Gentleman Spy).

The enemy had no music to compare with the popular Miller's. The Nazi Goebbels was desperately trying to rig up competitors. And he failed. The oom-pah couldn't make the grade. Miller was the favorite band for radio listeners, followed by other greats of the time, Artie Shaw, Benny Goodman, Louis Armstrong. British bands logged low. They tended to copy American swing but didn't match the explosive excitement of U.S. arrangements with their often "Hit the roof, Jack" climaxes.

Glenn's excursions to the field for concerts became infrequent. From the beginning, it was decided that while Glenn himself appeared to live with the band to Bedford, the band could come to him at the Queensbury Club in the West End, London, every weekend, and sometimes for Thursday matinees at the Theatre Royal Haymarket near Trafalgar Square. Meanwhile, to accommodate his in-German programs, he was given a convenient office at the Langham Hotel, close by BBC's Bush House on Regent Street.

The bar at his hotel, the Mount Royal, was named for him—still is—a tribute to his fame no doubt and possibly to the Captain's and Major's salary he left there with abandon. Back home in 1944 his records were still piling in the cash. Wife Helen and kids were well-provided for. So he could ease his stress well into the morning hours, alongside companions Brod Crawford, Tony Bartley, flying ace of the Battle of Britain (husband of Deborah Kerr), and Lt. Tony Pulitzer, scion of the famed American family. It's been suggested that Bartley flew Glenn that fateful night of December 16, 1944, a point vigorously denied by Bartley, a two-time winner of the Distinguished Flying Cross and a one-time pilot for Eisenhower himself.

Glenn's superior (two levels up), Col. David Niven, was not much in evidence prior to the liberation of Paris on August 17, 1944. Niven, one of Britain's pre-war stars in Hollywood, came home to "do his bit." It turned out to be "a bit more than a bit." As commander of the "Phantoms," his SIS job was integrating commando raids across the English Channel and coordination of Special Operations Executive (SOE) units parachuted in as spies to the Low Countries. These activities began in 1942 and prompted Hitler's secret *Erlass* of October 18, 1942, a death directive against all *Kommandos*. This from a (1952) search of Berlin's infamous Document Center containing Himmler's captured records. The scrawled notations preserved today (in Heinrich Himmler's own green-grease pencil) were "to kill Commandos in uniform or out, behind our lines or theirs." The name of "Miller" is margined.

Bartley wrote in his memoirs that on the eve of Glenn's departure from London, he warned his friend not to risk Paris. He was already an SS target. The SS, or RSHA, as it was known then in 1944, ran the department called *"Irrefuehrung"* meaning Dirty Tricks. Bartley was well enough acquainted with Nazi tricks to know there was a good chance RSHA spies might spot precisely and promptly where Glenn Miller would land—if he came to Paris—and when.

I'll get to David Niven's role and subsequent blackout of memory in the investigation that I, and others, made during the 1970s and 1990s. Admittedly it is difficult for a "now" generation to understand the near reverence the Glenn Miller "sound" generated as a war weapon. Heads of American radio, Sarnoff and Paley (NBC and CBS), knew it and knew what it could mean for victory.

A friend and collector of every number recorded by the GM bands, civilian and military, is Richard H. Lieve of Lucasville, Ohio. Better than anyone, he knows how to explain the power and the magic of "The Miller Sound:"

"If one taps a foot or a finger with the beat of a certain tune, the weak beat occurs when the foot or finger is in the raised position. The main melody of a tune is performed either by a certain section of the band, a solo played by a certain instrument, or by a vocalist. One will find, by the tapping of the foot or finger with the beat provided by the drums and guitar that much of the melody is played on the weak beat. The off-beat. The listener may not be able to explain why the syncopated style sounds better when comparing it to the same tune played in an "on-beat" fashion. The syncopated style is also more difficult to read since it requires the entire band to have a feel for the music being played. One member of Miller's band recounted that the band would sometimes practice a part of a certain tune for several hours until it sounded just like Glenn had heard it in his head. He was a strict disciplinarian who demanded excellence from all members of his orchestra."

A hint perhaps as to why Glenn's arrangements of catchy tunes captivated the German home audiences as well as the troops. His music possessed an originality, plus that "lifting" quality which makes you feel better than you really are.

Glenn "Germanized" his *Musik fuer die Wehrmacht* program by a heavily-accented but excellent Deutsch.[14] Speaking it correctly is a strong point of respect. For Germans, that is, if you want to be listened to. It would be Glenn's background that came in handy here and he spoke with confidence. He had American singer Johnny Desmond learn lyrics in German. There was none of that ugly *kraut*-business in the broadcasts. The phenomenal Beatles who came along later and organized their international efforts in Germany took pages from the Miller book. Getting an early hang on a foreign market, the Beatles sang their first songs in German, which delighted the original Hamburg audience. They recorded the German versions as well. If you haven't heard them, tune into any German station today; they're still top of the pops.

Glenn's broadcasts were to discourage faith in Adolf Hitler and his foolishness to extend the war, to play up the sacrifice of German soldiers and invite them to surrender, promising good treatment and an inevitable crushing defeat for the Nazis. Message in a word: Surrender! And You Win.

Second Lt. Don Haynes was far in the background during these days in Bedford. A tendency to aggrandize manifested itself when he was left on his own as straw boss of the band. When the City of Paris was conquered and jubilant throngs took the GI liberators to their hearts—literally to their bosoms, Haynes was not far from the action. He had taken up with a certain Lt. Col. Baessell, later termed by SHAEF personnel as a "drug and money" black marketer. They shared a deluxe apartment in Paris. With Morgan and his plane at the disposal of Baessell, Haynes had a free ride back and forth. Pilots who knew both officers have confirmed this to me in writing, just as Major May of the SHAEF Personnel office confirmed it in writing to Wilbur Wright in the 1970s (when Britian's Official Secrets Act lost its teeth) that Lt.Col. Baessell had actually been caught black-marketing, but the knowledgable personnel officer refrained from comment as to what happened to the erring officer. Baessell's untoward behavior prompted 28 references by Wright in Millergate (1990).

Haynes knew little if anything about Glenn's psywar programs. His was a band administrator's job, flying with the band and arranging details and keeping his volatile charges out of the MP's grasp. Whether he knew of his captain's (later major's) OSS flight coming up is questionable. Certainly none of the band members knew, as each was quizzed after the war and came up with blank stares of amazement. They knew of his "show for the Germans" but not the plans, rearing into being, to bring an "end to the war...in forty four." (It rhymed)

To understand Glenn's entry into a combat phase, it is vital to view SHAEF's preparation for the winter of 1944. General Omar N. Bradley, accepted as Ike's tactical genius, was now more interested in a quick peace, if possible, than in continuing the deadly slog through terrain like *Huertgen Forest*, and the unconscionable losses of the "Bridge Too Far." Bradley was called the "GI General" for his desire to save his men rather than expend them, a trait he shared with General Patton. In September 1944, ONB (Bradley was sometimes called by his initials, and Eisenhower by DDE) was presented with such an end-the-war plan (thru Ike) from top General George Marshall in Washington. The hush-hush deal was said to have been suggested by *Wehrmacht* generals who—as known from their past utterances—were ready to defy Hitler. These were not the SS generals personally avowed to the dictator but Junker generals of the professional army who saw the handwriting of defeat on the wall.

This cut-to-the-heart opportunity depended upon freedom lovers within Germany. In other words, a coordinated plan, secret until time of Departure, would smash from without and within. In fact, by autumn 1944 it was said that Berlin was merely a shell, with only foreign workers and government offices. All force was on the fronts (Eastern and Western) and the only true enemy to remain in

Germany was Hitler and his two SS armies. The idea was welcomed but doubted and put aside. Three American higher-ups did not put it aside: Allen Dulles in Switzerland, "Wild Bill" Donovan in Washington and Omar Bradley in Luxembourg City. They thought that Peace Now was a distinct possibility. Good Germans helping could assuage the failure of the July 20th Hitler assassination. It would revive Germany's pride and make it possible for a family of civilized nations at war's end. Above all, such a conceivable plan would save a few hundred thousand lives. Dulles redoubled his efforts in getting things going within Germany. Bradley set up a scheme which might lure the "baddie" SS Armies into Allied hands and then jump them. And a new kid on the block, William Casey, aged 31, a dynamite junior to "Wild Bill" Donovan, was put in charge of such an Army/ OSS operation. It was named "Operation Eclipse."

What was so attractive about Eclipse was a scheme bruited about by German General Speidel two years before in 1942. It proposed a get-together of enemy generals to finish off hostilities by joint action, arrest Hitler and declare Peace. Now Speidel was *Wehrmacht* Chief-of Staff of Group B Armies, Hdqrs. Krefeld, command point of the Western German front. He was close enough to the Allied front near Luxembourg to pick flowers. Secondly, his topper, a real general of the *Wehrmacht*, Gerd von Rundstedt, had long opposed Hitler by cautioning of "a war that could not be won." With Von Rundstedt Commander in Chief, as he was rumored to become (Hitler had no alternative to this brilliant man), the plotters were half way to working out a Peace plan already—it was said. Some hope for the idea filled the Pentagon. The idea was quasi-approved by the President, "so long as the Russians didn't find out."

Enter David Niven, knowledgeable of the in-and-out

business of spies.[4] Needed was a rendezvous for couriers to carry messages for both American and German generals. Luxembourg was well tamped down, and quiet. The front was hardly a front. One could fire a rifle into German territory, the city was that close to the lines. A thickly wooded area on the border had been hunting grounds for a Baron DeLannoy, his estate now deserted. On the hilltop was a castle, curiously the ancestral home of the Delanos, a family whose sons did remarkably well in America, one of whom now was President, Franklin Delano Roosevelt. The estate was splendidly isolated, perfect for a transit meeting point cutting through both ill-guarded fronts. Officer emissaries of U.S. and German generals began to exchange in the heart of the Ardennes, dagger point of the Bulge to come. A mistake by the Allies was realized too late. Someone had suggested enlisting junior German officers from a nearby POW camp for the runs back and forth. Reason: lack of German speakers among our own officer corps. A search for competent language officers in English began at POW camps. Volunteers—they would get special favors later on leaped at the opportunity. .

George Bailey, former director of Radio Liberty, Uncle Sam's piercer of the Iron Curtain by radio, is the author of The Germans (1974). I came to know George well because of his intense interest in the Glenn Miller effect on the war. I mention him at this time because of his knowledge of Operation Eclipse and some details he was able to furnish which General Bradley was unwilling to get into (after the war) when we met in Washington. Bailey recalled CBS correspondents at the time he was stationed in Paris, correspondents who knew from a trail of soldier recollections that Glenn had been imprisoned in a Pigalle bordello when the rest of the world was told he was dead.

This was my first indication of what had happened and George, close to the CIA, had an idea of why it had been covered up.

A most interesting sidebar to George's enthusiasm was his conjecture of how Glenn had changed since coming to England. At home in countless broadcasts he had been striving to make his music understood. Now, while reaction from troops was reminiscent—of girl friends and dates, of 78 RPM discs slung on the carpet, of family and friends, birthdays, high school loves, the "Apple Tree" and "Kalamazoo," his job now was toward the Germans—to make their innermost dreams light up, to think of living after the battles were gone. In a word—turn around those twisted minds on the other end of the hateful barrels. Yes, Glenn had changed. I thought so too. I think he had in mind the German democracy of today.

The Liberation of Paris emphasised the belief that we would win. If that is true, two generals should get credit: Omar Bradley on our side, Von Choltitz on the other. Hitler had ordered his occupying general to topple the City of Light—defend it in a fight to the death and destroy! Had Choltitz followed Hitler's orders, Paris might have looked like Berlin at war's end. Gone the great landmarks, the monuments, the tokens of history. Gone the superb art of centuries, all smoking on one vast desert of rubble.

General Omar N. Bradley had other ideas. With his closest friend, George S. Patton, they laid out an alternative to Ike. Bring Choltitz over to civility. Here was a golden chance of the war, to make "Paree" the symbol of inevitable Victory—a shout to be heard around the world. The Allied Command bought it. Choltitz listened. Troops were diverted from normal combat. Free French Army General LeClerc's fighting *Corps Francais* was brought up to participate not

only in the action, as they had, but in the glory. *La Gloire!*
Such a tenant of the French soul.

French and American divisions marched proudly down
the Champs Elysees and a throng the likes of which Paris had
never seen in its long and violent history roared welcome.
My own 28th Infantry Division was in the forefront.

"Paris Libre!" The shout galvanized London as well.
As fast as planes could get in the air, SHAEF and its 17,000
"deputies" came over. Ike claimed the Trianon Palace as his
General Staff Headquarters. The VIP hotel in the regained
capital was the George V. Other swank hotels; Meurice,
Ritz, Raphael, Lancaster, etc. filled with the multiplying
organizations.

With the decision that *divertissement á Paris* was
a historic stroke of genius, the feeling spread that the
Germans had given up. It would be only a matter of time
until they were hurled back into their "cabbage patches."
More good news—Radio Luxembourg was taken almost
intact. General Bradley moved his Tactical Headquarters to
Luxembourg City. Patton readied numerous mobile bridges
he had captured after Normandy to cross the Rhine. "Huns
on the Run" was the victory shout. Ike warned against such
runaway optimism, but his voice was faint against the din
set up in the U.S. and Great Britain.

Many of the Reich generals, including Number One,
Von Rundstedt, quietly joined the quest for Armistice.[18] The
"generals' deal" in Eclipse went ahead secretly and without
promise under the highest secret (Bigot) rating. President
Roosevelt "didn't want to know" and scornfully rejected
such a proposal in public. As if to emphasize his position
for "Unconditional Surrender," he let voices boil into the
political fracas of the 1944 elections. To satisfy the Hawks,
he authorized the Morgenthau Plan. He let his Treasury

Secretary Henry Morgenthau go on the air and boast, "We are going to level Germany to the ground, burn it up, and let anybody left be potato farmers." It was election rhetoric but bad news for our troops.

German will to stop fighting and surrender (helped in no small part by the Miller broadcasts) went into reverse. Kill us dead?! *Machen Sie uns Tod?!!* rebounded. Reaction came swift and angrily. Bad news for Allen Dulles's ears in Switzerland. The wily Dr. Goebbels urged with his high-pitched ferocity to millions of listeners (*Deutschlandsender*): "Now we knew the truth…. We know what is in store for us—if the Allies win. Our homes, our cities will be gone…. We are to plant and harvest potatoes on burned-out ground for hungry stomachs not our own." What seemed like a Sunday stroll to the cafes of *Kurfuerstendamm* in Berlin became rivers of bayonets. While agitator Morgenthau sat comfortably in Washington, Generals Patton and Bradley suffered. They had yet to cross the Rhine, much less the Siegfried fortifications. No greater mistake was ever made by a home-grown politico for the lives of American soldiers overseas. German soldiers ground their teeth, dug in. Radio Luxembourg's plan to stimulate an armistice wandered off course.

Filmmaker Leni Riefenstahl, who recorded those astounding Nazi show fests at Nuremberg, made fearful note of this Morgenthau Plan in her memoirs, <u>Leni Riefenstahl a Memoir</u> (1995). "We were all very worried about the Morgenthau Plan, especially the punishments the Germans could expect after the war. We were all pretty famished. I weighed about one hundred pounds." To die of starvation was Leni's fear of Allied retribution.

What kind of reaction would we face now in Germany? Could an underground be depended upon? It became painfully clear that some new guarantee was needed. But there is no guarantee in war. Those German generals ought to be taken up on their offer—to hell with the Russians, some said. "The only enemies are Hitler's two SS Panzer armies under Hitler's direct orders. Can't they be lured into our lines, surrounded? And trampled?" The pros and cons provided no ready answer. The capture of Radio Lux, half of the Nazi's dominant network system, proved a saver. Its power over enemy listenership gave reason to proceed, come what may, with Eclipse. And Bradley had it in his hands.

It must be strange to 21st century readers to recognize the crucial role of radio during World War Two. Hitler, early in the 1930s, set the stage. He set about making radio the most formidable means of communication between him and the *Volk*. Josef Goebbels followed his cue. And our two radio giants, David Sarnoff, head of NBC and Bill Paley, top executive of CBS, were sworn into uniform directly under Eisenhower. World War Two was a "front line radio war." (This was Manvell-Frankel's description in their splendid treatise <u>Dr. Goebbels</u> (1960).) But what-to-do now was equally enigmatic in Washington as Versailles, Berne and Luxembourg. The powers that be were momentarily aimless.

For a short span in the beleaguered history of World War Two, OSS Chief Casey, 31, was in charge of a million or so troops, Dulles, head spy who didn't even have a map on his office wall in Berne, was running the front. The army had a word for it: SNAFU. Situation Normal All Fouled Up. (Polite Meaning). "Get on with it," was the stern word from General Marshall, Ike's boss. He had another war to fight as well, across the Pacific. (From Persico's and Casey's books). But now, there was a glimmer of hope.

Those German officers who had surrendered or been captured were reporting good words from the *Wehrmacht's* Krefeld Headquarters. The secret plan seemed to be going ahead smoothly. The courier system devised to run back and forth, to meet at the FDR ancestral barony, then get past ill-guarded lines on both sides, was working smoother than expected. Bradley-Dulles-Donovan were encouraged.

Germany's best general, Von Rundstedt, was now in top place. So was General Speidel, Chief of the Group B Armies. Here, from Spiedel's Memoirs (1950) post-war: "Generals Rommel, Stuelpnegal and Von Rundstedt had agreed on a plan for armistice negotiations with Eisenhower and Montgomery. The plan would offer to evacuate German occupied areas in the west and withdraw all German forces behind the Siegfried Line in return for a cessation of bombing and the beginning of peace negotiations. Allied radio stations would explain to the German people the military and political situation and the crimes of their leaders...."

Ergo, who best to explain to the German people in their language? A voice they knew and could trust and could recognize? The answer was yet to come.

General Speidel's Memoirs continued: "On the Russian front fighting would continue as necessary to hold a reduced front along the Vistula, the Carpathians and down to the mouth of the Danube. Hitler would be arrested and tried and a new government would be formed."

Pipe-smoking, professorial Allen Dulles, FDR's spymaster into Germany from his post in Berne, also remembered these details. His chief undercover man in Berlin was Hans Bernd Gisevius who had firefighters and police under his rebelling wing, numbering 2,000. They were ready to assist any parachutists landing in the Berlin region, neutralize the

SS protecting the Hitler and Goebbels camps, and free the estimated one million forced laborers in the city's environs. Berlin, the capital, was vulnerable to Allied conquest to a flagrant extent, almost beyond imagination. Gisevius proposed: "Three Allied parachute divisions landing in the Berlin area, success to be made possible with the help of our sources here, and certain defecting local commanders."

Allen Dulles sent this information on to Washington with the added recommendation of Gisevius' trustworthiness, plus these comments:

"This same opposition group is reported to feel that the War has been lost, and that the last hope of preventing the spread of Communism in Germany is the occupation of as large a section of Europe as is possible by the Americans and the British, and that helping our armed forces enter Germany before the fall of the East (Soviet) Front is the only possible means of accomplishing this." The Secret War Against Hitler (1988), William J. Casey.

The sticking point was which of the Nazi army's General Staff would go along? It boiled down to one fact: the generals on Germany's side anxious to end the war quickly were Regular Army generals, Junkers, professionals. Opposite: the diehard SS generals who would follow Hitler's orders to the death of all their men.

Eisenhower's desire was to trick the enemy to make a modest attack somewhere along this fluid autumnal line-of-battle—"Out into the open where we can get at 'em." (News published in Britain and America.) Omar Bradley came up with his decoy, a simple enough plan—lure the SS divisions into a "counter-offensive," (by order of Von Rundstedt) get them moving forward, and vulnerable, surround them on our side and close the gap, ever tightening the noose. If the remaining "regulars" were on the other side of the front, they could be summoned by Von Rundstedt to quell any public opposition, and arrest Hitler. That was the generals' deal if they wanted Peace Now.

What would the Soviets do? That was the Germans' worry. There was in the Ardennes a rest area for tired troops, a gap of 60 to 80 kilometers wide with about one soldier to every three hundred yards to protect it. Also, this was the area thru which the Nazi army of 1940 had poured—conquering France and the lowlands. Best place for a lure? The negatives were plentiful—unfriendly mountain roads, soggy and ill-networked, an illogical ground for tank-led offensives. But the decoy could be just that, supposedly unguarded, with Patton's and Hodges' Armies alert, ready to jump for the kill.

But could Gisevius and another Berlin spy, Kolbe, be trusted? Dulles was sure they could be. Still, for such an overpowering operation on which a civilization might depend, one had to be sure. Washington was cautious. Laborious checks again. Leading U.S. spy historian Joseph Persico writes in Piercing the Reich (1979): "The conspiracy leaders in Berlin had accepted, as soon as Hitler was killed, they would have to surrender unconditionally to the Russians as well as the Allies. Though Gisevius was on Himmler's wanted list, he still had powerful protectors, among them Count Wolf Heinrich von Helldorf, the Berlin Police Chief, and Arthur Nebe, Chief of the Reich Detective Service, both co-conspirators."

Persico added: "Hans Gisevius was one of a rapidly vanishing species in Germany, a plotter who—at least for the moment—still lived."

Those who want to read more about Operation Eclipse may get Casey's own view in The Secret War Against Hitler (1989). In the book he let one secret out of the bag he probably wished he hadn't. He admitted that he "knew well" the Second-in-Command of Britain's Secret Service (which funneled all intelligence secrets)—a fellow by name of Kim Philby. Later Philby proved to be a spy who fled to Russia. At the same moment, an intimate friend of the Soviet leadership was sitting at Roosevelt's side, Alger Hiss. Both were later exposed as Soviet tools. Thus, we can see that most messages that passed in the realm of super-highly classified were known by the Red Army potentate. Stalin had access to all but not Ultra and Bigot. He must have been pleased at the Battle of the Bulge, to find all three of his adversaries (Britain, U.S. and Germany) horn-locked in a battle over territory he coveted and intended to occupy.

Operation Eclipse was not yet secure when the 1944 elections put Roosevelt back in office. It might have slipped into oblivion had not a physically-agile and mental giant stepped into Paris two days after the city's liberation, leading a cordon of physicists and an armed guard. Samuel Goudsmit, Dutch-American, small of stature as Alan Ladd and as handsome, had a mandate from FDR and the Pentagon.

The Nazis were easily at least two years ahead of the Allies in the development of atomic energy to make a bomb. At least in the early 1940s, this was a proven fact. What now? Adolf Hitler in recent speeches had been bragging about, "a new and awesome secret weapon to which there was no retaliation." Goudsmit was FDR-directed, under strict military control, to find the Nazi bomb, if it existed, and get the Air Corps to destroy it. This was to be done immediately, even at risk, as Nazis now had means to strike New York and Washington in proximity, etc. The Nazi submarine force was already trolling America's east coast, close enough to observe traffic lights and hear horns blowing. Goudsmit personally was charged with this overriding mission (approved by Manhattan Project) because of his undoubted patriotism, his brilliance as associate to Einstein, Fermi, and other leading atomic scientists, but mainly because he had been a close friend of Werner Heisenberg, Germany's leading physicist. He knew his haunts, could recognize him. Heisenberg, pre-war, had been offered scientific haven at the University of Michigan, approved by our government, but he had chosen to refuse, preferring to work in his native Germany. Thus he was now, willing or not, a subject of Hitler. Goudsmit, member of the "atomic genius club" had a better chance than any to locate Heisenberg and put him out of commission. Undeniable fact–wherever was Werner Heisenberg, in or out of Germany, was the "feared Nazi bomb"—life or death for millions.

The Dutch-American took up Paris residence at the fancy Hotel Prince de Galle, using the back entrance, *Number 12, rue Quantin Beauchart.* Washington had given him three months to locate the awesome weapon and to find Heisenberg. That was from August to November. Just on time, following numerous leads through clues known only to high level physicists, Goudsmit stated flatly that there was no German atomic bomb. He had in hand Heisenberg to prove it. He wasn't believed. Nor was Heisenberg, himself, believed to be telling the truth. What Goudsmit had found, pictures showed, was a half-built atomic reactor. The Dutch American produced Heisenberg's entire team of all the great German physicists. He still wasn't believed.

Eclipse got the final signal to go. It was now up to the generals.[26]

Hitler knew it all. His plan to combat the pending inner-revolution was to bring 25 divisions on line and crush the

Allies through the Ardennes, a plan he called Autumn Mist, possibly because he needed lots of mists to keep movements secret. And he further kept them secret by changing dates of attack. Major Miller's unexpected orders to Ike's palace, for the second time, arrived when he was in Bedfordshire to lead the band in a farewell tribute to the people of Bedford. By a curious "coincidence," printed in The Bedfordshire News, November 15, 1944, exactly one month before the ill-fated "accident." "He left the concert early," wrote The News, "taking a small plane, a single-engine Norseman, EC-64, piloted by Flight Officer W.O. John Morgan." Was this the germ of the concept describing Miller's later disappearance?

Morgan was said to be flying to Paris but actually his destination was Bovington Airfield, departure point of the three-a-day service to France, a corridor patrolled by P-51 fighters across the Channel. Glenn's presence in Bovington on that November 15th day was established and proven by a photograph. He flew to Paris only via Bovington, and from there took the regularly scheduled, guarded flights over. All of his trips to France were from Bovington, never Twinwood.

Bovington was a huge military field, the UK air connection to France. Manifests were prepared at Hotel Langham, destroyed after a safe landing. No voice paging was permitted. If you weren't in your assigned seat by takeoff, you lost the flight. Space was precious. There were long waiting lists. To be absent was disobedience of a SHAEF order. The witnesses that saw Glenn on the November 15 flight were a BBC technician aboard and an AAC pilot. (Interviewed by Wilbur Wright.) Bovington was decommissioned after the war.

It is documented by Robert Payne in <u>The Life and</u>

Death of Adolf Hitler (1973) that the "Armistice" date was altered several times. Hitler changed his mind repeatedly for what Von Runstedt called Little Slam and what Bradley called "a counter-attack." As it turned out in the final fatal thrust, it was Grand Slam, comprising four armies instead of just the SS Panzers the deal called for. Despite his two trips over to get into the Plan, Glenn knew little more than bare bones. He knew he would be flown to Paris for instructions, then guided through a lowered flak curtain to Group B Headquarters near Krefeld, and placed under protection of General Von Rundstedt. At that exact moment Operation Eclipse would begin. As soon as the advancing SS Panzers Divisions had been cut off by Patton's and Hodges' armies, the Armistice would be sounded. That was Glenn's job. He would be flown to Berlin where the undercover insurgents would have taken over the radio facilities. He would have with him a box of recordings, his own music, messages recorded from Ike, plus repetitious instructions and warnings to Germans. Simple if it worked. This system had been used throughout the war when the Nazis took over country after country. So it should work in reverse. Radio instructions were necessary to calm the public, reduce chances of resistance, make the operation a success. Both Ike and Von Rundstedt were addicts to the game of bridge. Hence, some bridge words were chosen which would speak volumes. Little Slam was a light attack, Grand Slam meant full force. And there were other terms more familiar to Glenn. In his own flanking maneuver, Odin 7/13 was the code standing for Glenn Miller, the alphabetic count of his initials. Odin meant God of Flight in archaic Nordic legend.

Much of this information was not collected until the 1990s when email contact was made with Bulge survivors on the German side, and with Goebbels' secret diaries, untranslated, kept in Archives at the University of Trier. They proved the premise of duplicity without question. Goebbels referred to these "Eisenhower messengers," captured officers of lower rank, who almost uniformly surrendered once they reached their own lines, and were led to continue the Dirty Tricks going back and forth. While true in most cases, it was not in all. Those who had opted to help us were suspect from then on, and no doubt "sent to the Russian front." Deceit continued to be the keyword which was to undermine Operation Eclipse.

Meanwhile, the musicians in Bedfordshire were preparing for their own move to Paris. What with dancing, drinking and the overtures of local girls, Lt. Don Haynes became a star. His band managing was good, much to Glenn's satisfaction, but The Boss was not around Bedford to keep an eye out for misbehavior. Glenn's and Don's wives back home were best-of-friends, both of impeccable morals. If Glenn had discovered Don's cheating, it would have been the end of an amicable relationship.

At his hotel home in London, the Mount Royal, Glenn prepared himself as best he could for his role in Eclipse. His was a sidebar operation, Odin-7/13, but vital to the whole operation. He certainly knew the overriding value of Odin 7/13. The thrill of working out from *Deutschland-Sender* in Berlin in partnership with Marlene Dietrich at Radio Luxembourg excited him no end. This was why he had volunteered. He knew that their two voices—calm and dispassionate for they were saving lives—would amount to exactly what he had offered to The General, "Wild Bill" Donovan. Some kind of a hero he would be... and yes, he would experience combat.

Samuel Goudsmit's mission (Alsos) had achieved success,

but success with a frightening shadow about to unfold. Goudsmit had traced the enemy's nuclear organization through its Paris, Strasbourg, and Dutch branches to discover the *Kernphysik* (atomic physics) sites were in two locations, both behind the German lines. One was near Berlin, the other in Bavaria, at a hamlet called Hechingen. The latter was the test site for a planned minor explosion. Goudsmit and his physicists also discovered why his one time friend Heisenberg had not succeeded with a German atomic bomb. Work had been impeded by Hitler on the rationale that "Einstein and his Jews had propounded propaganda." Hitler's "awesome new weapons" turned out to be the V-I and V-II, the missiles which struck London. Although Eisenhower transmitted Goudsmit's findings to Washington, they were not accepted. The awesomely bright and handsome Dutch-American, miffed at his honesty and loyalty being questioned, put it all in a book, saved it for post-war. Almost immediately after publication it was taken off the lists. Not until a new edition of <u>ALSOS</u> (1983) appeared long after his death was the truth about the German A-Bomb known. ALSOS first published 1946 by American Institute fo Physics. Book withdrawn shortly after publication. There were two more attempts to publish prior to the 1983 edition of ALSOS which is considered by critics to be objective.

It can be surmised that in his Paris trips, Glenn secretly visited the Supreme Commander at his villa, a few miles from the Trianon Palace, a magnificent site overlooking the Seine valley. He was certainly at the Trianon itself. He never commented, not even to his pal Brod, about being there. Yet it is obvious he would have visited the villa, for secrecy if nothing else. In its remote location, the chateau at *32 rue Alexandre* would appear impregnable. A select company of riflemen with machine guns at ready would surround the U-shaped road clustering the house. The three-storied stone-walled villa had one door on the street. General Marshall had overnighted there. And Churchill. It had to be safe.[17, 23] The guards knew famous Glenn. Who didn't?

Was Samuel Goudsmit correct in his assumption that we had nothing to fear from a German A-bomb? Strangely enough, we had nothing to fear—as FDR was so classically quoted as saying—but fear itself.

Glenn must have had a premonition of something not just right. His statements of "going home a hero" and "wanting to see combat" were widely reported and quoted after the war. They contradicted his underlying worries. I believe his boasts were for public effect. A few days before his derring-do to help end the war, he went to the studio and recorded a Christmas message for Helen. I have to thank Ed Polic and Sid Robinson for preserving the last scrap of Glenn Miller's words—their authenticity is beyond doubt:

"Hello, Helen dear. Merry Christmas. I beat you to the punch on that one. You don't get a chance to answer. I'm following a pretty tough routine because Don and Paul were just here and made records to send to Joy and Polly and they had theirs all written out, but I thought I'd rather just sit down and talk a little while. Course, you can't answer but I can imagine what the answer'd be. Don't know when we're gonna get home. Looks like it's gonna be quite a little while yet, but if this makes Christmas any better for you then that'll be such a great pleasure for me.

"Sure dyin' to see Steve. Got the pictures. He sure has grown. Great little guy. Ah. Tell him Merry Christmas for me. And Jonnie Dee, course she won't understand but I'm tickled to death that she's there and I'm dyin' to see the pictures and get letters from you tellin' me about her. Ah,

Paul and Don send their greetings, and ah, oh, there's not an awful lot to say when you're so far away on Christmas, you know. Well, this is a couple of 'em that we've missed together, the next few will make up for all the time that we've wasted and we'll have our family with us, really have a wonderful…. Ah, a million sweet kisses and god bless you and keep you and the kids 'til we come home. Merry Christmas, dear."

The Glenn Miller puzzle was at hand. But we don't have to be satisfied with CIA Miles Copeland's enigmatic posture: "Miller was on his way to some kind of engagement. He was taking a plane from some unknown point to an equally mysterious destination." (Official CIA Files of Miles Copeland.)

We have learned after years of search the location of this "unknown point." We learned it from Gen. Maxwell Taylor's own pilot in London and from Joan Heath at Buc Field in Versailles. We now know the "mysterious destination"—*Fichtenhain Airport* near Krefeld, Ruhr; thence to *Tempelhof Flughafen* in Berlin, once Gen. Von Rundstedt had conceded a condition of Armistice, and Von Helldorf's underground police had secured powerful *Deutschlandsender* with the 101st Division and 82nd Division paradroppers in Operation Eclipse. Glenn's risk was commendable in my estimation to end the reign of the most hated despot of the 20th Century. Medals and a Memorial at Arlington testify to Glenn Miller's valor in <u>combat</u>. The U.S. government has finally conceded his place in history as a combat hero. But it is not enough.

Glenn's initial assignment to a conquered Berlin to speak to a defeated German nation was not his only assignment. He was carrying a personal message to be delivered to General Walter Dornberger, who undergrounders in Berlin (known as Black Orchestra) would know where to find.. The message to be relayed personally was from General George C. Marshall in Washington, and was of such extraordinarily private nature, it had to be borne by an individual of trust, one the Regular Army Dornberger could value. Of course Glenn fit the bill. The offer proposed that Dornberger's unit of rocket scientists, in entirety, including the genius Wernher Von Braun and all their families, slip away secretly from Peenemuende and all entangling Nazi controls. They should make way to the American front and surrender. If not done forthwith, the group stood to be captured by the oncoming Red Army, about a 100 kilometers away and advancing. Marshall promised sanctuary if the scientists surrendered to the U.S., and gave his word, even though the action broke immigration and deNazification laws. Thus, whoever presented the idea general-to-general had to be considered a speaker for the top U.S. Defense Chief in America. Miller, an icon in Germany, handy to Eisenhower could fill that bill. It would be easy for Dornberger to spurn a less personal offer which would smack of an entrapment or a plan to thwart V-1's and V-2's causing so much damage to Britain. Marshall knew the scientists had nothing to do with the actual firings of the destructive missiles. That was a Nazi function. Marshall respected Dornberger as a World War One officer of repute. And Marshall knew that the thinkers and designers of these long-range ballistic missiles adapted to combat had little choice. It was fall to the Russians for them, or come aboard. So, Glenn Miller had good reason for worries about getting to Dornberger as he prepared for his trip. This was a mighty, earth-shaking assignment..

    This was one general-to-general deal which worked and was successful. We know now from dozens of web sites on the Internet, information passing freely that has come to light, that it worked, almost beyond expectation. For the most part it was provided by Marshall himself or by his numerous biographers. On the other side, there are Dornberger's diaries and numerous studies by those who have looked into his amazing escape with Von Braun and 500 of the scientific family, including wives and children. They trekked across the breadth of Nazi-held Europe from the Baltic to Austria, harassed at every turn, threatened with Concentration Camps, even mass murder.

The following jotted extracts from Marshall's papers and diaries provide an unexpected new look at the busy, busy general running two wars—East and West. He was the only top-flight U.S. official who had the presience to lure Germany's ballistic missile designers away out of pending Soviet clutches and into U.S. hands.

NOTES FROM DIARIES OF GEN. GEORGE C. MARSHALL AND BIOGRAPHIES:
- May 1943. A "black shadow" observed by Allied photography over Peenemuende, a test site on the Baltic Sea. See British report: "An airplane without a cockpit." (Actual language of observation)
- May-Dec 1943. Studied organization of German origin to build space vehicles. Begun 1930. Move from Kummersdorf (Berlin) to Peenemuende (Baltic) 1936. Command by General Walter Dornberger, WWI officer of mettle and distinction. Varying success. Little progress in beginning. Addition to staff Wernher Von Braun in 1932 spelled longer projectile flights.. From Peenemuende, 200 KM surveillance over water possible within German territory.

So such mileage probably feasible. Danger England.

Army exerts control of scientists with little Nazi interest. British reluctant to discuss or share information.

- Aug 16, 1943. RAF Operation Hydra. 500 Heavy Bombers attack Peenemuende. Strike mostly ineffective as firing sites mobile. In and out of shelters, exposed momentarily. Noted: Building of bomb-proof caverns with Nazi labor indicates missiles intended military use.

- Dec 29, 1943. Have demanded complete intelligence Peenemuende from Sir John Dill. Not forthcoming. Secretary of War Stimson asks "full information" from Rocket and Test Site Peenemuende. British reluctant share knowledge.

- Jan-Jun 1944. Some British Intelligence made available. Need study increasing capability Space rockets. Mileage impossible estimate due to Von Braun closed-circuit TV system. Difficult not to be alarmed over German progression of missile as weapons More and more large sites observed by photography. Some 25 foot walls with 1000 feet cavern space for advancing projectile site. Can expect the worst.

- Jul-Dec 1944. V-1 and V-2 rockets rain on England by hundreds then thousands. No defense solution. American cities now faced with possible naval launches. Solution: Get scientists out of Germany. Here. Regardless risk. To hell with how.

- Dec 1944. Operation Eclipse to be in effect. End war possibility. Send message through to Dornberger. He can escape to us. Soviets aiming on them as priority. Message greatest importance. Eisenhower will use surest method delivery once Armistice holds.

END OF CHRONOLOGY

Ike's method of delivery by Glenn Miller failed, as did the planned war's end, with the total disruption of Eclipse by Hitler's Autumn Mist. Still, the message must go forward, Marshall insisted, even as Rhine is crossed and Germany is invaded and the war boils to its sure end.. Ike assigns Col. David Niven to carry the word to Dornberger, not failing to mention it was Miller carrying the general-to-general offer before he was murdered. Of course we know from history that Niven got through. It's become history as Marshall, Dornberger and Von Braun tell it. Niven could not have advertised his feat more clearly than by absenting himself from SHAEF at the same time for eight days with no later explanation, and to totally avoid mentioning the name Glenn Miller, refusing ever to discuss him and leaving him out completely of his movie books and public appearances. Glenn was his friend. That's BIGOT secret.[4]

Dornberger wrote in his diary when the Nazis discovered his plans to escape the V-1 and V-2 barrage at Peenemuende: "I had to endure a whole series of humiliations, a chaotic flood of ignorant, contradictory, irreconcilable orders from that black shirt, SS Kammler. who Himmler appointed to supervise us. Kammler was neither a soldier nor a statesman." But Dornberger outwitted him, pretending to go along when Kammler said he was arresting them, delivering them to the new RSHA center in Oberammergau, SS Headquarters in the Bavaria Alps, for sentence and disposition.

Wernher Von Braun and the associates were the brains Marshall wanted, but he needed a general, Dornberger, to get them out. He got them all, which resulted in "Operation Paperclip," the move to America. Thus dawned America's space age.

CHAPTER **4**

Getting a Hand on Slippery Eclipse

No secret can be kept forever—wise men back to the Greeks have postulated, "Secrets… neither of universe nor of man can be kept." Thus, while the insinuating, faceless form of "Operation Eclipse" worked its way to realization, the heavy clamp of secrecy groaned and became not-so-secret. In fact, one wonders today—how could this gamble which cost 80,090 U.S. casualties be swept under the carpet with such guile and aplomb?

Yorkshire-born Charles Whiting, 19, was a stripling parachutist with the 52nd Lowland Division. On the eve of the breakthrough of Hitler's hordes which he terms "American-European Pearl Harbor," he awaited orders for his unit to drop on Berlin. Did he know of Eclipse? Know it?— he was in the middle of it. Whiting went on to become the most knowledgeable journalist and historian of the Greatest Land Battle of the War in any language. Of 51 books to his credit, more than a dozen are on The Bulge. He was selected as Technical Supervisor for the great TV series, *Band of*

Brothers. He gracefully joined my search to find out what happened to Glenn Miller.

Whiting never landed in Berlin. Nor did Uncle Sam's 101st Airborne or follow-up U.S. 82nd Airborne. All were due. But they never took off. Eclipse went on the wrong road and crashed. Naturally Whiting knew of the operation about to enfold him. And he learned of Dirty Tricks which fouled it. Some of Whiting's credits are noteworthy. He covered the Nazi surrender at *Rheims* on May 7, 1945, then went on to report the Nuremberg trials. He interviewed *Wehrmacht* General Jodl, Col. Otto Skorzeny and others of the evil hierarchy who took the war six months longer to die than it should have. In a personal note to me, he wrote longhand: "I know about Operation Eclipse. The Nazis had it well in advance of it being put into operation. Jodl told me. General Gavin (82nd Airborne) told me there was a spy at Ike's Headquarters. I think there were more."

Secrecy—that was the problem in a SHAEF overstuffed with 17,000 "hangers-on." Bradley complained about this to me post-war. The top-notch Bigot classification, which he revealed to the world in <u>A Soldier's Story</u> (1978), still wasn't high enough. There was "Ears Only"—coded wire transmissions which were voiced without recording. These predominated during Eclipse, unfortunately leaving no record.

Charles Whiting in his book <u>The Spymasters</u> (1976) tells how this unfortunately bloody chapter of war started, and how news of it was so peremptorily squashed.

"On 16 December, 1944, the massive bombardment which began at 5:45 a.m. on the "ghost front" was followed by an attack launched by three German armies, totaling half-a-million men. This revealed to General Sibert, Bradley's head of Intelligence in Luxembourg City, just how badly he had been fooled. While the OSS and SOE had been toying with their incredible schemes to bring the war to a speedy end, their men in the field had suffered an incredible defeat. Why was it that the two surviving copies of the highly-classified "Top Secret" intelligence digests, which Eisenhower's Supreme Headquarters prepared regularly for distribution to its subordinate army groups, were destroyed after the war "for security reasons," as general Sir Kenneth Strong, Eisenhower's Chief-of-Intelligence maintains?

First indications of a cover-up. Now let's look at the guts of "Eclipse" as it developed from German General Speidel's Valkyrie of 1942. The Allied coordination included: Berlin airdrops and massive assistance from the German underground, guaranteed by Allen Dulles in Switzerland. All of this was never made public in detail to establish accountability. Add to this Ike's postwar admonition to the War Department about wiping out details of the Ardennes disaster. Make no mistake about it. Ike was The Boss in Europe in 1945—and in Washington! Hadn't he won the war?

Students of history and professors alike can doff a hat to Charles Whiting for finding the greenest peas in the soup of what happened to accountability at the Bulge, and also a tip which gave away the German secret of possessing Heavy Water, the essential component for an atomic bomb. He uncovered this story which gave the Allies a start in winning the nuclear race. Here's history back in the early Forties. Scene: Germany's Rhine (Rhein) River, on the southwest bank of the Ruhr complex. As Whiting tells it:

"*Un ouvrier*—A French worker—swimming across the Rhine from the north, climbed out, encountered by chance a passing person, asked for dry clothes. The worker had come all the way from Norway where he had hefted huge casks of water from Ryukan to the island of Peenemuende in the Baltic Sea. This was obviously an unimportant incident, yet it reached the ears of an OSS operative embedded with the populace. Somebody looked up Ryukan which turned out to be the biggest hydro-electric concentration in all of Europe. What was going on there? Hauling casks of water when there was water all over the place? Scientist Dr. Stanley P. Lovell, who was in on the Manhattan Project, went to see Gen. "Wild Bill" Donovan who at about this time was enlisting Captain Glenn Miller into OWI/OSS services. "Remember what Hitler threatened?" Lovell reminded Donovan. "We are perfecting a weapon to which there is no answer," he said. The deduction was that the barreled contents could only be heavy water, essential for the construction of an atomic bomb. Such proved to be the case. The Nazi's source of heavy water was eliminated."

That's how a French worker, asking for dry clothes, did his bit to win both wars—thanks to Charles Whiting's reporting diligence.

For the contents of Operation Eclipse we are indebted to many. William Casey, whose mandate it was, coordinated with Sir Stewart Menzies, head of SIS (Secret Intelligence Service of Great Britain). In Casey's book, Eclipse turned out to be plotted by the Brits as well as Americans, and proof gathered since verifies this point. Major Miller's secret flight to Krefeld was coordinated by RAF Croydon, as the reprinted wires here evince.[1] In The Secret War Against Hitler (1989), Casey wrote: "We had five captured generals ready to turn tail." Then he implicated the British in the failed quest. "Neither Bradley's nor Montgomery's headquarters had any hard intelligence pointing to German intentions of attacking the Ardennes." This minor point is extremely interesting given that the Brits laced into Bradley for Eclipse's waterloo, which had not a little to do with their demand during the Bulge agony for Montgomery to take over all American forces and send Bradley home. It was a close shave. Bradley threatened to tell all, which was plenty, if he went home. He was pretty safe, and he knew it. He stayed, fortunate for the crossings of the Rhine and end result on the Elbe.

As recently as 2004, Zbigniew Brzezinski, a U.S. anchor of intelligence, referred on TV appearances with Wolf Blitzer (CNN) and Bob Edwards (NPR) to Casey's "generals." On nationwide broadcasts, Brzezinski pointed out that the Nazi generals proposal in 1943-4 to overthrow Hitler was "similar to the effort made by the Pentagon and certain Iraqi generals to eliminate Saddam Hussein."

Author Casey with hindsight could afford to be bitter that the Plan he was running went sour. He admittedly didn't know of Hitler's treacherous double-cross, named Autumn Mist which sprung a surprise on well-intended Eclipse. Wrote Casey in his memoirs: "In September, 1944, the war was all but won. We believed the end was near. Back in Washington, Gen. Marshall was urging Eisenhower to use this immensely powerful force (German underground after the failed July 20th Hitler assassination attempt) plus our own airborne in one great operation to finish the war in 1944. If Eisenhower had only decided one way or the other, the war could have ended six months before it did."

William Casey's blame on Ike is not entirely deserved. Of all persons, Kay Summersby, Ike's driver-cum-persona, defended him. That is to say: no-one knew Ike better than she. Writing in her second book on their relationship "Past Forgetting" (1977), she made the blunt point, "The general is on a tight leash. He is not his own master. He is always surrounded by political people who practically dictate his every move." Miss Summersby's bitter barb could well have been spiteful. Still, with masses of people convinced the war was as good as over, US politicos wanted it over. These were mostly Republicans luring Ike to head up their ticket after Peace was signed. General Patton had no qualms in joking about this, much to Ike's discomfort.

The Ike-Patton relationship has always presented debated overtones. They countenanced one another, but there was no friendship and a good deal of envy. I picked up some of this discord from my friend General Bradley who was always Patton's champion. In pre-war, George vastly outranked Ike; in fact, Ike once requested, in writing, a job on Patton's staff in Hawaii. So the tables turned. Ike was a smiler; George was a doer. As it turned out for victory, both got their jobs well done. But why wasn't Patton buried at Arlington? Why was his body left under a cross in Luxembourg? General Patton's disagreements with his chief Eisenhower over strategy, discipline and supply, are not the subject of this book. My sympathies when they erupted were almost always with Patton because of his close friendship with my boss, General Bradley. Little known by the U.S. and British public, revealed in Butcher's <u>My Three Years with Eisenhower</u> (1946), is Bradley's Battle of the Bulge account wherein Patton offered to resign with Bradley, go home and tell the public what was really transpiring in the field.

There's an old army expression: "Rank Has Its Privilege… and it's often Rank." The "Should We Trust Von Rundstedt" axiom was not Ike's, nor Bradley's or Donovan's to decide, but was an ever-confusing wrestle between Marshall and Roosevelt. The General of All U.S. Armies in Washington keened by the Nazi atomic threat, wanted Europe out of the way, to concentrate on Japan. FDR was sweating out the Teheran Conference and Stalin with its "unconditional" surrender premise, and there was the fretful policy for post-war Germany—"the potato patch debacle." Marshall was immersed as well, in something he was to become world famous for, aid packages for Europe, eventually to be known far-and-wide as the Marshall Plan.

One of the most respected of World War Two historians to cover Eclipe afterwards is Joseph Persico <u>Penetrating the Reich</u> (1979). Here he details Operation Eclipse unfolding:

"Fritz Kolbe (a spy known as George Wood) led an underground group, the *Reichsbanner*, a veterans' organization of Social Democrats in Berlin, who stood ready to help the Allies take over Berlin and beat the Russians to it. The offer was made to Dulles and was guaranteed to:

- Provide site maps for U.S. paratroopers for safe drop landings.
- Provide a cadre of scouts and guides to avoid Nazi defenses in Berlin.
- Provide a temporary headquarters at 28 Unter den Linden (belonging to Herr Bauer of the group.)"

The Bauer item of a "hiding place," if need be, was confirmed years later in a talk to me by one of the Social Democrat group. It was to be Glenn's safe house until our paratroopers had secured *Deutschlandsender*, Germany's multi-transmitter center for Reich broadcasts.

Persico concludes and fails to hide his disdain: "In failing to exploit the anti-Nazism which Gisevius and his co-conspirators represented, the Allies may have let slip the best hope for an earlier ending of the war."

Allen Dulles backed the intercession until it became too late. As A.C. Brown's <u>Wild Bill Donovan</u> (1984) describes: "Dulles sent this proposal by the conspirators to Washington with comment, 'The Black Orchestra', self-adopted tag of the Berlin underground, is ready to help our armed forces get into Germany under the condition that we agree to allow them to hold the Eastern Front." Almost in desperation, he repeated a nine-general agreement of May 13, 1944 which even provided the "how to." There was the three division jump on Berlin with underground help, simultaneous amphibious landings on the Bremen/Hamburg coast, and the isolation of Berchtesgaden (Hitler's abode in Bavaria). Quite apparently, everything waited on the generals' deal, Little Slam or Grand Slam.

And then it was all too late.

Professor E.H. Cookridge, ranked with Trevor-Roper as one of the distinguished chroniclers of World War Two, comments cryptically, Gehlen, Spy of the Century (1972): "Captured from an American officer toward the end of the Ardennes battle—a document containing an outline for Operation Eclipse." This was certainly the coup fatale—that the Nazis knew it all, down to the last detail, including Odin 7/13 Glenn Miller.

One final comment on the fate of Operation Eclipse centers on one man who claimed it could have worked. This erstwhile enemy, who came to our side after the war, mocked the Eclipse failure as "Donovan's War." He was Col. Otto Skorzeny, an enigmatic soldier-of-fortune who considered himself "Wild Bill's" opposite, and, so convinced accusers at the Nuremberg trials. But for his services being needed by the OSS—which turned a blind eye to his crimes—he might have been hung. He wasn't put to the rope as the Soviets were pressing. He was aided in "escape" from his cell (OSS connections) and was off to Cairo to abet U.S. fortunes vis-à-vis Nasser. Skorzeny had rescued Mussolini off the Gran Sasso Italian mountain range, using a decoy (a familiar face) to get him past guarding soldiers. Eisenhower decried him as "the most dangerous man in Europe," My Three Years with Eisenhower (1946).

Four out of five Americans I've talked to have never heard of Eisenhower hiding from Skorzeny killers out to assassinate him. Yet they've heard of a rampaging soldier dressed as a GI dropped behind our lines. Reason: the latter was advertised; the former was not. [see Chapter 5]

Eventually Skorzeny wound up as a business man in Madrid after the CIA discontinued his hire in Egypt and Argentina. I met him there in Madrid in the early '70s. It was at a lunch cooked by Hitler's ex-chef, Papa Horcher. Of course, everybody knows that many Germans fled to Spain post war and took up residence. In Spain, we talked about his book, Special Memoirs (1957), published only in Britain, because he mentioned his attempted coup on the young Shah while I was there in Teheran (1943). Two years earlier the young Shah had assumed the throne (September 1941) and was self-proclaimed King of Kings, though this followed the abdication of his father after American and British forces entered Iran bent on protecting Iran's oilfields from the advancing German troops. Skorzeny's book twitted the Allies for their "weak-knees" at the moment when victory loomed: "I often wondered why Allied divisions were not dumped in the vicinity of Berlin in the winter of 1944," he wrote. "All of the Ministries were concentrated here (Berlin). It was a real possibility to end the war. 'Wild Bill' Donovan and his Merry Men (sic) were quite capable of making a job of it."

Gen. Bradley wanted to make that decision work but his hands were tied. Washington had to okay the go. Bradley recalls in A Soldiers' Story (1978) one of the misfires of Eclipse.

"Radio Luxembourg delivered this announcement: 'An SS Colonel had delivered to Von Rundstedt in Cologne orders from the German High Command for an immediate counter-offensive. Von Rundstedt rejected the order and protested that he could not obey it without leading his command to destruction. An altercation followed and the SS Colonel was shot. The Field Marshal, it was reported, had ordered

Wehrmacht troops to disarm SS units. He thereupon appealed to the German people in a public broadcast, urging them to rally to his side that he might conclude an honorable peace with the Allies."

Somebody had jumped the gun, Bradley admitted to me later in Washington. "A shame," he said. "I hate to think of the lives we tried to save and nearly did." Bradley's "lure" front for "Little Slam" had changed to "Grand Slam" in the bridge-playing generals code to establish armistice. We had been duped and General Omar had reason to fret.

My British colleague, Charles Whiting, <u>The Last Assault the Battle of the Bulge Reassessed</u> (1994), found some consolation in the Nazi double-cross: "It made America's spymasters swear that there would not be another intelligence failure, at least in Europe. From then on the intelligence war with Germany would be fought with that kind of harsh bitterness that only Americans can achieve when they feel their innocence and inherent goodness have been betrayed."

The ensuing Battle of the Bulge fills a hundred or so history books, and there's no need for repetition here. We finally turned the tide, and total surrender came six months later. But in one respect the war never ended—the war to discover what really happened to Major Glenn Miller, O-505273 AC. The two competing theories: (1) loss in a single-engine plane over the English Channel and (2) being hit by a loose bomb jettisoned by a Lancaster—have been so soundly rejected by students and scholars that their probabilities are ludicrous.

I can claim to be the very first researcher into Glenn's vanishing. And along with others listed here, I'm among the last. This book is predicated not in comfortable fiction but in facts. That Glenn Miller was involved in Operation Eclipse, given the dates and the testimony is undeniable. That he gave his life in combat is admitted, and you don't win that

Bronze Star unless you can prove <u>combat</u>.

The big blank in official responses to inquiries about Glenn Miller is not helped by the Freedom of Information Act. A wartime generation and a Vietnam generation have tried to get to the files. Both are more-and-more convinced that the blank pages were set out for protection of reputations. At the time, perhaps hiding behind a cover-up was all-important. Given grounds, Americans heroes of heritage can commit no sins. But isn't it equally important to finally salute a real hero lost somewhere between the frontispiece and back cover of the Great War?

If a similar wall to the Vietnam tribute in Arlington (with 58,000 names) could be raised to honor the dead and dying of the Battle of the Bulge, it would stretch twice as far. We don't remember those guys and gals because the battered and headless bodies lie elsewhere. I've seen those crosses, thick as a snowstorm on endless green hills. I differ from the account of one Madison Avenue lieutenant who penned three different versions of how Glenn Miller died, and who has never been named in official investigative correspondence— only as "an officer in the band."

In November, 1952, The Document Center—so called— of Heinrich Himmler's secret RSHA Files (initialing for a lengthy German word meaning Highest Office for Reich Security) was made available to me. It was in Berlin's suburb of Zehlendorf in a maze of underground chambers roofed with green lawns overhead. Left undetected by the invading Red Army which first took Berlin, it contained condemning files of the Nazis' tortuous doings and was a *Kultur Archive* as well, designated as *Ahnenerbe*. As a Major on Active duty in 1951, I had orders to go through its files and, in a secret report to USAREUR (US Army Europe) Headquarters in Heidelberg, detail what I saw...

CHAPTER **5**

Nazi Files: Miller, Lampshades and "Kultur"

BERLIN - What an odd place to shiver and think of the uncle who raised me in the Blue Ridge Mountains of Virginia! "It's a braw, bricht, moonlicht nicht," he would say, never forgetting the bracing chill of a Glasgow dawn before he immigrated to the pacific breezes of soft blue hills. The same tails of northern ice chewed at the goose bumps of Major Hunton L. Downs on U.S. Army Active Reserve duty. A polar blast was hitting this city, and raising a "braw, bricht" of red on my neck as well. It was November in Berlin, 1951, a few years past the Nazi debacle. We were a besieged city, surrounded by the Soviet Red Army.

I was in the American Sector, waiting in front of the Harnack House, my quarters, for an OD sedan to pick me up. It wasn't far to the notorious Document Center, a trove of captured Nazi papers. The find had been overlooked by the Russians, and discovered by accident when a German mower of a lawn without a house slipped on a hole and fell down camouflaged stairs. *Voila.* There was the underground library of Herr Heinrich Himmler, room after room of classified Nazi papers, all the dirty do's of five egregious years. My job was as secret as was the location. Our U.S. Mission didn't want anyone to know the papers were there, particularly the Russians in their Sektor and Germans still undergoing Denazification. I had to be Johnny on the spot by 7:00 a.m. Everything was in German, of course, and even with my capable German, it was necessary to be absolutely accurate, so a certain Frau Blum was to be my translator, she being cleared from Nazi tags. She would be in the car to pick me up. What we were to see on my two-week assignment were the files of *AMT IV* and *AMT VI* of the *Reichsicherheitshauptamt*, better known as RSHA, combination of the infamous SS, SD, Gestapo and other groups, all thrown into one basket. My report was for the Intelligence Division of USAREUR, then presumably sent on to Washington.

Frau Blum wasn't any foolishness. She was a survivor, and an intellectual as well. We passed a few blasted blocks and some noble mansions trying to hide their luxury in green foliage, and there we were in Zehlendorf. The car stopped. I couldn't see anything except a frost-tipped green lawn.

With that subtle irony of which Berliners are famous, Frau Blum said, "The Russians when they took over here were blind. They could only see the houses next door for looting. There was nothing on this lot but a lawn and sunflowers." With a laconic gait she led the way to a barely concealed entrance, a step down into the ground. Further steps and there loomed on the same eye level ceiling fans. Then, literally tons of bins with plaques in German script on the walls. Several U.S. hired Polish guards were having coffee and trying to keep warm. A swift "Attenshun" was called. My ID was examined, a quiz on my serial number (0-386244) completed satisfactorily. Pages from a pad of instructions were handed me. It was colder than above ground but an old Nuremberg porcelain stove was beginning to redden. Hanging bulbs shone wanly. Most of the bins were in shadows.

My job was to pick areas of Communications Espionage with which I was fairly familiar, and combine them into a report. Frau Blum would find the areas I was to look through, then translate whatever I wanted from the myriad of papers.

The Sergeant of the Polish guard presented me with a greenish-tipped grease pencil which he said, jokingly, was one of a stock used in signature by Heinrich Himmler when he signed death orders for the KZ (Concentration Camps). I don't know why, but I took notes with it... perhaps my way of getting even. All of the infamies were here in bins, carefully ordered with a catalogue in German. On one wall over the bin that Frau Blum and I started on was the bland admonition attributed to Martin Bormann, signed by Adolf Hitler:

"Insofar as we don't need them, they may die. Fertility is undesirable. Let them use contraceptives or practice abortion. The more, the better. Education is dangerous. It is enough if they can count up to 100. Every educated person is a future enemy. Religion we leave to them as a means of diversion. As for food, they won't get any more than is absolutely necessary. We are the masters. We come first."
ADOLF HITLER

The translation was by Frau Blum, and she stared at me as she voiced it, as if she were on stage, rehearsing a well-practiced line. She spat the author's name.

Several of these minutely scribbled green-pencilled pages

remain in my possession—not for sale on Ebay. On to work. My note pages flew. The notes had Ike's villa at St. Germain en Laye, 32 rue Alexandre Dumas down pat. His car limousine was an olive, drab-colored Cadillac with three flags flying. Even the date of his promotion to Five Stars was indicated: December 16. (They missed it by one day). There was even a weather forecast prepared by SS spies in Paris – to be included in the overview plans assassinating Eisenhower (which I read in captured documents, Berlin 1951). The reading was not from Berlin or from Model's headquarters at Fichtenhain (near Krefeld), but from Paris! The reading: *"Mist Sonntag bis Mitwoch* (Sunday to Wednesday), low clouds and reduced visibility in the mornings. Winds not to exceed 17 to 22 knots. Choppy water in the English Channel with breakers."

The weather factor in the Glenn Miller Mystery has been a long bone of contention as to whether that single-engine Norseman E-64 flew on to the continent or fell into Channel breakers. No one had ever published an official weather forecast for Dec. 15-16 as it pertained to the English Channel where Glenn was said to have gone down. I finally found one from the Nazi-held Channel Island of Jersey. Overlooked for half a century, it helped establish credence for a key witness to Glenn's presence with Ike at Trianon Palace when he was supposed to be dead and gone.

We went up for air and a walk. The Polish guards had been replaced by Berlin garrison soldiers. The Document Center was too hot a capture to let press or anyone but secure personnel in on the secret. The Polish guards were considered exceptions. They came from the hordes of refugees who had crossed into Germany post-war. The ones here, sharp in their black uniforms with V-emblems sewed over the right breast pocket of their uniforms, had received strict training at Munich's McGraw Kaserne before assignment here.

I was surprised to run across the name of "Miller" in the documents. It shouldn't have been, knowing of his psywar broadcasts monitored by General Sarnoff. The notation I made from Blum's interpretation was "MILLER – CAUSES LOWER TROOP CONFIDENCE IN COMMANDERS." Alone, this would be enough to submit him to a special decree, a *Fuehrer Erlass* "From henceforth, all enemies or so-called commandos, even if they are in uniform, whether armed or unarmed, in battle or in flight, are to be slaughtered."

Virtually every paper I picked up was classified in the German system. *Geheim* and *Sehr Geheim* (secret and very secret). There was only one level higher in Nazi classification, I learned—*Chef Sache*—which meant "*Fuehrer*'s Own Will." Other *Erlass* decrees were issued to be executed by a Hitler staffer such as Bormann, Hess, Goebbels, or by Himmler's RSHA. *Sehr Geheim Erlass* as it pertained to commandos was margined near the reference to Glenn Miller. There could be no mistaking that Major Miller was a *Kommando* in the Nazi appraisal, liable to be done away with.

My green pencil flew. A name Otto Skorzeny, without all the usual title formalities the Nazi's loved, cropped up often. He had a lot to do with Communications involving the *Abwehr* and Hitler's private wishes. "Special Treatment" popped up in Skorzeny's file often. "Special Treatment," it became clear, was a synonym for Death. One such in the Nazi system was *Sisyphische Hinrichtungen*. Sisyphische Executions. Following exactions of the ancient Greek gods. Sisyphus, famed from Homer on as the craftiest of men, ordered prisoners condemned to an eternity of torture pushing a huge boulder uphill and never reaching the top. At

Malthausen, U.S. captured flyers were made to do the same, struggling uphill boosting a huge boulder in front of them until they fell exhausted or were crushed. For them, eternity was shortlived. Skorzeny, I was to learn from Captain Harry Butcher's diary, <u>My Three Years With Eisenhower</u> (1946), was Hitler's appointed executioner of Ike during the Battle of the Bulge. When I ran into Skorzeny at that fancy lunch in Madrid, we talked about what I had read about him at the Document Center. He was fascinated that I knew more than he did about Himmler's journal dotting. We had only just that one thing in common – IRAN. He was flown to and paradropped near Teheran to organize an execution of the young Shah. At the time I met him, I didn't know of his intent to kidnap and use Glenn Miller.

In <u>My Three Years With Eisenhower</u> (1946) Butcher describes Eisenhower as alert to the danger of Otto Skorzeny. Butcher chronicles SHAEF at that perilous mid-December moment. "A character named Skorzeny, who reputedly rescued Mussolini, is said to have passed through our lines with about sixty of his men and had the mission of killing the Supreme Commander. One of their rendezvous points is said to be the Café de la Paix in Paris. There German sympathizers and agents are supposed to meet Skorzeny's gang and furnish information about General Ike's abode, movement and security guard."

Rules in the Polish-guarded Document Center were strict. Investigators were not allowed to take away papers, or to photograph them. This was evident as Frau Blum's silvered fingers ran through crinkly, yellowed papers. Some were crumbling, oppressed by the war's conflagration and neglect. Then, too, much of this information could be used to convict or excuse thousands of erstwhile Nazis, some at the moment protesting their innocence of crimes. I was curious as to whether my wartime job of beam-guiding the bombers from the Ploesti Oil Fields (Bari-Tiflis-Teheran-Cairo-Bari) had reached this far in Nazi intelligence. It hadn't. I found no trace of the reference. There were no spies in my outfit.

I had a persistent desire to see the file of Frau Ilse Koch, who had lampshades made from the skins of her KZ victims. There was no notation in the file of that notorious beauty with the horrifying hobby, but there was her photo. She was pictured as a better-than-good looking *Hausfrau*— as indeed she must have been—rising to be selected as a *Triblinke* commandant. One of the Polish guards told me in German that the green pencils I was using were the real thing, from Himmler's abundant, readily available supply.)

I had skipped through about one-tenth of the Communications bulk in two weeks and had done my job, but I had to know the meaning of *Ahnenerbe* (Culture!) How could such a horror-manufacturer as the RSHA have had a Cultural Department? It was there! Besides tracing the symbol SS to a magical, runic stroke of lightning, the Nazi generics had mostly to do with supremacy of Aryan values to those less pure-blooded. How much cold could a human being stand before freezing to death? Could freezing be adverted by coition? If so, how many of the opposite sex were needed? This seems dangerously close to waterboarding and is perhaps where the idea originated and developed . Testing was done at Ravensberg and Auschwitz. With POWs of both sexes. *Kultur!*

I went back to my "pseudo-civilian" position in the American Forces Network Europe to supervise news and program content. However, the lost bandmaster never ranged far from my head. Miller music and Miller news were everywhere in such an atmosphere. Many officers and

GIs of the war had chosen to stay on in service, and gotten themselves assigned to the Occupation. Those connected with SHAEF and the Battle of the Bulge were at first disbelieving that Glenn Miller had any other job but lifting a trombone. They listened to me, and I found myself in some trouble trying to prove the government was all wrong about the missing Major. I would have been the object of a vengeful Gestapo, I thought, if the other side had won. The Army was tolerant. The (OSS) CIA was not.

An overwhelming majority of soldiers in post-war USAREUR, U.S. Army Europe (Headquarters: Heidelberg) worshipped Glenn Miller. Many thought he was still alive. The Twinwood sham never-ever found GIs as believers. That is, believing in this announcement released as PR: "On December 15, 1944, Major Glenn Miller was seen off at Twinwood Airport in Bedfordshire, England, headed for France in a single-engine plane with a pilot and one other passenger, and was never seen again." The more this became credo, the more it was disbelieved. The government's policy was "like it or not, that's all you get." There was no evidence offered other than the diary of the band's administrative officer, who the government refused to name in official correspondence: Lt. Don Haynes.

Captain Bill Loveridge was assigned to the Network from the CIA in Washington. He told me confidentially that he had seen "the file" and it was Top Secret and never to be released. His only comment: "It's not the same story. It's too hot to handle. Don't push it."

The official OSS had by then changed names. Following the war, it was reorganized and renamed the Central Intelligence Agency. It was based at Langley, Virginia near Washington where stored facts of those three blind weeks between Dec. 23, 1944 and Jan. 8, 1945 were undoubtedly buried. Letters to a dozen federal agencies by early British and American researchers, asking, asking, asking, got no answers.

In retrospect, one of America's great ambassadors, George F. Kennan, in Moscow during the Cold War, had roughed out provisions of the Marshall Plan. He said that, "the need to hide so much secrecy in government is not only foolhardy but wasteful of resources." Kennan's quote: "It is my conviction, based on some years of experience, first as a government official and then in the past 43 years as an historian, that the need by our government for secret intelligence about affairs elsewhere in the world has been vastly overrated. I would say that something upward of 95% of what we need to know could be very well obtained by the careful and competent study of perfectly legitimate sources in information, open and available to us in the rich library and archival holdings of this country." George Kennan's Memoirs, 1925-1950, (1967).

Trouble was, information about Glenn Miller's demise was not "open and available." Ambassador Kennen was a close friend of my next door neighbor in Berlin (1963-5), Dr James B. Conant, ex-president of Harvard. Thanks to Conant and George Kennen, I learned to pull a knotty, bunched up string straight and clear from a twisted heap.

One guy who knew about Glenn and kept his mouth shut was my direct boss in Heidelberg! I didn't know it until one of the searchers I was in touch with, Dale Titler, sent me a SHAEF copy[8] about Colonel Dupuy, then head of Public Relations for SHAEF. He's the one who had released Glenn Miller's death notice (Christmas Eve, 1944) to the world's press. Dupuy wanted his memo "returned to him and did not want to see any release before it went public." And he wrote it down on the memo, an act of self-protection. Was this the same guy as my boss?

He was! Col. Dupuy knew of my interest in Glenn Miller, but was cautious. Why had he brushed off such an international story, and ducked to get out of the way? I had to ask him. Was Dupuy afraid of an investigation which could deal with hiding a murder? A nasty situation for Eisenhower, not to mention for Dupuy himself. I was stepping on eggs, I knew, and valued my job. Dupuy was a quiet executive, a career officer sweating out his 20 years. If he was a wheel in the big cover up, he had been smart about it. No investigation, if one ever developed, could convict him of anything. Familiar ground... nobody wanted to know. Colonel Dupuy knew the rules. If Twinwood was a cover-up, criminality could easily evolve from charges of complicity in demise of a fellow officer.

Rather than bring out a copy of the Paris memo, I hazarded an innocent approach. I just asked him what he knew about Glenn's death—inasmuch as he was there in Paris at the time. Without blinking an eye, he fed me the official line (well rehearsed no doubt). "There was a war on, you know. Miller was only one of many missing officers." The condemning memo stayed put in my notebook. Until now.

The British Forces Network ran its own show from Muenchen-Gladbach near Cologne. Every now and then, we had a joint meeting, either in Frankfurt, our headquarters, or in theirs at Muenchen Gladbach along the Rhine.

Miller was raised from the dead at our 1954 get-together. The BFN program directors brought along for the 10th Anniversary of Glenn's '44 disappearance a Most Secret transcription of *Musik fuer die Wehrmacht*. It was etched on a wax disc, a needle-recorded transcription. It had been swiped by the boys from secret BBC files at Bush

House, London. The British GIs presented it proudly for playing. I was exonerated. That I had heard these programs in warfare had solicited the usual "Oh yeah...sure." Here was Glenn's warm, comfortable, unmistakable voice telling Germans in their own language to give up, to disbelieve the Nazi propaganda, to remember their families at home and relatives in America. They were to know that German POWs were well treated. (And they were!) The BFN directors also told me about a well-known British writer digging into the Miller mystery. He was an RAF flyer who had touched down at every RAF base in Britain. This was Wilbur Wright whose work I was to oversee years later. When he heard that Twinwood was open that particular December 15, 1944—sworn to by the government—he decided to check. And found out it was <u>closed</u>. This is what Wilbur was able to prove from Croydon RAF Headquarters:

"A signals square outside the Tower will indicate that the airfield is closed and no radio contact is possible while flying is suspended. There would be no fire or rescue vehicles on standby, and no pilot would risk a landing there, save in dire emergency. Further, the standard method of controlling the descent of an aircraft through cloud was ground VHF radio linked to a radio DF facility, enabling the Controller to guide the aircraft down into visual contact. No pilot could descend through cloud and reach the airfield without radio assistance from the ground, from an open and fully-manned Control Tower." (Imperial War Museum.) The Glenn Miller Burial File (1993) Wright.

And now I have proven, the Public Record Office has proven, and the British government has proven what Wilbur proved all those decades ago.

After the BFN meeting, I addressed correspondence to the British Broadcasting Company, Regent Street, Bush

House, London. "In my studies of the Glenn Miller Mystery, I propose consideration of several factors which contest the belief, widespread, that Major Miller went missing over the English Channel in an E-64 single-engine Norseman plane on December 15, 1944. In the event of an investigation, the following are factors to be considered, and should be weighed against what was declared publicly in 1944-45 with little evidence to back a contestable claim."

I listed the following points:

- Britain's MET office reported weather "temperate, cloudy, clearing, warming over the Channel. A PM report. This contests the witness's story.
- Flight path, Bedford to Paris, 20 minutes over water. Clearing.
- Other planes (Col. Corrigan) flew the England-to-Paris path that same day without difficulty (December 15, 1944).
- No SOS calls registered, no Mayday, no radar reports of loss.
- No flotage, no land wreckage reported, then or now.
- No search initiated by SHAEF or Britain's Help-at-Sea units.
- Glenn Miller's brother, Herbert Miller (on BBC in 1954) stated that there had been no Military Inquiry. His request to open the file of papers related to the accident was refused.
- Miller was seen in Paris after December 15, 1944, according to several witnesses, Millergate (1990), none of whom were officially interrogated. Rumors motivated CBS in Paris to search for facts.
- Testimony by a U.S. Officer who has seen the Glenn Miller file of OSS (now CIA). He tells a far different

story from your announced release. Name available: Captain Wm. Loveridge.

- Miller, because of his psywar German broadcasts was a *Feind* (enemy) of the SS, subject by Hitler *Erlass* of October 18, 1942 to capture and death.
- The Miller family requests for investigation (Helen-Herbert) refused by authorities. Since made public on BBC.
- Availability of a Miller broadcast in German from British Forces Network. British servicemen can testify as to psychological warfare contents.
- Glenn Miller biography by George T. Simon confirms Miller's connection with OWI/OSS.
- According to one soldier-witness (MP in Paris at the time), Miller's body was found near-death in Pigalle section of Paris. Soldier threatened with rank loss if he told.

Hunton L. Downs – July 1956

I received no answer to my letter. The details of the last item above need clarification. In fact, the occurrence spurred me on to breach official sternness and risk rebuke— as I was still working for the U.S. government. Terre Hautian Mary M. Downs had been my secretary at Armed Forces Radio Service in Los Angeles. We married. We were cleared for government jobs; she easily caught on with the 15th CID Detachment in Frankfurt to make a few extra bucks. CID is Criminal Investigative Division and works like the FBI. I had applied in 1956 for Vietnam with the State Department, and she was going with me. A farewell party was in order, and we made it at our house.

The booze flowed and it was time, maybe, for confessions. My wife's commander, a major, admitted that he found his job bleak and bloody. His troupe consisted of five or six in number. One of them, a Technical Sergeant Roscoe X (I omit the last name) was feeling his oats. When the subject of Glenn Miller came up, as it always did, I tape-recorded what was said in an interview for David Wright, Wilbur's son, years later. (I had no recorder with me at the party, nor would Roscoe have confided had he seen one.)

DW:

Colonel Downs, you mentioned that at an early stage after the war, you got interested in solving the Glenn Miller mystery. You were in a good position, in Europe, working for U.S. Army broadcasting. Did you ever get close to that secret file with the documents proving what really happened?

HD:

Yes, a number of times. I came close. I wasn't allowed to see it myself but I did find one officer who had read it, a Captain Bill Loveridge of CIA. He verified what a lot of us involved in Miller music thought, that something stank about the story put out, Miller going down in the Channel, then keeping the loss quiet for five days. Bill wouldn't say much, "Just don't believe it." he told me referring to the official story. Through my wife's intercession... she was working for CID in Frankfurt, I got to a sergeant who was on MP patrol duty in the Paris Montmartre the night after the Ardennes broke. He had been radioed to pick up a dead or dying Major at the notorious Sphinx cabaret, a high class bordello up near the top of Montmartre. He was pretty sure it was Glenn Miller, although he had been beaten up and was barely conscious. Kept saying something, he told me, like *Fashim Yeah-ge... Fashim Yeah-ge.* And *Telek...telek!* To the sergeant it was like alien-speak. And to me as well. When the sergeant reported the incident, he was clamped to secrecy. I asked him what they had done with Glenn. Did he live? The sergeant wouldn't say anymore and seemed frightened at what he had told me. Wouldn't answer and avoided me ever after until he was ZI'd. I don't know what ever happened to him, but I heard he tried to sell his story in the states after the war and was leaned upon pretty heavily.

DW:

Any more leaks while you were in Germany?

HD:

A few more. I looked up what those words could possibly mean, and got some good advice from a German airman. Fashim Yeah-ge is about as close as you can get to Fallschirmjaeger, the Parachute Brigades of the Luftwaffe. Telek? I don't know what to say about Telek. It might have been a type of glider. I'm tempted to think it could have been "Tell Ike."

DW:

I'm told, Colonel Downs that you are one of the few who have actually heard these *Musik fuer die Wehrmacht* broadcasts. How did that happen?

HD:

When I was Program Chief for the American Forces Network in Europe, Frankfurt, my British counterpart in Cologne came for a visit back in the '50s and brought one of the old acetate recordings, still marked Most Secret. I thought then that I wouldn't stop until I got Glenn into a more favorable light than what's been given him. He was a hero, and if Telek was Tell Ike, he deserves a high medal for trying to warn his Commander- in-Chief. That's when I met you here in London and you and your dad had the same idea.

Never mind that Glenn had been clubbed on the head. And what about the brothel? It was on Roscoe X's beat.

The Sphinx, it was called. He didn't remember the address, didn't want to. He ducked me for the rest of the evening, and I never got his last name. But check it out anybody. He was in the 15th CID, Frankfurt Detachment. The date was Spring, 1955 in USAREUR. Maybe DOD will answer you. They didn't me when I tried to locate him.

There was another fingerprint: an admission. Ike's aide-de-camp Harry Butcher had written a book shortly after the war which was a collection of diaries, My Three Years With Eisenhower (1946). The book makes no secret of friendship throughout the war between author Butcher and his CBS pal Stephen Early, promoted to be Franklin D. Roosevelt's press secretary. Early is in-and-out of Butcher's pages on Ike and is credited with forty two references. What caught my attention was that all the references mentioned in detail occurred either before, and after that mysterious 3-week blight of news when Glenn went missing. That was the period of the German breakthrough. Early's name vanishes as completely as if he had dropped out of the world. What had happened to him? Where was he? Had he anything to do with Glenn's disappearance? Something was fishy. It prompted me to ask—"Where was Stephen Early?" I got an answer forty years later when a long-buried document came to light in the 1990s. The document bore Early's name. It not only involved Glenn Miller. It was what happened to Glenn Miller—the way "Early" framed it. This was the original telegram dated December 22, 1944, Early-to-Ike, announcing Glenn's "death." Stephen was the guy who fixed up that phony story of John Morgan's rusty crate going down with Glenn aboard. And then made it disappear.

The telegram from "EARLY" to SHAEF's Commander-in-Chief was signed just that—EARLY. No title, no rank. No military man would dare send such a critical report without including his rank. This report to Ike of VIP Glenn's disappearance was sent with the confidence of FDR's press secretary, supposedly to ease public dismay at home. Could the truth have been told right then on-the-spot? Without shaking up the core of our front against the Nazis? To be fair, Early had a horrendous decision to make. Glenn Miller murdered? Why? What's this about a whorehouse? Why weren't we concentrating on an enemy breaking through at the Ardennes? Why were we caught off guard? Where was Intelligence? What!!! A confidence deal with the Nazi generals? And double crossed? SHAEF trusted the Nazi generals?!!

I can't find fault with the Morgan plane decision. As it was, the Channel debacle saved the day, and Stephen Early perhaps could be commended. But all these years later, after Ike had won his prize of the White House, to ride on a risible story—and do so with a straight face—is not a matter of patriotic pride. Besides, with the truth out, and both governments know the truth by now, let's stand up for Glenn Miller.

Wilbur Wright tried to track down a certain Colonel Early who was declared by elements of SHAEF to have taken over command of Morgan's outfit. This was meant to exclude FDR's man from complicity. It didn't work. No one in the London Bedford area has ever spoken to this so-called Colonel James F. Early. Wright tried three times, and came up with empty doors. I tried hard to find him. A recent discovery on the Internet, updated 1951 (!), assigns one full page with picture to Col. James F. Early, said by some to be a mover and shaker in the Miller Affair. Some dates in the on-line profile do not match facts, nor is he mentioned in one edition of the manufactured Don Haynes' diaries. Col. Early was promoted to Brigadier General, the buzz sheet proclaims, after his Service Command duty in England.

Eating up some leave time before the Vietnam transfer, I thought I might gain re-access to the Document Center, and therein find the evidence which would explain everything. Sorry! My credentials were not good news to the Germans. The Center was closed—it had been turned over, intact, to the new German Federal Republic. Where were Himmler's documents?

What Hitler did to humiliate the generals on both sides and destroy a good proportion of the world's youth in so doing was gravel in my craw which wouldn't go away. It was a bit of luck to me that Butcher brought his book out, My Three Years with Eisenhower (1946), too close after war's end. He gave away secrets that a judicious delay might have scoured into silence—such as the Early absence from pages during that news blackout, December to January. Also, for instance, he told of Ike's condescension for the world press. When Ike went into the field with troops, he thought it sufficient for "two cars only...to transport the correspondents, the Signal Corps photographers and the conducting officer." And Harry admitted to "Ike's news blackout" when he wrote: "Great alarm was being caused, particularly at home, because the blackout was interpreted as a SHAEF device to withhold bad news. Ike felt this was something the public simply would have to stand for a few days." The "few days" turned into three weeks when all the wrecked hopes spun into view. Ike made his blackout freeze permanent when on December 18, 1945 he addressed his letter to Secretary of War Robert Patterson: "I am unalterably opposed to making any effort to publicize at the time any story concerning the Ardennes Battle or even of allowing any written explanation to go outside the War

Department." (Eisenhower Library at Abilene, Kansas)

A decade later when I returned to my quest after Vietnam—this time as a foreign correspondent—my friends and researchers were still at it. More whispers abounded about the blank three weeks, and a good deal of what was covered up had been brought out into the open. Unfortunately, Glenn still lay in the Channel as far as governments were concerned. But with an even larger contingent of voluntary researchers—now American—the doors began to revolve.

To counter those previous stultifying shrug-offs, I now had opinions from honest and brilliant reporters. These were writers who dug in and knew facts when they saw them: Trevor-Roper, William L. Shirer, Robert Payne, Peter Calvocoressi, Charles Whiting, M.R.D. Foot, Peter Gross, Joachim Fest, F.W. Winterbotham and others. They did the spadework which gave this book a frame.

Two of Hitler's most fascinating and adventurous evildoers provided the final blueprint to solution of the Glenn Miller Mystery. Their *Irrefuehrung* set up the Dirty Tricks in autumn 1944 which blanketed Versailles in fear, put Eisenhower in a tank between home and office. Who were the evil- doers? These were bright, daring officers, Colonel Walter Schellenberg and Colonel Otto Skorzeny—Nazi to the bone in careers, they were contrite at the ending. They pretty much ran things as far as Glenn Miller was concerned.[15]

CHAPTER **6**

Hitler's Last Gasp: A Three-pronged Double Cross

The man was six feet four inches tall, hiding a swagger his stiff manner couldn't conceal. The brawny figure resembled a genie coming out of a bottle. In effect, he was a genie, Adolf Hitler's genie. In 1940, he'd been among a few stalwarts of the SS to stand before the *Fuehrer* and be selected as a personal bodyguard. He was questioned: "Where are you from?"

"Oesterreich, Fuehrer."

Hitler liked what he saw. The fellow Austrian was given the envied job. Otto Skorzeny was a sergeant. He was to rise to a colonel, do secret work in Paris, in Moscow, in Rome, Iran and Yugoslavia. Under arrest at war's end in Nuremberg, he managed an escape, worked for the CIA in Egypt and Rio de Janeiro, dying finally in Madrid.

A film producer in Wilmington, North Carolina asked me recently to do a screenplay on this buccaneer. I wouldn't. Otto Skorzeny was not a nice guy. He was a murderer.

He accompanied the conqueror of France to Paris

in 1940, strode with his Chief down the Champs Elysees
(along with Albert Speer), and had his play of the town.
A lieutenant now, he got the plum job of working in the
Zeppelin Kommandos, charged with airdrops between
the Eastern Front and Moscow; the idea being to cut
communications and disrupt supplies. According to
Skorzeny's admission, he got close enough to Moscow to
see the towers. This boldness suggested to his mentor Hitler
that, with luck, Stalin could be done away with. In his book
Geheim Geschwader (1995), Luftwaffe Captain F.W. Stahl,
head of KG200, a secret air arm, gives an amazing account
of *Operation Geheim Geschwader*. He came within a
breath of succeeding, fouled only by a sudden rainstorm.
The assassins who got inside the Kremlin to hide for the
planned moment were caught. They were wearing dry
raincoats when it was cats-and-dogs outside.

Skorzeny, the one go-to-hell guy Hitler trusted, got
the job of running missions from secret "outstation Olga"
(part of Frankfurt/Main airport now). He was to have a
partner, a politico, the Deputy to Heinrich Himmler, Walter
Schellenberg. Their association was called *Irrefuehrung*,
meaning Dirty Tricks. This is spelled out in Stahl's
biography (published postwar but taken quickly out of print
in Germany); also by E. H. Cookridge in Spy of the Century
(1972) foreword by Trevor-Roper.

Walter Schellenberg, the youngest and most engaging
of generals, became Hitler's Chief of Counter intelligence.
Before Himmler, he was aide to Reinhard Heydrich in
Prague. When this infamous hangman was assassinated by
British agents, Schellenberg segued over to work for the
weak-chinned Himmler whose *AMT IV* and *AMT VI* of RSHA
(*Reichsicherheitshauptamt*) ran all the horrors we associate
with Nazism. Alan Bullock, in his foreword to Schellenberg's

Memoirs (1956) published in the UK, had this comment: "*AMT IV* was entrusted with counter espionage work for the Gestapo in Germany and the occupied countries. He (Schellenberg) took over and organized *AMT VI* (as well)." Bullock's footnote: "RSHA – *AMT IV A-4B* was responsible for the rounding up, transportation, shooting and gassing to death of at least three million Jews."

The war was a chess game for Walter Schellenberg. Pawns were sacrificed to get at the queen, and in one too real case Walter's audacity caught a near Queen—the Duchess of Windsor. She and the Duke were playing hide-and-seek in Spain where their attitudes tipped toward the Nazis but their allegiances belonged to the Crown. Schellenberg had the job of kidnapping them. The idea was to set the Duke on a British throne for Germany. British agents beat him to it, moving the Royal Pair to Bermuda. The 30'ish Nazi also drew up a list of Britishers to be executed when Hitler took over London. These numbered 2,300 (according to William L. Shirer, America's top war historian), and included H. G. Wells, Aldous Huxley, Virginia Woolf, besides Churchill and his entire cabinet plus Americans Paul Robson, Bernard Baruch and John Gunther. Only George Bernard Shaw among famous British artisans escaped the would-be scaffold and nobody has ever explained why. Perhaps because Shaw had gained recognition as a dedicated pacifist.

A well-suited pair, one could say, for "Dirty Tricks." Schellenberg, as one of the documents in this book indicates plainly, signed the lure, a captured wireless copy, dooming Glenn Miller and his mission.[21] This usually smiling Deputy to Himmler had a pair of machine guns mounted in his desk, aimed toward the door. They were encased in a drawer, hidden of course. In his postwar confessions, he stated, "They were for 'friends.'"

October 11, 1944—Skorzeny is turning the corner of *Wilhelmstrasse 61A-67A*, the high government quarter of *Wilhelmplatz* in Berlin. This is a two-story white palace, marble, one of Albert Speer's designs for a world capital. There is space in front for a pair of idling, brown Mercedes sedans lofting black steel Nazi flags. At attention is a white-coated traffic policeman in a kiosk, a curious contrast to a brown tail-coated guard in velvet collar at the massive doorway. <u>Skorzeny's Special Memoirs</u> (1957)

But Hitler is away. He is at the Wolf's Lair of East Prussia—down in the bunker where he was nearly assassinated on July 20, 1944.

Skorzeny hears footsteps behind him and swirls quickly. It's only a breathless messenger, seemingly glad to reach his quarry. He blurts out, "The *Fuehrer* demands your presence immediately." Or in German – *"Der Fuehrer will Sie sofort bei Ihm sehen. Heute!"*

One of the Mercedes is whipped to the curb. Twenty minutes to the airport in central Berlin. A plane will be waiting.

Skorzeny watches the passing wreckage of a once-noble metropolis. Except for nearby factories where foreign workers are changing shifts, the streets are virtually empty. One could imagine his thoughts as he viewed these unfortunates and compared his current luxury with his previous soldiers' ration card as a sergeant: 10 pounds of bread and cake, two pounds of meat per week, a half-pound ersatz coffee. He just had lunch at fancy Horcher's on Unter den Linden, a favorite of Air Marshal Goering.

At 8 p.m., 2000 hrs, he is sitting in an outdoor corridor at the *Fuehrer's* deep-down bunker behind three rings of barbed wire, minefields and a lone path through the dank trees, cleared of armament—for Hitler's daily walk.

Rastenburg, or the Wolf's Lair as it was called, was unpleasant in all its aspects, a mood which seemed to fit the dictator during the failing days of the war.

Promptly, Hitler called Skorzeny into the cell-like room. Gone were the hangings of Europe's finest art. Behind the desk hung only the oblong-framed portrait in blue of Frederick the Great.

The door closed. The two were alone, as Skorzeny later described it, "For five hours, well into the night." This was an honor for the colonel. It was "prime time." The *sehr Geheim* secret plan of *Wacht am Rhein* had been adjusted to *Herbstnebel.* Autumn Mist was unfolded. Skorzeny was needed for the plan to succeed, as was Schellenberg, for a delicate *Chef Sache* (top priority) mission which could not be put into writing. It was three-phased.[20]

The plan, as later proved, was genius in conception. It was Germany's last chance to save itself from ignominy and, possibly, disaster. It conceivably could enact a future to regain France, Belgium and Holland. This Hitler explained to his aide.

1. A breakthrough in the Ardennes (where Hitler had struck to conquer France in 1940), using at least twice the force the Allies could reasonably expect. Divisions could be mustered from armies North and South, transported secretly by rail, with all wireless suspended for fear of alerting the Allies. (This actually happened as planned, disabling the famed Bletchley Park Ultra monitors which contrived to capture nearly all Nazi headquarters orders, even from Hitler himself.) The plan was to split the Army Group forces of Bradley and Montgomery by driving a wedge to Antwerp, the West's major supply port. Possibly grabbing Paris was not out of the question.

2. With Eisenhower dead, or as Hitler's prisoner, courtesy

of Skorzeny, the job of SHAEF Commander would naturally fall to British General Montgomery. Known for his delaying, "nipping up" tactics, the new Chief would by habit delay the confusion. That is to say, he would take several weeks to react to the SS Panzer armies' thrust.

3. To abet the confusion, Hitler planned an operation called *Nachtwind* (Night Wind) which would send some 3,000 bombers to devastate the RAF and AAC bases. (In actual fact when the strike did occur, Montgomery's own C-47 was bombed out of commission which might have added to Monte's delay in taking over. *Nachtwind* suggested Divine Wind, reminiscent of Japanese Kamikaze.)

The 3-pronged attack was in earnest. It was the only way Hitler thought he could save his own neck, and avoid defeat for the Nazis. To disguise Skorzeny's thrust into Versailles to kill Eisenhower, a Brandenburg Division of parachutists, dressed as American GI's, would land behind U.S. lines to disrupt supplies and communications— the same as Skorzeny's *Zeppelin* squadrons had done in Russia—and to some extent camouflage the real mission. Skorzeny's killer attack on Eisenhower would be possible by utilizing KG200, the secret unit of captured U.S. planes. Allied intelligence during the war never learned of this Nazi arm which repaired downed Allied planes, kept the markings, and used them to advantage in crossing over fronts and landing in enemy airports for spying purposes. A squadron of B-24 reconditioned Liberators would be employed for the Brandenberg drop, hoodwinking the Allies as they passed unchallenged overhead. Skorzeny, along with Schellenberg, in control of KG200 plus the recently absorbed *Abwehr* intelligence, could set up plots to disarm enemy suspicion in London. It was a fact that by fall 1944, German military intelligence was out of Admiral

Canaris's control and in Dirty Tricks' hands.

A lot to absorb, Skorzeny must have ruminated, "in five hours." But he was up to it, as he was with the Mussolini capture. A frown might have crossed his face as he left the East Prussian command post for officer quarters. In Moscow he had used a decoy to get to Stalin, a trusted courier of the Kremlin. In Yugoslavia to reach Tito, he had enlisted a family servant. In the isolated mountain top Abruzzi to get Mussolini, he had kidnapped an Italian general of the mountain top forces off the Via Veneto in Rome. Who would he use to get past guards at Versailles? The thought must have needled him until he met up with Walter Schellenberg, after which Odin 7/13 evolved. Major Miller was already wanted. They would get him and try to turn him to their use.

By November, this three-phased overall plan of attack was underway. Hitler's Plan was Grand Slam, unbeknownst to Von Rundstedt, who was recommending Little Slam. At Bletchley Park there was no signal intercept of a pending attack. Not per se. But top officials would claim, thirty years postwar, that massive new troop locations opposite Bradley's Gap had been spotted and that there had been unusually heavy rail traffic from the Eastern Front. The Allied generals, with their up-to-now invincible SLU (Special Liason Units) for this intelligence, relaxed. It would be a winter of back-and forth with the odd joust of muscle, the G-2 Intel guys guessed. SHAEF gave Eclipse a good chance to work. All were aware that Nazi Sepp Dietrich's SS Panzer Army stood at the gate. But then we had our Patton. If Sepp came in and got swallowed, war was over. Von Rundstedt had promised and he was a gentleman, wasn't he?

The triumph of Bletchley Park and its ability to break the top Nazi codes is renowned in history. There were

388,188 messages broken (PRO – Britain's Public Record Office count, 1941-5) Little known, if at all, was the role of SLU's in achieving victory. These were small radio receiving units attached to every major command in the field, forty at war's end. They spelled out tactical decisions of the enemy, Hitler orders from battles in North Africa to the final Elbe in Germany.

Except for one classical goof (the Bulge), SLU's told our generals where the Nazis were, and when and where to attack their weak points. Some commanders paid little attention (Montgomery, Mark Clark). Others made the tips pay off (Alexander, French General Juin and SLU's greatest booster George Patton)—From F.W. Wintherbotham's The Ultra Secret (1974).

Otto Skorzeny assembled his sleazy warriors. He sent them to POW camps to familiarize them with GI jargon. They brought back uniforms and jeeps. There were gliders aplenty to carry the besiegers, even the captured jeeps could fit in a glider. Each invading glider was towed by a JU-52. Even a tank could go inside the 200-foot- wingspread- wide Gigant, but the macro-glider was ruled out for this exercise. It would be too easily marked as German. Surprise would be lost. As for Skorzeny's carriers, two or more would suffice. The captured American B24 Liberators would be fitted for passengers. They could land without problem at a French airfield such as Villacoublais near Versailles. The B-24s had been used before to embed spies for the German underground *Zeppelin Kommandos*.

Robert Payne in his remarkably detailed history, The Life and Death of Adolf Hitler (1973), summarizes the jittery situation on this anticipating Western front: "The mustering yards of the armored divisions for the Ardennes offensive were the woods and forests of the Eifel region. There with the autumn mists clinging to the trees, they were able to assemble in secrecy. There was a low cloud cover, and no allied airplanes detected them."

The opposing generals, faced with the possibility of two competing orders of battle, were bridge-playing addicts. What they called Little Slam involved sucking in the SS Divisions, then chewing them up by our armies as Junker generals who wanted the war over surrendered and arrested Hitler. Bradley called this lighter attack a counter-offensive. Grand Slam meant a major strike with several armies, not expected in the dead of winter. Code breaks gave no indication—at least not read as such—of the juggernaut Hitler planned. Grand Slam called for a juggernaut breakthrough as far as Antwerp, Aachen and Paris. Little Slam was essential for Eclipse. SLU's (code breakers of enemy movements) at every top general's right hand gave no indication of a mighty thrust, only hints that a lot more enemy was standing by than had been there the weeks before, Bradley's G-2 did call a warning, but he was ignored in the pervading atmosphere of over-confidence.

As Robert Payne would later write, "Hitler kept postponing the offensive. In October, he spoke of an offensive in November, and in November he spoke of an offensive at the beginning of December. On December 7, he postponed it to December 14. On December 12 he postponed it to December 16. (Date it actually started). It was the last throw of the dice, and he spent a month shaking them in his cupped hands."

Payne writes so well that it would be easy to underestimate the extensive research by the author and the near-amazing extent to which history sometimes reveals so many of its details, including what Payne describes as a speech by Hitler (to his generals) "that must be counted among the most impressive speeches he ever delivered."

A side comment here. Who would have guessed that Payne's exact detailing would explain why Glenn had to make so many trips from London to Paris to "arrange one concert?"

He had to be ready whenever the balloon went up. Why the Hitler delays? Payne: "On December 12, Hitler invited all the generals taking part in the offensive to a briefing in the underground bunker at *Adlerhorst*, near *Bad Nauheim bei Frankfurt*. Stripped from their briefcases and weapons, they were driven to the secret command post which deposited them before a double line of SS guards near the bunker entrance. There was something frightening and intimidating about these guards who descended into the bunker with the generals and then stood guard behind their chairs. General Beyerlein, soon to be leading a panzer division through the Ardennes forests, was so terrified of the glowering SS officer behind him that he was hesitant even to reach for a handkerchief."

Payne writes of the tense atmosphere as Hitler presented his generals with the juggernaut plan, termed Grand Slam, and demanded it be followed to the letter, even down to platoon action. When forces reached the Meuse, they would cross it and get to Antwerp as directed. Each general's SS guard, standing behind the chairs, was instructed to follow that general even to the bathroom. Any deviation from any detail of Hitler's plan would result in instant death for that general. This proved to be the last of Hitler's start-stop-postponements for Autumn Mist. His jiggling of the dates, as Payne documents, was cause for Major Miller's own frequent change of plans, flying to Paris to fulfill his duty assignment.

Eisenhower, Bradley, Dulles, Casey, Donovan, Miller, all

expecting a Little Slam and a New Years Day in Berlin—were taken completely off-guard. That memorable day of December 16, 1944 commenced at 4:30 a.m. with a mighty barrage across the 80-kilometer-wide decoy front. Eclipse was off. *Herbstnebel* was on.

Thus Glenn Miller, about to become a hero, became a Mystery of the Century. As later confirmed by Charles Whiting, five days elapsed with Otto Skorzeny missing from Nazi ranks for the exact same number of days before Glenn Miller's absence was explained. After that came the news blackout of three weeks ordained by Eisenhower, and not cleared to this date. Hitler's three-point plan faltered but damn near succeeded. And then flat-out failed.

There was *Malmedy, Bastogne,* the great Patton run and "Nuts!"—all woven into what could be called, "the war's greatest land battle." The Bulge tightened and bent inward. Charles Whiting describes what he saw as the "turning point" which Americans should have celebrated, and would have, had the news clamp not dampened individual exploits of bravery.

Joachen Peiper, officer of Panzer 1st Division, was near the point of the breakthrough advance. He led the way forward to cross the river Meuse. (He was the Malmedy executioner.) With 13 Panzer tanks, he was within clear sight of a virtual free run to Antwerp. The obstacle was a railroad underpass at Trois Ponts, Belgium. From Whiting's The Battle for the German Frontier (1990):

"Peiper had not reckoned with four young American anti-tank gunners—McCollum, Hollerbeck, Buchanan and Higgins. If the achievement of their lives had been modest up to that point, the way they died was to give them a kind of immortality, for they were going to change the whole course of the Battle of the Bulge."

Acknowledged as the most prolific of Bulge historians, Whiting gives details of how the four held out with "one puny 57 mm gun," stopping the attack cold until one shot from a long probing *Wehrmacht* cannon found the mark. "The little gun and its American crew disappeared in a ball of flame. Behind this valiant crew were U.S. engineers striving to blow the last bridge away, the bridge which could give Peiper the clear sweep to Antwerp. He was only yards away from achieving Hitler's triumph. A Captain Yates yelled at his dynamiters—"Blow her!" The engineers slammed down the charges. A dull roar, a burst of flame, and the bridge across the river Ambleve existed no more. Peiper would never reach the Meuse." He himself confessed this at his trial for murdering U.S. POWs. He was convicted, sentenced to death, but later (in de-Nazification) freed. The French caught up with him, killed him, and burned his body.

To conclude this historical moment, the *Wehrmacht* was driven back by the 30th Division of Yanks as the entire Bradley group of armies came charging in to flatten the Bulge. I have often wondered what medals those four heroes received, if any. They were on the ground where my old 28th "Bloody Bucket" division was torn apart on that fatal day of December 16. Dying, too, were a few of my war buddies from Scranton and Philly.

As a correspondent again in Europe I was able to dig more gracefully, knowing there wouldn't be clucking disapproval of army brass over my shoulder. Some Skorzeny papers turned up while I was in London trying to break down barriers. I learned more from them about that five-hour private meeting with Hitler—plus Hitler's orders to kill Ike. Skorzeny sketched his own plans as follow up, and outlines one of these provisions in Skorzeny's Special Missions (1957):

Skorzeny has admitted in print his use of decoys to reach Benito Mussolini, Stalin, Tito and the Hungarian Chief of State Horthy.

Would not Skorzeny have tried the same ploy to get to Eisenhower? The thought nagged. The clues came together in the mid-nineties. Fellow researchers joined expressing their belief. Who better to get past guards of Eisenhower than a face familiar to all guards, a face and figure in uniform of Glenn Miller. GI's, would you stop him?

A shot in the dark, I knew, but proof piled up in two faxes sent to me care Wilbur Wright's doorstep in Southampton;[43] documents from Cheltenham GCHQ from a persona not to be identified with them. Their authenticity was incontestable. One was signed by Schellenberg (from Krefeld, Germany's Ruhr, dispatched to Berlin). The other was from Berlin to Krefeld, signed Bergmann.[21] Several distinguished historians have by now (2008) acknowledged that Bergmann was a sobriquet for Bormann. Joachim Fest the fine German historian acknowledges this; in fact, he led me to find the proof.

E.H. Cookridge in <u>Spy of the Century</u> (1972), biographer of the famed General Gehlen who was fired by Hitler, came over to our side, and successfully organized Intel for Allen Dulles, writes that Bormann was well known as Bergmann. "His wife, there at *Wolkenstein* in the *Groednertal*, lived in hiding for several weeks (after he disappeared) under the assumed name of Frau Bergmann. She was seriously ill, until she declared herself to an American headquarters in Bolzano. She died shortly thereafter."

These reproduced OKW (*Oberkommandwehrmacht*) telegrams dealt with a lowering of the flak curtain guarding the Ruhr to allow a small plane through for landing. The wires were signed copies from an original teletype. Both dealt with "7-13 Odin" and were within the same time and date frames. That they were from high enough authority to close down Germany's Western flak curtain was plain from the *Waffen* SS and the *OKW* seals. Bergmann (Bormann) in Berlin had enough clout to give this order. His signature was followed by *Oberst*, which indicates the highest officer in command. If 7-13 was an alphabetic code for G-M, and Odin stood for a mystical hero on a flying horse, and both were proven true, Glenn Miller was not only the subject but predicate as well. The wires indicated a complicity (false on one side) to get Glenn in hand and let Allies believe he was on his way to Berlin. It didn't work out that way but in affirming Glenn was on his way to Berlin was proof to us that Eclipse was going through. A false affirmation, a subterfuge, of course. With Radio Lux in Allied hands and *Deutschlandsender* in Berlin on the way—46 million German listeners—RSHA pulled another trick to feed our overconfidence.[33, 34]

Joachim Fest, the notable German writer-expert on World War II, (Face of the Third Reich (1970), Hitler (2002), Plotting Hitler's Death (1970), and more recently Inside Hitler's Bunker (2005) on which the German movie *The Downfall* was based, had led me to find that Bormann was Bergmann. Did Fest know why Hitler's right hand man had chosen that alias? It was the same as *Haemmel* (means flesh) was code-name for Schellenberg. Martin Bormann was a would-be "mountaineer" and well-known for his title acquisition of *Berchtesgaden* property, including Hitler's own *Berghof.* Finally, at that time, after discovery of the *OKW* wires, we could be sure of their authenticity.

Points which came to light only in the late 1990s. "If the 'generals' plot' really existed," a GM Society spokesman nailed me up, "why don't the German files prove it?

Germans kept records." Yeahhhh!! Records... where were the Nazi files? Gone, burned, bombed, hidden, or just plain denied. Our governments both were intent on holding their secrets fast. Could there be any document left to evince an "Armistice by Christmas 1944?" The historical town of Trier within shouting distance of that viciously exploded front provided answer. But it didn't come easy.

Here, my Saigon duty came in handy. My chief in that woebegone part of the world was Robert Lochner, son of the famed Louis P. Lochner, ace AP reporter and bureau chief in Berlin during the Hitler years—who later edited the <u>Goebbels Diaries</u> (1948). Bob was Public Affairs Officer, USIS (United States Information Service), in Saigon, and by now he had advanced to head up American radio, RIAS (Radio In American Sector), in Berlin. His contacts were invaluable. One was the *Buergermeister* of *Trier*. I received permission from "Hizzoner" to look at the original German hand-written diaries in *Deutscheschrift*.

The <u>Goebbels Diaries</u> (1948) were easily available in any library, but not the private diaries in German, un-translated, consisting of Goebbels' notations of critical days, events of December 1944. I found a student at the University of Trier who could do the reading and translation. Sure enough her research found that Goebbels twice mentioned in his secret diaries the couriers between Versailles and Krefeld (via Luxembourg) as "returning with serenity and joy to their homeland, bypassing the treacherous generals." So, Hitler was aware of the threat to depose him.

A happenstance. The Imperial War Museum in London gave me secret messages tying in Glenn Miller's flight Odin 7/13 to that night of December 15th into 16th. RAF and British radar both had the flight plotted.

Pursuing the old RSHA documents was getting harder

and harder. With archives no longer in Berlin, I tried at rumored RSHA vaults in Koblenz and Aachen. Not there. Thumbs pointed to Freiburg near the Swiss border, home of all secret material left over from the Third Reich. It took nearly a year to arrange a meeting there with the top guy, Intendant Dr. Kehrig, Oberst a.D.u.d.R. There were two witnesses for me on the mission, Renate Heiss (now Wendt), who got the Trier diaries out in the open, and Cathe Baker, my Southampton assistant.

"Sorry, those *AMT-IV* and *AMT-VI* incriminating files have either been destroyed *nach dem Krieg* (after the war) or been taken to Washington," Kehrig said. Polite as he was, nothing could stir Kehrig's statement. In other words, whatever there was on Glenn Miller to be found in RSHA (including the little notation I ran across doing Reserve Duty in Berlin) was now in some graven file in Washington. It was by chasing-around-Germany's secret libraries that I found help from F.W. Stahl, former captain in the Luftwaffe and head of ground operations for Schellenberg's and Skorzeny's *Irrefuehrung*. I got a copy of his out-of-print book <u>Battle Wing 200</u> (Germany only), and then came helpful email correspondence with members of the 26th *Fallschirmjaeger* Regiment of the 9th *Fallschirmjaeger* Division. Their public search in the Berlin area produced one ex-*Greif Soldat*, the last survivor of the group which captured, tortured and left, head bludgeoned, Glenn Miller. The man spoke only with shame, near death himself.

KG200 (Battle Wing) was as secret in Nazi classification as any level under *Chef Sache*.[32] Formed February 20, 1944, KG200 commanded a fleet of German aircraft plus captured B-24s and Boeing B-17s (Flying Forts). The latter were made air-worthy again and used to fly over Allied fronts to land on Allied airfields to deposit spies, Zeppelin operations, etc. In crossing German lines, a special identifying code allowed overhead transit without challenge. These shadow planes had been newly refitted with parts and German transmitting equipment, but retained their original markings. It became plain to see how one such plane with a US-appearing crew could land on any Western field, exit personnel and take off again without question. One U.S. pilot, Robert Baker, a captain, remembered in the winter of 1944 one such B-24 from his outfit, the 310th Ferrying Command. It had been reported lost over Germany but was found abandoned at French Villacoublais (December 16, 1944), near Versailles, What this spy plane, in Baker's 1998 recollection, was doing at Villacoublais is not hard to ascertain.

Baker, incidentally, was one of the pilots authorized to fly either Miller or the Miller band to concerts around Britain. He knew Glenn personally and put to rest that recurring rumor of Glenn being ill and close to death: "He looked as healthy as the next guy, bearing in mind the slim wartime rations, the usual stress factors of doodlebugs, air raids, etc. Except of course, when he hung one on the night before, when he looked like shit."

I was back in London from the investigative tours of German libraries when Charles Whiting, the Skorzeny biographer, rang to tell of a proven fact he had discovered which linked Skorzeny with Glenn Miller. Checking his collection of Nazi documents in the Autumn Mist attack, Whiting confirmed again that Skorzeny had been absent from his duty base, starting December 16th, for exactly five days before reporting back. These five days coincided with Miller's five days "missing" before the report to the world by SHAEF as "lost in flight."

"In flight" means a <u>passenger</u>. "In flight" didn't deserve a Bronze Star. <u>Combat did</u>. What about it, Congress? Isn't dying to save your Supreme Commander worthy of a Congressional Medal of Honor? Otto Skorzeny was there in Versailles. Now, that's doubly proven. Harry Butcher wrote that Skorzeny was in Paris and Versailles, trying to close-in on them to kill his boss. In fact, he wrote a whole page about it in My Three Years with Eisenhower (1946).

The signed telegram proving FDR's aide Stephen Early was the author of the "Twinwood" mess came to light 48 years after the event. "EARLY" sent the message to Ike. It had been buried, released only when Wilbur Wright wrote to President Reagan to see Glenn's personal 201 File. He received papers, including this one, when Reagan ordered Glenn's 201 papers, classified Confidential, be sent to Wright in Southampton. The secret stuff on Miller wasn't available. Ronald Reagan: "It would seem my presidential security rating is not sufficient to look into this highly classified file."

I have seen the RR letter, one of the prized possessions of the Wilbur Wright estate. What emerges is that Glenn Miller, the OSS psywar broadcaster, formed a vital part of Operation Eclipse, and was himself Odin 7/13. It's for sure that he was killed in action, that he flew to Krefeld in an authorized AACS plane of at least two motors, that somehow he was conveyed to Paris where his body was found outside a notorious brothel, dead or half-dead, that German propaganda, then and later, intimated his whoring, and that a New Jersey document (his last residence) has placed his death in Ohio. (There is a Glenn Miller memorial at Wright-Patterson Airfield, Dayton, Ohio.) But New Jersey later voided the document. On orders?[7, 13]

Trying to nexus two ends of the story, I got a phone call from my researcher, Karolina Krauss in Paris. "I have found the old Sphinx," she said in a calm voice. "It's in total disrepair, hidden, glass-broken, covered with obscene graffiti... also, the Secret Service guy who can tell you about it." She took a deep breath. "The Sphinx brothel where Glenn was found belonged to the Nazi SS. The Party owned it, bought it in 1935. Hitler approved the purchase. Eva Braun visited... all fact."

CHAPTER **7**

Clearing a Besmirched Hero

Claude Igagnon was dapper, middle-aged, past his prime but didn't show it. He drove us to *Montmartre*, and through its narrow twisting cobbles as if he didn't need his eyes. He weaved into just the niche he was looking for—a 45 degree cant upward which he backed into. And I hoped his brakes would hold. He and my beauteous researcher Karolina Krauss, both French, took off afoot to pinpoint the elusive Sphinx. I followed them. It wasn't more than ten minutes before we upped-and-downed—shouldering past cheese shops, postcard kiosks and not-quite munificent couturier shops. Then, there we were! *Voila!* In the lurid Place Pigalle, heart of the juicy entertainment district. Up an alley which nobody paid attention to, it was so tiny, and we saw a boarded-up seven story, 19th century building. Its surface was flaky. Birds cooped in the open windows. Its once handsome frontage had turned with time to dust and rust. Claude Igagnon, a retired officer of France's secret service *Duexieme Bureau*, had dug up ancient records

from the local *Arrondissement*. This once-proud street of
Paris was *Montmartre*. The law stated that old buildings
are 'atmosphere', not to be torn down. Hence, the Sphinx,
unused and dilapidated, was still there. The word Sphinx
is puzzling usage for a house of ill-repute, perhaps not too
far off its original Greek meaning: "a mythological creature,
half woman, half lion." This particular Sphinx was an R&R
(Rest and Recreation) site for German soldiers and the
cheaper crowd of wartime and pre-war Paris. A far more
refined edition of "The Sphinx" lay across the Seine in
Montparnasse. In fact, Parisian writer Alphonse Boudard
listed seventeen Sphinx bordellos in cities across France. In
accordance with a 1946 law, all now are closed.

Without the immense help of *Musée de l'Erotique*,
the documents I was able to scan, and sometimes copy,
could not have led to the true Sphinx story as it concerned
Glenn Miller's death. Where else but in Paris would a noted
museum on sex be open day and night—with no violence
or reported incidents? Such is true of this popular *musée*
today. There's no attempt to hide the sex; it's just there in
Pigalle in all of its "*gloire.*"

A German news agency in 1998 put out the story:
"Miller died in the arms of a prostitute from heart failure"
(*Frankfurter Zeitung*). This "news"—as I mentioned
previously—was gleaned from an email out of Washington's
secret U.S. file. What file? What agency? Whose signature?
What heading? Nobody seemed to be concerned in finding
out. Nobody official seemed interested in finding out
details in this free-for-all-message battening down the fate
of Major Glenn Miller. Nobody in Washington or London
or the recipient, German journalist Udo Ulfkotte. I spoke
by phone with Udo several times, and I gathered he wasn't
particularly fond of stepping on his good relationship with

Washington's spy services. No help there.

This foolishness was about to be stood-at-attention, thanks to the Paris *Musée de l'Érotique,* a five story building around the corner from the- gray-uniformed enlisted-men's "Sphinx" in *Place Pigalle.* For years, rumors and stories about Le Sphinx had referred to the more refined establishment with choicer ladies at *31 boulevard Edgar Quinet, Montparnasse.* That one is a story in itself. A few edge of chair details later.

The expert on Paris brothels, I found out, was noted French author Alfonse Boudard. His extraordinary book La Fermature (1986) on brothels past and present throughout France is the definitive work on the subject. When I phoned him, with difficulty, through his publishers Robert Lafon, he was in the hospital suffering from cancer.

He knew of course of the Glenn Miller rumors but could not verify any substance other than the time (mid-December 1944) when the two brothels had been rampaged by gangs, first by German sympathizers, then by French *revengistes.* The latter tore the place up and sent the German Madame Freda scurrying for her life. My surprise was that I learned for the first time (from Boudard) that Sphinx was just the common name for all whorehouses. The stories which had been rumored involving Glenn had mentioned just the one. Boudard cut the theory flat: "There were Sphinx brothels in virtually every French city. It was the common word, even when the establishment was embellished with a more enticing name. There were no ads, of course, nor any signs on the door, so who would know the name? Even the fancy ones, famed internationally before the war, had no ads."

Le Sphinx Pigalle in year 2002, the one I was looking at, had torn plankings and broken windows. The entrance was barred. Obviously, the wrecked "hotel" had been a house of joy, with rude graffiti decorating the once-busy turnstile. But of Glenn Miller there was nothing to show except for one mighty fact: in the building codes were proofs of this Sphinx's sale to the Nazis, through a consortium of French bankers, lawyers and German money men—a sale to the political party NSDAP in *Muenchen, Deutschland.* The "godfathers" guaranteeing this acquisition were named: Heinrich Himmler and Hermann Goering (the latter, according to strict records kept at the Montparnasse address, was "a most frequent customer").

For those of you with a bent to know how a fancy French brothel worked, I'll depart from the Miller theme just for moments, as you may be as curious as I was. The fancy Sphinx across the Seine at *31 Edgar Quintet* is no more. It was torn down after hosting such celebrities as King Farouk, Gary Cooper, Marlene Dietrich, and Eva Braun, all pre-war. The register today is part of the *Musée de l'Érotique* and the bordello's fantasies way back then were incredible. The broken-down Sphinx we are looking at was for German ranks that arrived in busses, were given freebie coupons good for a half-hour to accomplish their R&R. When Paris was liberated, the house reverted to whoever got there first with a bevy of ladies to sell. While strictly off limits to Allied soldiers and officers, it was often fought over by French or Nazi sympathizers. This could explain the easy access of Skorzeny's assassins dressed as Americans, even off limits, toting an unconscious Glenn Miller, drugged or beaten. The Skorzeny plan placed the assembly point for the Ike assassins at the Café de la Paix, only blocks away. This *Montmartre Sphinx* was classified in the *Arrondissement* files as a "hotel." On the *Montparnasse* side of the Seine, the Madame of the fancy Le Sphinx, Marthe Lemestre, was known as "Martoune." She wrote of her life in <u>Madame Sphinx</u> (1945—published only in France) with details that even today are newsworthy. Read it in French and you will get a whole new look at our 1930's movie stars, even the dollar-ribbed business mastodons of those days, including William Randolph Hearst, an X-rated Citizen Kane. Martoune admits that in 1940, when Hitler took over the city, she was fired and replaced by a German Madame, Freda. Martoune took refuge on the Riviera where she continued a pretty good business, she claimed, keeping in contact with Parisian clients, and "thus keeping their joy coinage out of Nazi coffers."

To compete with the classy houses of that time, One Two Two and Chabanais, (in existence since World War One) the fancy Sphinx had to offer every delectable sweetmeat of sex. Still, it remained third choice. Martoune won her spurs to run the place by one simple suggestion: "Get the showgirls from the Folies Bergère and National Theatre. They'll get five times as much by us, and it won't interfere with their matinees and evenings." The word spread, the cash registers rang and Le Sphinx was soon Number One. The girls were not tied in; they could come and go as they liked; even work on landing a husband which many did.

French author, Alfonse Boudard, died in the hospital. I saw him just once. His book on "les maisons" (the houses) is no longer in print. France, a proud nation, looked down upon the old city rife with brothels. Brothels and the books about them went zip. Nevertheless, helped by the indefatigable Mlle. Kraus, I dug up a copy junked in a disposal bin at the ratty Paris flea market. The manager of the "antique" shop, Mme. Goutier, disdainfully sold it to me for 25 francs, less than half-a-buck. Called *La Fermature*, the book is now a rare collectible.

The even rarer book, <u>Madame Sphinx</u>, a friend of

Karolina found in a second-hand bookstore in Nice. Marthe Lemestre (Martoune) kept scrupulous records. Here is a typical example of the roaring Thirties and early Forties, a description one will never find in U.S. journalism:

"Since I got to know *tous les gens* (many people) in New York and Chicago, I continued to receive many American actors and music hall stars. Just as soon as they arrived in Paris, all of the Hollywood celebrities would come to Le Sphinx. We had great ceremony with a very young Clark Gable. I received Gary Cooper, John Gilbert, John Barrymore, Errol Flynn, Cary Grant… Tyrone Power.

"I remember also the visit of Eva Braun, the fiancée of Adolf Hitler. She was beautiful. She came to the Sphinx one evening with some German friends. She was coming back from Hollywood, I believe, where she had gone to work in a film, or to try for a role. She was stopping off in Paris. She and her friends drank and sang German songs the entire evening. I remember her with a glass of champagne in her hand, surrounded by a circle of admirers." <u>Madame Sphinx Vous Parle</u> (1972) Lemestre Martoune in French only.

Martoune was a good accountant. In her text: "An average of 1,000 bottles of champagne was consumed each night in Le Sphinx (four stories) and the alternately called Panier Fleuri or Cheval Blanc (seven stories) at the Montmartre." Henri Escoffier was our occasional chef. Maurice Chevalier and Edith Piaf often were our featured singers. The wine? Taittinger champagne."

Musee de l'Érotique does not, NOT, include Glenn Miller's name as a celebrity. It proves in fact that Glenn never voluntarily visited the place, but was a prisoner there and thrown outside to *le trottoir* (sidewalk). Boudard's study, precisely detailed, (<u>La Fermature</u> (1986), confirms Nazi ownership of both places. As for German press reports that

Glenn Miller had died there "in the arms of a prostitute," we can best look to Boudard's succinct comment: "The only client who ever died there of a heart attack in the arms of a prostitute, since the opening of the houses to their closure, was an ecclesiastic, a Cardinal, whose feverish body was quickly moved to the nearest Cathedral, his demise thusly recorded as having expired in the course of duty."

The Sphinxes – to any who might be curious when visiting Paris—are hardly worth looking for. Few remnants remain. The fancy one at *31 Boulevard Edgar Quinet* was torn down to make way for an industrial complex, and the one where Glenn was taken is in Montmartre: at *2 rue Coustou*, Pigalle.

Ex-World War Two soldier and writer John Edwards discovered this brothel connection in 1973. He wrote of it at length in 1976. His evidence went out to the world press, a release of which hit the *New York Times*: "There was never a proper official inquiry of Miller's death," Edwards stated, and concluded, "I have evidence that Glenn Miller was murdered in Paris. He died of a fractured skull in the city's red light district of Pigalle. I also have the name of a man who played in the band with Miller who states that it was common knowledge that those close to him knew very well he was murdered in Paris." But Edwards never located The Sphinx, nor mentioned by name the band witness.

After the war, the band manager Don Haynes chased up and down the money streets of New York and the corner offices of Hollywood studios. Three different versions of his diaries were in hand (take your pick). He was finally successful. People were curious about Glenn's disappearance and Americans flocked in the '70s to see the movie, *The Glenn Miller Story* starring Jimmy Stewart. Its story was attributed to Haynes, our errant diarist, and was believed around the world.

The one who clamped the truth on the Miller-Sphinx connection was a Britisher. "You couldn't make it up," wrote Arnold Smith of Bucks County, England. "It was so wild… all of a sudden." This British GI was the witness who saw the body of Glenn Miller thrown out of The Sphinx. "I was playing pinochle with guys from an MP station next to my hotel. The majority of guys were combat vets and we had a lot in common. One evening at around 11 p.m. an urgent call came over the radio. It was early December 1944 and we all thought the war was damned near over. I was included in the group and we mounted the waiting jeeps. We were only about two miles from the scene. When we arrived at the site, the French police were there as were other MPs. I stood aside as a stretcher was being brought down with a blanket covering a nude body. We watched as the body was loaded into a GI ambulance. The dead man, an army officer said, "was none other than Maj. Glenn Miller."

Smith's account, checked and verified by him personally in 1998, settled the question. But there was more, lots more, surfacing by then which required investigation.

Flight Lt. Wilbur Wright, Battle of Britain ace, had since 1946 collected 4,000 pertinent documents on the Miller case. I read them all over a period of months, commuting from Gloucestershire where I lived, to Southampton (port where the Titanic left berth). There in Southampton, I met my studious secretary-to-be, Cathe Baker. She worked off and on for the Postal Service of the Royal Mail.

Of extraordinary interest to Cathe was the case of Joan Heath. Joan was the SHAEF driver who drove Glenn to his destiny that night of the breakthrough. She took him from the goodbye-and-good-luck handclasp of General Eisenhower at the ornate bar of the Trianon Palace to a two-motor plane waiting in the suddenly fallen snow at nearby VIP Buc Field. On duty as well in the bar were two pilots on soft drinks. They got up and left with Glenn. "Miller was flying home," Ike told her later. "Unfortunately, he was lost." That was the recollection which haunted Joan all of her life. Lost? How? Glenn was on duty. He couldn't have been flying "home." All the way to the United States? By himself? Nonsense.

The crusty snow was deep on Buc Field that night, a point Joan reiterated time after time in telling her story, but that detail was brushed aside and taken as a slur on the truthfulness of her story. There was no snow on the ground in Versailles the next morning, so there couldn't be snow at Buc—so was the reasoning. Sixty years later, thanks to meteorological expert Bill Pike, the snowfall was verified by UK's Meteorological Service Command and, recently, just in rereading Butcher's book on Ike for the umpteenth time, I encountered an outright reference to snow on the precise date Butcher was there in Versailles (December 16-17, 1944), his office within pitching distance of where Joan Heath's car was parked. This date matches Joe Dobson's testimony of when Glenn Miller left London. What crushed Cathe, though, was the British driver's last glimpse of Glenn. He sat alone at a square window and waved a kiss to her as the plane took off in the slush. And aloft. Farewell, Major Glenn Miller.

This was the same night, just hours before the crush of Hitler's Autumn Mist armies devoured the front: December 16 to 17, 1944.

Joan was threatened for telling this story, and the threats followed her all her life. But she stuck to her guns. Her boyfriend (to the end) was Vic Porter from Teddington, Middlesex. He was an RAF acquaintance of Wilbur Wright.

The file Cathe was so concerned about contained all of Vic's letters to Wilbur describing the "heat" put on Joan officially, even up to her death. Politely put, that meant No Publicity Please on any resume of Glenn's last moments and Ike's awkward, rather carefree explanation to her. Then she passed away.

Karolina and I debated the seeming improbability of Miss Heath's testimony. From all sources, she was impeccably honest, her memory excellent. She hadn't tried to sell a story or even claim publication. Her recollection of the aircraft and its details couldn't be challenged. But its square-window features, the stairs up to the double-pilot crew could also apply to an Afro-Anson. Either plane could have made it non-stop to the St. Omer checkpoint, thence to Krefeld, Germany.

Eisenhower's comment to Joan that "the news" of Glenn's disappearance had been kept quiet because Major Miller had gone "without permission," is highly questionable. Ike was insinuating that the man who had saved his life was AWOL, Absent Without Leave. AWOL was a despicable offense in wartime, punishable by death. In my own 28th Infantry Division a soldier gone AWOL was shot for doing just that—the controversial Private Edward Slovik—an execution Ike would have had to approve.

It is surpassing logic to believe Major Miller was on his way to a Christmas vacation in America, "carrying bundles for his wife and new son." (They were tapes for broadcast according to Brod Crawford). Of course, he couldn't tell Joan of his mission when the war itself depended on his security. What was Glenn to say: "I'm off to meet with General Von Rundstedt about ending the war?" His bundles, it emerged in 1974 conversations with Brod Crawford, were transcriptions to be played on the *Deutschlandsender*, possibly terse messages from Eisenhower and of course Miller music which wouldn't be available in Berlin. In the Manvell-Fraenkel biography Dr. Goebbels (1960), this pair of writers describe how the Nazis took over a foreign country when language changed with the borders:

"Berlin radio reporters arrived in Hilversum (Holland), thirty strong, the day after the Dutch army surrendered. With them were enough transcribed programs in Dutch to last two weeks. All music by British, French or Jewish composers was barred. When news was resumed, the Dutch announcers were told they might say anything they pleased (in front of squads with loaded pistols to discourage adverse comments). The Dutch people, recognizing the familiar voices of the old announcers were greatly reassured. The trucks of the German radio unit contained two months of recorded programs labeled from England."

The system was equally practicable for letting Germans know what was expected for their necessary armistice and surrender. Today, we forget that during World War Two radio was the surest, quickest, often the only means of mass communications. It was certainly faster than foot as I found out in a day long chase in the tiny bucolic town of Versailles, trying to locate Ike's SHAEF encampment. No correspondent had ever put a finger on it much less been there. It was known only by WWII writers as a Versailles hotel. "You mean the old U.S. Headquarters?"—A tourist official shrugged my question at the town's office on *33 rue Royale*. We were directed to *Place du Marche, Notre Dame*, thence to *Avenue de la Reine*.[16] "Turn left until you hit an arcade of trees," we were told. SHAEF turned out to be the fabled Trianon Palace, a historic French crown of culture where the Versailles Treaty ending World War I was promulgated. Not an encampment, but a jeweled

French monument. A hotel? No wonder Ike kept this place quiet! France has hotels and hotels. In olden days a royal type of "hotel" had a far different meaning than today. Hotel then meant a cherished piece of architecture— gripped to history. Today, in the classiest sense a hotel can be a palace and a hotel, too. Versailles' noble Trianon stands alone as a gem hotel, and for the Westin chain of hotels, it is a palace.

The colonnade of trees which proved we were on the right track extended welcoming branches for a quarter mile to greet us. Mlle. Krauss and I were led to a gilded gate which is normal French decor for a national park. We virtually tiptoed past the elegance and into the "lobby." This huge airy space was once the Trianon ballroom. Massive, dangling, crystal chandeliers seemed to own the place. We walked softly not to scar the exquisite antique flooring. Film crews are not allowed with their rude dollies and tracking devices, but the politeness and efficiency of the palace employees soon made us forget we were in a palace. "Leave it to Ike," Karolina said. "He knew how to put up with tough field conditions." We went into the bar and salon where Ike's new five-stars were toasted. I refrained from thinking of the princely quaffs of ice water given frozen GIs spading up frozen ground to soften it up for foxholes.

It became easier to understand how in a social atmosphere of a few ranking officers, their underling juniors and some enlisted lesser ranks, all living together, could come to a family level-just keep your distance-much as in Buckingham Palace with lords and their servants. Living the posh at Trianon Palace back to 1944, one can visualize more readily the scene Joan Heath described. An estate night—quiet—the plush bar—soft quartet music—

officers—at tables or bending the elbow. Or maybe just sitting awaiting orders.

High ranked Ike-jacketed staffers would have been there, exchanging chat, the Commander in Chief enters, with Glenn Miller at his side. No big deal. Joan Heath is on night-driver duty, sitting at a table. A half-stir of legs for an Attention... Ike waves. At Ease...Glenn is well known. He and the CIC go into a corner.

Buc Field is a mile away, a treacherous drive for Joan on the uneven farm road in total darkness, even with a skim of snow. But she makes it without difficulty. A single macadam tarmac looms, a dug out hill to accommodate a strip. There is a tiny tower, no lights, but staffed. Two figures tumble from inside. A single two-engine Bobcat plane reflects half-painted headlights from the sedan. Crumbly snow, shivering at the cusp, is near melting. This was Joan's quick view. Today Buc is still there, albeit modernized, serving French VIPs—chromed, lit, extended. No more hill. Still only for VIPs. Where's the romance? Gone with Joan Heath.

I made a date with Managing Director Madame Gouvenou for a chat. Of course, she was a child at the time, knew only a few stories passed on by the generations.

With anticipation that I might hear some details of 1944-45 army life at the Trianon—and of Glenn Miller—whom she didn't recollect except as a great music maker, we agreed to a later sit-down over coffee. Karolina and I left her and the magnificent setting for Villacoublais Airport, a short drive away. (American spelling: Villacoublay.)

Villacoublais was enormous and still is. It has been a major field for the French military since World War One. One could compare it—if smaller—to Andrews Air Force Base or Wright-Patterson. The U.S. was given a permit to use it by the French, which back in 1944 meant damned-near the whole thing. Unlike Buc, there were plenty of strips to land on. Back then, there were no scarf-buckled engine jockeys to wave you into a stall. You just parked and went about your business; and took off again with a tower okay. It didn't matter how you spelled Villacoublay. There was easy U.S. transport available—jeeps, ambulances, 6-by-6's. Several vet pilots have told about their luck in landing at Villacoublais, sometimes in emergency. It meant a night in Paris.... Whoopee, a needed vacation. There is sufficient testimony among Glenn Miller researchers to prove that Lt. Col. Norman Baessell—claimed by officialdom to be aboard the "lost Miller plane"—went out of his way to land at "Villa." He had an expensive flat off the Champs Elysees and a circle of girlfriends. Eisenhower's G-1 (personnel) deputy Major May (1993) admitted by letter that Baessell was into high-jinks, black marketing, and was good riddance when he "disappeared." There is a compact of theories among researchers about how Baessell disappeared, having nothing to do with a dive in the Channel. He is said to have been seen in Rhodesia after the war, and if government perusal of records had so allowed publication, he pulled down a pension well into the 1950s.

Madame Gouvenou's discussion of the Ike years at Versailles proved more interesting than informative. She had little to add about Glenn being there, only employee's gossip. "Eisenhower had made a deal with the French generals (DeGaulle and LeClerc) to protect the palace from becoming an 'army camp'. She knew all about that. She explained that if Ike had tried to take over Marie Antoinette's nearby Petite Trianon (where most press believed he was), – there would have been a different war at hand. And General Juin was reported to have said, not so light-heartedly, "The French Resistance will pull out of the Alliance if Eisenhower insists on taking over Marie Antoinette's Petite Trianon!"

Such a threat sounds petty today, even ridiculous, but it was a no joking matter then. French culture can rise above reality. A story circulated in France (Le Monde) after the war, and picked up by several British historians, had to do with French generals DeGaulle and LeClerc, commander of France's 2nd Division, getting in a deadly argument with Eisenhower in this very SHAEF Headquarters where we were sitting. Ike wanted to pull the French 15th Army back after it had liberated Strasbourg, and send it to aid Bradley's decimated forces at the "lure gap." That would have meant reoccupation by the Nazis of that magnificent city and widespread executions of French-Germans who had helped win it by covert underground activities. *Non!!!*...the French generals would not have it. Yet Ike was insistent. He was the Supreme Commander. DeGaulle and LeClerc stood up, gave their ultimatum: "You do that and we will immediately close all French railroads and shut down electricity for the country." Story told me by *Marachal de France* Alfonse Juin when I interviewed him in Paris in 1962, several years before his death. I was Voice of America Bureau Chief in Munich at the time with cities of responsibility: Paris, Brussels and Berlin. Juin was much liked by Americans, in part because he led a ragamuffin group of French-African troops at Monte Cassino, following Patton's attack philosophy, to win the way clear to Rome over and past a rugged German defense. The French generals of the Resistance got their way. Strasbourg stayed *libre*, thanks to its liberators.

The Trianon Palace's charming directrice did remember "Ike's tank." The story had been told so many times she didn't remember when she first heard it. It happened at the beginning of the Bulge battle when Germans in U.S .

uniforms (*Greif*) were roaming France to kill or capture Eisenhower. For his own protection he rode from Versailles palace to his villa at St. Germain en Laye inside a tank. True to his promise, Eisenhower wouldn't allow his Sherman treads to smash up the gilded gates or go inside the courtyard to sludge the antique décor. He was *très bien* as a Supreme Commander, Gouvenou said. He kept his word.

Karolina went to Ike's little village to locate his house, "the villa overlooking the Seine." Even without perfect instructions from the Mayor's Office and the City of St. Germain en Laye's Tourist Office, she could have found it. Anybody can today, just head for the ridge overlooking France's great river Seine. It is on an S-curve just as the highway turns sharply downhill. It matches General Bradley's description exactly (from his book); and also the description of St. Germain's founder—back in the 17th Century: St. Germain said that his town had, "A view like the Bay of Naples." Anybody who knows Naples and its astounding views can imagine what he meant.

Karolina and I met up the following day for a thorough search of the impressive villa's grounds. They belong more properly to a castle—high stone walls surrounding four acres of bastioned bunkers seven stories deep.[23] The house looks like a suburban property of a middle class family, nothing very impressive, but seven stories underground meant somebody was afraid of bombs, and so it was, the occupant before Ike—German general Von Rundstedt. At this writing (2008) the stone villa belongs to the City government and is closed to the public but for once a year. I wondered why it remained closed when it could be a clever tourist attraction. The official reason given is that the villa has bunkers and medieval dungeons deep into the ground. They are shaky, and outside, rather dangerous approaches sheer off cliff-side alongside its kilometer-length high wall. Considering its 300 years' history, it reminded me of an urbanite's country manor built on top of the Siegfried Line.

The Wilbur Wright estate (after his demise February 24, 1994) gave me permission to study and utilize the entire file he had collected, much of which went to the Imperial War Museum, London. The estate also gave me Wilbur's last words about the Joan Heath affair. As he was the researcher closest to Joan and Vic, I include his words from deep respect: "I am often asked my own personal opinion of Miller's fate and here I must go along irrevocably with Joan Heath's account. At 76, she is still alert and active with an excellent memory of her days at SHAEF driving Air Marshal Tedder. Her account of Ike's party is corroborated in his biographies, and she successfully identified the Cessna Bobcat. We confirmed that 112th Liaison Squadron at Buc Field used Bobcats exclusively to ferry around VIPs—including Winston Churchill and his wife. We know that no Bobcat or west-bound transatlantic flight was lost in December 1944, from the 112th Squadron history and records at Maxwell AFB Historical Center. Joan has been interrogated a number of times and has never changed her story or the essential details." WILBUR WRIGHT (1992)

In 1998, after a thorough check of available British military records at Bletchley Park, RAF Croydon and those few "transients" available from SHAEF Versailles, I issued this statement, upon request, to ex-AAC airman Sid Robinson, brother in law of Tex Beneke, the Miller vocalist. Robinson heads a massive research organization across America to get to the bottom of the true Glenn Miller story. He asked for this information on Miss Heath, and I was happy to give it to him:

WAFF-MT driver Joan Heath was one of five girls

sent from Bletchley Park in 1944 to drive Senior SHAEF officers, and was assigned to be the personal driver to Air Marshal Tedder. Actually, she drove most of the top brass, as required, including Eisenhower on occasion and Mrs. Churchill when she paid a short visit to the Western Front Headquarters. My letter to Sid follows:

"The problem with Joan started shortly after she drove two generals to the "Little Red House" on *Luneberg Heath* for the surrender of the German Army. War over, her memory of the night Glenn disappeared (and Ardennes offensive commenced) differed drastically from the official accounts. Joan stuck to her guns. The US and UK governments were not happy. Each time she recounted those few fate-laden hours of an impromptu party seeing Glenn off, with Ike and a few officers in attendance, she was leaned on. "Shut up about that" became "Shut up or else." Little by little, as the years wore on (she lived to be 80, still with a clear mind), friends were persuaded to drop her. She became frightened to tell of it. Vic Porter of 30 Springfield Road, Teddington became her only friend left. Thanks to Vic, her final years were filled with some peace. She rebuffed all press inquiries, confided only in Vic. Fearful of signing her name, she lived in dread of two years imprisonment for offending the Official Secrets Act in spite of the fact that the Act lost its teeth in 1973, thirty years after the incident. There was nothing secret about her being at the impromptu party, nothing announced as classified. She was ordered to be there as a driver. The evening was made Top Secret later, as were all of Glenn Miller's movements which clashed with his being lost over the English Channel on December 15, 1944." This information to Sid and his correspondents was as up-to-date as possible (1999).

Some of the gap had slackened. Glenn could be proven

as far as Paris. What then happened until he was picked up, beaten over the head at a Nazi-infested Pigalle brothel?

If Odin 7/13 had gotten to Krefeld per the telegrams, how did he get back to Paris? By captured plane? By *Greif* parachutists? I wrote to F.W. Stahl and asked him. He said he didn't know. "I and my crews," he wrote me in German, "would have no details about the agents on board to be delivered to enemy lands, about their tasks or who was dispatching them." He refused to answer any questions about Glenn Miller, cut off correspondence. F.W. Stahl made a fool of US security, dropping off spies at will at every Allied airport during 1943-1944, and he was solidly involved in Autumn Mist with Skorzeny. I didn't press him. P.W. Stahl's book <u>Geheim Geschwader: KG 200</u> (1995) told what he wanted to be known. I tried to interest him in a trio approach to tell all about Glenn's capture and what had happened—a trio of himself, Charles Whiting and me. He turned me down, no reason. Poor intelligence seems the bugaboo of U.S. fortunes in war and peace, even today. Poor intelligence may be why we get into so many wars.

There was only one more thing to learn about the villa at St. Germain en Laye. There is a hole in the sturdy meter-thick stone wall that wasn't there before World War Two, or even during Von Rundstedt's residence. One can walk around the wall in fifteen minutes, unlike the Trianon Palace, which for me, took two hours. Whoever punched the hole knew where it led to, the only interior corridor where entrance could be gained to the main house. Diagram of the house and grounds show this, and German architects are presumed to have drawn the diagram.

The hole is 70 to 80 yards from where *Boulevard Victor Hugo* and *Avenue Alexandre Dumas* conjoin. The number of the house is 32. The "boulevard" and "avenue" in no way resemble what we think of today as a boulevard or an avenue. The house (upper right corner of the sketch) shows the complexity of the huge estate.[23] The bunker complex served as an underground shelter for Von Rundstedt seven levels deep. It is unknown if Eisenhower ever inspected the levels when he took over. But he knew that his opposite commander had lived here and that details of the entire compound would have been surveyed by the Nazis down to the last micrometer. Did he know of the endless secret passage through the bunkers with only one roadside exit? Or that entrance, if hammered through? That's where we found an attempt to dig a body-sized hole from the outside in. It was not successful. The blast or excavation only penetrated half way through the meter-thick stones. Was this Skorzeny's second chance to get at Eisenhower? That story no one will ever know, but the odds favor an interrupted attempt.

Karolina and I walked around this medieval stone castle without one car ever appearing – probably a half mile jaunt. The hole we found was the only attempt to break in. We asked a St. Germain resident for the story of the hole. She shrugged. *"Je ne sais pas. Cela...c'était fait pendant la guerre."* I don't know that... it happened during the war.

It's hard to query this selection of a home away from home for the Commander in Chief. Security seemed to be the least of considerations. There must have been reasons. It was far afield. . Ike didn't want press, so nobody in the Press Corps knew about it. As his driver Kay Summersby noted in her book <u>Past Forgetting</u> (1976), "General Eisenhower only told the press what he wanted them to know. They never came to the house or to his office."

Lesson learned from the Bulge battle with one win and 80,090 losses.

But the Bulge turned our Allied Command from a naïve, trusting bunch believing in "gentlemen generals" into a crafty, conniving, hard-assed elite who outfought and outthought the Germans the rest of the way.

Charles Whiting is the only accredited Bulge historian who was both journalist and soldier in 1945. He interviewed most of the principals—German, American and British, at war's end. Here is his comment as published in The Spymasters (1976).

"Today any researcher attempting to find out about the British Secret Intelligence Service and its associate, the US Office of Strategic Service, meets the same barrier of silence that the enemy, Admiral Canaris of *Abwehr*, must have encountered over thirty years ago. Mouths ordered closed, stayed closed. Both General Sir Kenneth Strong (Ike's staff and bridge playing partner) and Admiral Sir Norman Denning, a wartime Intelligence leader and post-war Head of Intelligence, preferred not to recollect anything 'at this distance in time'. When approached, Field Marshal Sir Gerald Templer, the last head of SOE's (Special Operations Executive) German Section SIS (Secret Intelligence Service), 'could not imagine' who could assist me (the researcher), and hadn't the 'vaguest idea who might help'. Sir Hugh Trevor-Roper, a Regius Professor of Modern History at Oxford, offered: "I do not know whether we had any personal sources within Germany, and I, myself, would not have believed anything they said anyway."

A mumble-jumble of words adding up to nothing, all heeding the goodly number of U.S. Officers and Enlisted Men paying sealed-lip service to the Supreme Commander's "Shut up about the Bulge." Several "in the know" became heads of the new CIA when it was established. Thus the "Miller thing" never escaped its folders. Upcoming directors: Allen Dulles, Walter "Bedell" Smith (Ike's former Chief of Staff), William Casey, William Colby and Richard Helms. All were involved in knowledge of or operation of Eclipse and Odin 7/13. Three of these individuals are reputed to be among the most enigmatic characters in American political history. Compared to other issues shadowing the three, including: Casey (Iran), Colby (Phoenix), and Helms (Watergate), keeping the "Miller thing" quiet would not be difficult.

There was good news to balance the blemish of cover-up. Sid Robinson of DeQuincy, Louisiana was making time. He ran across Robert Cloer, editor of the world-wide AACS Newsletter (Army Air Corps members). Airman Cloer acknowledges that as a crewmember, he personally flew with the Miller band from Bedford to Paris on Monday, December 18, 1944, and maintains in his printed story of the incident, "The Miller fake is the biggest cover-up of the war." Air servicemen during World War II belonged to "the Corps" before it became the Air Force.

Robinson let me know that several of the cobwebs were swept away. Gen. Maxwell Taylor's vet pilot, a Captain Joe Dobson, had told the same story to anybody who would listen since he came home from the war. Challenging the more conventional story, Sid reports that Dobson had met up with Major Glenn Miller at Northolt Airport much later than the date and time Miller was said to have disappeared. True? A letter from John T. Garner of Frederick, MD to Sid Robinson declaring the he, Garner himself, had seen Miller at the Shuttle takeoff point in Bovington on December 16th, 1944. This letter, referred on to me from Sid, added a witness to others offering proof that Miller's flight from the King and Queens Airport in London was to Bovington, not directly to France. Bovington's weather was okay for a landing, while all of France was inclement, closed to air travel. Glenn Miller's last flight from England originated at Bovington. Not Twinwood. It didn't start with a single witness at Twinwood. It started at London's Northolt Airport with several witnesses. Yet another confirmed it later, Joe Dobson's copilot, Glen Ellerman. Sid Robinson and Richard Leive were the moving forces in locating the whereabouts of Dobson's copilot that foggy day of December 1944 at Northolt. The copilot could verify Joe Dobson's told-and-retold story. It was Glen Ellerman, Dobson recalled. He was reached by phone shortly before Dobson's death, and confirmed to Sid both the story and the citing. Sid related this to me both in letter and by phone.

Haynes' fabrication of Glenn's departure story upon which a false history has been built up—and believed—is hereby junked. In contrast, this is a credible report. As Miller's wife Helen would acknowledge, Glenn always took the shuttle to-and-from Paris.

Film scenarist Don Haynes claimed that he, himself, jiggled Miller's orders around, changing them at will. I dare anyone familiar with Base Operations in the heat of warfare to walk in and change orders, just like that. And for an officer two ranks higher than he was, it was a good way to get sent home. A guy could be court-marshaled for even trying such a trick. A general or two did get sent home for more trivial offenses. Don Haynes ran the band dates, not Glenn's life.

Captain Dobson (DFC) was awaiting weather clearance for Rheims, France. Fog at Rheims was mishmash… no landings. Bovington in Britain was open to Paris or Versailles. Glenn was going to Paris, not Rheims. He was at Northolt along with 22 officers from the 101st, all 22 of the division's brass preparing for the drop mission on Berlin connected with Eclipse. Gen. Maxwell Taylor was at the Pentagon for that critical decision. While Glenn took off on the 16th, Dobson and the twenty two had to wait for the next day's clearer weather in Central France. All of these movements are proven by 101st orders.

Another Sid Robinson scoop was the testimony he got from Captain, now Colonel, Harry Witt, Retired; a thoroughly precise officer, a senior pilot in the unit to which W.O. John Morgan belonged. Witt, a pal of Morgan's, was at Villacoublais that day, logged in and waiting for Morgan's arrival on that fatal day of December 15th. Morgan's flight was chalked up on the board. It did not leave from or land at Twinwood. Captain Witt waited and waited. The Norseman did not arrive, on time or late. When it was two hours overdue, Witt got worried. He checked. Warrant Officer John Morgan was flying solo. He had no passengers. No Twinwood stop-off... no Baessell... no Miller on board. He flew a hurried-up reconnaissance looking for Morgan. He was turned back by the weather around the Seine. He flew again the next day, looking. Nothing. Col. Harry Witt presented to Robinson all the proof of his search, as he did in a communication to me.

Truth was closing in. Glenn wasn't in Bedford. He was London to Versailles, flown by a command Colonel. That means total flight resonsibility. He wasn't with colleague Don Haynes to be picked up willy-nilly by young Morgan. He was with twenty two officers of the 101st Airborne, participating in a mission to end the war, a mission in jeopardy. For at Krefeld, thinking he was an armistice mediator, he would be met not by protecting German general Von Rundstedt or by Admiral Canaris, both sympathetic to the "generals' truce," but by Dirty Tricks killer-kidnapper, Otto Skorzeny.

CHAPTER **8**

USA Comes To Bat: Guys Who Were There

Unbeknownst to me and my British cohorts (busy excavating the Miller mess) a skein of Miller questioning had spread across America, led by the Beneke family's Sid Robinson. Sid had been a trooper in China, Burma, and India during the Big Two. He conjoined with members of the Euro/Asia AACS still alive, and some of the soldiers from the original "Band of Brothers" E-Company. He became close to Don Malarky and "Wild Bill" Guarnera plus two of the Miller band members, Trigger Alpert and John Best. Sympathetically, all lent bravos to get to the Truth. That didn't count about one hundred others from all over the world, mostly vets, who were corresponding with him regularly, eager for new findings, often adding their own vitally important details.

Samuel Goudsmit, the President's choice to find the German A-Bomb, found only Heisenberg and his lame 1944 fizzle. Samuel wasn't believed until war's end proved him right.

But government wasn't ready to admit it was wrong. Eclipse was well on the road. Little Slam ready to cut the war short and save countless lives. Bradley's suck-in plan had Marshall's and Eisenhower's approval. The limited SS armies to be sent forward into Bradley's trap would be chewed up enough by Patton and Hodges to allow the armistice plan to go through.

The 50-odd mile stretch Bradley had opened up, virtually "inviting" the SS Panzers to come through (and be hit), seemingly offering little defense. It was poor tank country, hilly with winding one-way roads.

What we didn't realize was that Hitler had spies at SHAEF who knew our plans intimately, and when we were expecting the least, the Germans hit us with everything they had. We were caught waiting for the signal that Eclipse, with its lesser amount of men and munitions, would be starting – a signal we obviously never would get.

Several versions of Haynes' diaries do exist. One was sold to Universal Pictures as basis for "*The Glenn Miller Story.*" Confronted with publishing untruths about the Glenn disappearance, Haynes limped publicly, admitted some "lapses of memory" but stood by his statement that an Army Air Corps Court of Inquiry had been held in January 1945. "There was no such inquiry," Herbert Miller, Glenn's brother, declared flatly in 1974. He told an avid BBC-TV audience in prime-time after the news that he had pressed and pressed since the end of the war to get such an inquiry served—and in vain. There is actually no official record of an inquiry for reasons that you can now understand because they relate to legalities and possible criminal prosecution. In perusing the great Wilbur Wright library in Southampton, England, one objective of that fine author became clear. Wright's overriding theme was his continual amazement at why he was being rebuffed time-after-time. He simply couldn't dig it. Why the cover-up? What was wrong?

He held letters from every federal institution in Washington that he contacted, including the White House (letter from President Reagan). I list them just to show how much Wright's puzzlement in his book <u>Millergate</u> (1990) is apparent. His was an excusable fury at being denied what should properly belong to public knowledge fifty years after any reason to sublimate news of American goof-ups was gone. In fact, the goof-ups might have steered us away from dirty whirlpools we dove into in current conflicts.

Among agencies who didn't want to know, or wouldn't want to open their files—re: Glenn Miller were:

1. National Personnel Records Center, St Louis, MO—However, the NPRC rendered me an unclassified Glenn Miller 201 file in 2000, but sent a blurred one to Wright only after presidential intercession.
2. Casualty and Memorial Affairs Division, Alexandria, VA
3. USAF Inspection and Safety Center, Norton AFB, CA
4. Military Field Branch, National Archives, Washington, DC
5. Department of the Army, Casualty and Reference Branch, National Archives, Washington, DC
6. Headquarters, Army Air Forces, Washington, DC
7. Maxwell Air Force Base, Alabama
8. U.S. Army Military Personnel Center, Alexandria, VA
9. U.S. National Archives, Washington, DC
10. U.S. Total Army Personnel Command, Alexandria, VA
11. Department of the Army, Adjutant General, The Pentagon, Alexandria, VA

A note here about the Freedom of Information

Act: Following one of Wright's inquiries, a Freedom of Information and Privacy Act Officer, Mary Anne Quintard, wrote him (Nov. 1991) that, "Due to the number of documents to be reviewed, a brief delay is expected." She wrote him six months later in May, 1992. Wright received mostly blank or blurred pages of the requested Glenn Miller 201 file along with this note: "In applying the FOIA balancing test we conclude that the privacy interests of others weigh against public releases, etc. etc." Wright then wrote back, declaring, "The entire package was worthless and contained no new information." If Wright's put down was because he was British, not American, it divulges a shameful standard. Wright was an RAF fighter against the Nazi Blitz when Britain stood alone against the common enemy, fighting for us when we weren't as yet in.

Interestingly, on this same subject, Peter Grose, biographer of Allen Dulles (who became head of the CIA) found difficulty in getting to basic information given classifications above "Confidential." He so states in his impeccable study of Allen Dulles, Gentleman Spy: The Life of Allen Dulles (1994). Dulles was called "America's top spook." The higher secrecy grades, Grose had to conclude, "... are commandments of policy, to remain forever dust." With my batch of Glenn's 201 file (clean ones) came this note: "Attached are some copies of documents from Major Miller's record containing information which is normally releasable by this center under the provisions of the Freedom of Information Act (FOIA)... In the case of Major Miller, we can only assure you that there is no part of his military personnel record which is kept separately, or which is classified with the current or previously used categories of Bigot, Top Secret, or Secret... We hold what appears to be a normal military personnel record, with a period of time not well accounted for." (Signed) Charles Pellegrini, National Personnel Records Center, St. Louis, MO. March 15, 2000.

So the wall is still up in the 21st Century, intended to remain so unless works like this one and Dale Titler's or U.S. reprints of Wilbur Wright's famous books can receive a go-ahead to be read in the USA. Titler, a well known American author about aircraft, wrote me in the '70s:

"For the past eight years, I have been involved with research on a documented volume on the circumstances that surround the death and disappearance of Glenn Miller in December 1944. I have amassed considerable documentation on the subject, enough to positively conclude that Miller, his pilot and passenger did not perish in a crash into the English Channel while on a flight from England to Paris. Among more than a hundred persons with whom I've corresponded and personally interviewed, was Bernie Quinn, formerly PIO (Public Information Officer) with SHAEF at the time of Miller's death. One account he said came from you in 1955, written when you were in the Persian Gulf at the time of Miller's disappearance but he had heard an account that Miller was murdered in Paris with a French woman. There were dozens of rumors and stories that circulated in the ETO after Miller's disappearance. But this one seems to predominate—in slightly varied versions—and stands out among them."

Dale Titler, still alive, and Bernie Quinn, now deceased, knew (because they were there in Paris) how Parisians absorbed themselves in the mystery. There was only one slight error in Dale's account. There wasn't one woman blamed in the death—there were prostitutes under RSHA brutality who told the authorities, "Glenn died in a whorehouse from a heart attack in the arms of a prostitute...."

etc." And Uncle Sam, for want of no better excuse, ducked and tried to hide behind John Morgan's disappearance in a single-engine plane over the English Channel!

I clued into the AACS network, an organization of veteran pilots and found some who actually flew Glenn Miller. They spoke up and got on the same jet trail as I was on. Joe Dobson was the big break. He was the bemedaled captain who regularly flew Gen. Maxwell Taylor, two star commander of the 101st Airborne. The airborne bragged about a bond between this legendary division "Band of Brothers" and Glenn Miller. He was their idol. He made a special trip to Newbury in England to entertain them— many of the 101st wrote to tell me. Here is a recap of some of their confidences. They prove Eclipse was in preparation and that a jump on Berlin, key to the operation, was on the verge.

In London, preparing to jump on *Deutschlandsender*, the gathered officers of the 101st knew from Glenn's presence that he would need their protection. This is no foolish surmise. Pilot Charlie Towne, a friend of Sid Robinson, wrote to the researcher whom he knew well, that he, himself, had flown elements of the 17th Airborne to participate in Operation Eclipse. This from Sid: "My log book shows I flew the original Argonia from Châteaudun to Fairford, England on December 12, 1944, with a formation of 45 ships, carrying the 17th Airborne (to its Eclipse mission). Noted historian Charles Whiting adds, "My own 14th Air brigade was alerted toward mid-December to prepare for a drop on Berlin." In short, the Mission for Ike was three-winged and scheduled for December 16, 1944. Glenn was not dead. He was key to a Win-the-War operation. Letters back and forth from SHAEF Special Service officers and those in Washington prove that Glenn had invited Don

McKay, his New York business manager, over to Paris for the year-end celebration

Interesting telltale: this London "rehearsal" for victory required no artillery officers. The brass was there, but not the artillery—it wasn't needed. Naturally not. This was to be a drop-takeover, not a long range firefight. Artillery Officers were left behind in France. Of course they were sent to Bastogne when plans changed where they formed a rugged defense.

Captain Joe Dobson (Distinguished Flying Cross) opened the door to the final solution of the Glenn Miller Mystery. His recorded testimony set Glenn on the track of a vital duty essential to the Supreme Commander and the fate of the war. On the day we interviewed him, Dobson was near-terminal, confined to bed. This was in 2002, long after the war. He was ill, but insisted on doing the tape. His wife Peggy was there to hold the mike and correct any slips of memory. This is Joe:

"At 7 a.m. on the 16th of December General Higgins got a message from General McAuliffe ordering the group back to Rheims immediately. I went out to Northolt Airfield arriving at about 9 a.m. on the 16th of December and was out there until about 4 p.m. Weather conditions were so bad that it was unsafe to fly.

"It was upon this day (16th of December, 1944) that I encountered a Colonel and Glenn Miller under the control tower of Northolt Airfield. To the best of my knowledge the time was 8 a.m. of the 16th December. To the best of my knowledge they took off. I saw them taxiing off. I went back to the Northolt Airfield control tower on 17 December, 1944 and at about 10 a.m. the weather cleared and I called General Higgins to come out for takeoff. We departed Northolt at about...PAUSE... on the morning of

December 17th, 1944, and returned to Rheims."

This is the story Joe Dobson has told everybody since the end of World War Two, at first to wife and friends; then he was warned to shut up, to which he paid no attention. After Sid Robinson's interview with Dobson and his wife (she, too, was taped), I received the following memo from Sid.[42]

"Joe was staying at the Regent Palace Hotel in London. General Higgins and his staff stayed at a luxury hotel across the street from the Regent Palace. Joe said it was the Savoy. Joe never knew the officer with Miller by name. The name Baessell was not mentioned. The officer said he was a command pilot (Baessell had no license to fly). Joe saw the two men climb aboard a small plane. He saw the plane taxi down the runway and disappear. I took this to mean that the airplane eventually took off from Northolt. If they went on to Bovington that day they would have had to take off at Northolt in order to get to Bovington. Joe was not aware of a third person in the party."

This was a big break—it established responsible, accurate evidence that the Channel take off from Twinwood in Bedford was treacherously wrong, and that Glenn Miller was alive and on his way to Paris under far more serious circumstances and at a conclusively later date than the world had been led to believe. Sid dispatched me the above note after the meeting with Joe and Peggy, and I telephoned the Dobsons to confirm the dates and wordage.

The note and testimony (tape recorded) is now part of the Glenn Miller history. The highly-decorated and responsible pilot Captain Joe Dobson is an integral part of Bastogne heritage, so his word must be taken over an unnamed officer of the band—never identified officially, merely as author of a movie.

Some loggerheads still swear by the "Twinwood farewell"
of December 15th. Whoever claims that as "expertise" is
a generation slow to the mystery's solution and is copying
long discarded rumors. The airport of RAF Twinwood
was doubled with neighboring RAF Cranfield airport, two
distinctly different fields with different missions. The two
kept their own weather patterns and strips—but the same
rules applied to both, and were tight. This was Top Secret
country, close to Bletchley Park. If one airport was closed
for a day, the other was marked closed as well. This British
security lasted through the war. Such congeniality and go-
to-hell atmosphere portrayed in the Haynes' diaries—better
described as partying—would never have been condoned
at Twinwood or Cranfield.

GI Sergeant Broderick Crawford, whose pictures were
playing on the Champs Elysees of Paris in 1944, was one
of the top American film stars of that decade. I met him
in 1979. It didn't take long for me to become acquainted
with him at the palace of *Vaux-le-Vicompte*. We were
working on a Laurence Olivier film directed by George Roy
Hill, titled *A Little Romance*. We were to work together
for three months traveling from Paris to Verona to Venice
in the shooting schedule. That's when I learned from Brod
that he had been Glenn's buddy and virtual roommate up
to disappearance. Crawford knew what happened. Would
he go back on the oath-of-silence he had sworn to? Would
he tell me what happened?

I suggested a dinner one night at the hotel where he
and wife were putting up, the *très élégant* Raphael Hotel
on Avenue Kleber, just off the Arc de Triomphe. Brod had
been assigned a billet there during the war. The hotel was
for U.S. field-grade officers. Brod was a sergeant in the Paris
MP's, but wore tailor-made uniforms. "How come you could

stay at the Rapfael?" I asked. "Tell you tonight," he winked, and went looking for a "loo" on the grounds of the French palace where we were filming.

There was no such thing as a round, open-to-the-air urinal in these palace grounds. One had to sneak into the wonderfully preserved rooms of Louis the Fourteenth, inspiration for the later Versailles. I've always chuckled at the derivation of the word "Loo." During World War I toilet locations were signified by the simple double zero "OO". The French, of course, pronounced it with the article "l" before the zeros.

What I didn't know about Glenn Miller came pretty fast that night. I didn't dare look at the *sommelier*. A bottle of champagne was priced $100. Brod saved Warner Bros. this bill as he had underarm a fifth of vodka, had it planked on center table in a silver, hotel-embossed bucket. "Mill got me a room here when he stayed. I hadda look after him... Ike's orders!"

We went through his Hollywood years, fascinating enough, then his being assigned to Glenn's contingent at Yale, then to England and France. "Like Ike figured, I'd better be here in the MPs as a kinda guard. Mill had to slip over quiet-like from London every now and then. He was on a mission for Ike."

It wasn't long before he was talking about "me and Mill and Croz," idols of his past whom he had consorted and cavorted with from Hollywood to London to this City of Light. Brod had a small part in *A Little Romance*, so he had plenty of time to yakkity-yak, and his stories were mostly of his being made an honorary major of Paris and how he and his American wife were still celebrities, trompin' the Champs (Champs Elysees) and being noticed.

It was hearty talking with him, if saddening. He couldn't

go long without a sip of vodka, and I wouldn't drink with him on duty, as he offered behind the giant statue in the impeccable 17th Century gardens of the palace where we were filming. Finally, once again at dinner, he mentioned Glenn's "mission."

What kind of mission?—I wanted to know. Brod shrugged. He didn't want to talk but I waited. Then he burst out: "We were pals but Mill shut up about whatever it was Ike asked him to do. I had better sense than tryin' to string him out. Ole Mill had a sewing machine mouth when he wanted not to say somethin'."

This one-time great star and superb actor rambled on, not about Glenn, but about Paris and movies he had done around Europe, Italy, and how he had met his wife. I never got her name, just Mrs. Crawford. She kept a slit eye out on that bottle which was more half-empty than half-full. Brod kept on. "Mill was his favorite nickname. I never used it until we'd been about a year together. Why'd he pick me? Dunno. Liked me, I guess. He was a very formal gent, not like me. Nor Crosby. But ole Croz had it together."

I looked at the pastiche of the Hotel Raphael and could understand how Glenn could fit in here. The Hotel was a class act and so was he. And he loved class. Reason his band was top of the others.

I remember the weird feeling I think Brod and I both had just then. We were taken back to living in another epoch, not World War Two but at Louis XIV's *Vaux-le-Viscompte*, hundreds of years ago. Then dining here at the Raphael like Louis XVI court companions—and through it all we were discussing the future...in World War Two. I think that's why he began to talk. It was strange, forbidding.

We walked over to the Arc de Triomphe only a couple of blocks away. The Eternal Flame lay flickering in the wind.

I asked Brod when he last saw Glenn. It was then that he said something which sent a shock up my spine.

"The Bulge had started but Glenn was no where to be found. But I knew he'd been here in the Raphael suite. We had adjoining rooms. He'd unpacked and the box was gone, a box he'd had with tapes and records. Broadcast stuff, I guess. German manufacture… Magnet… something."

I said, "Magnetophon… first German tape recorders. I used one. They were about a hundred-year-jump ahead of wire recorders."

Brod looked at me, shivered in the night air. "Let's go back to the hotel. I need a drink." We said nothing. His lips were moving. When he whispered Amen, I realized he had made a silent prayer for Glenn. What Brod said that night I've relayed to my fellow researchers. It supports exactly what Joan Heath wrote.

My Glenn Miller meeting with Britisher David Niven came, of all places, in Rhodes, Greece, the island of the Adriatic where the Crusaders based. We were doing a picture, *Escape to Athena*, with a lot of stars, Telly Savalas, Roger Moore, Sonny Bono, Elliot Gould, Stephanie Powers, Claudia Cardinale and Niven. It was kind of a celebration picture, a holiday for all these stars from one agency, William Morris. The pix was a send-up on war pictures where Niven played a nice-guy Nazi officer collecting artifacts, where occupied villagers lined up willingly to be shot and where Savalas danced in a Greek wedding and Bono cooked spaghetti. Despite the hokum, Elliot Gould filmed one of the best motorbike chases through cobbled winding streets ever made.

Remote David Niven didn't seem to belong to this gang though son Jamie of WM talent agency had set up the frolic. When in the course of human events (a la Hollywood)…

there is always a lull during the sharpest action. When villagers attacked the Nazi prison to free our notable cast, I learned from a wise old Best Boy on camera that David was one of the ghost-like "Phantoms" in World War Two, an honest-to-God Commando. Commandos were the British equivalent to our OSS! I jumped. Glenn Miller had been tabbed by the Nazis as *Kommando*. I knew vaguely that David Niven had had something to do with Armed Forces Broadcasting in England, but his Commando connection was for me unknown. There he was, on the set now in front of me, a surviving *Kommando* on that list Hitler had condemned. As Glenn had been.[4]

I had my chance to get close to him next day when he was waiting for two extras to finish their takes. He knew I was military and I told him my record. When our talk hit on the Bulge, I asked him how well he knew Glenn Miller. The conversation took a cold shower. He frowned and said only, "I was his superior at the Troop Broadcasting Unit in London." He quickly changed the subject. I thought little of it at the time but a few years later, when I discovered he was in the thick of the breakthrough at Spa and Radio Luxembourg, that he had known Glenn in Hollywood, that they had done concerts together, were both on secret missions, had disappeared for the same five days – and in his two books of memoirs The Moon's A Balloon (1971) and Bring on the Empty Horses (1975), and in an autobiography, he had never mentioned Glenn Miller, not even his name. I wished I could have had that interview back. Niven was in the know. And he knew what it meant to keep his yap shut. Like now.

Putting all the two's together and coming up with a few fours, I figured out what must have happened. Wilbur Wright in Millergate (1990) had noted David Niven's expressed alarm, as Niven recalled his concern of the Bulge breakthrough, for the safety of Marlene Dietrich at Spa. She was there "on a USO tour" when Hitler's giant fist smashed through the lines. "Knowing what they would do to her, if caught," are the words Niven used when telling how he had phoned his old army buddies in England for help to get her out, and had been turned down flat. They were too busy themselves. Niven proceeds (in his book) to the end of the Bulge as if nothing more than a few ho-hums had occurred. What had happened to Niven as Reich artillery was pounding his ears? He just "disappeared," seemingly a favored duty status during that part of the war. "What did you do in the Great War, granddaddy" (as the line goes). "Oh, I just disappeared." The mystery of Niven's whereabouts during this interval is explained only by his Reich penetration to finish the job Glenn Miller had started on—personally getting the vital message from General Marshall to General Dornberger to get the German rocket scientists out. But I suspect also, never proven, that the unidentified telephone call wife Helen Miller received in New Jersey on Sunday, December 17th, as reported by Herb Miller who was there with his sister-in-law, was from close friend in Hollywood, David Niven.

Not even his family, his wife Hjordis nor his son Jamie, would ever discuss the tragedy. Why? We continued to try to find answer—just to the "Why?" if nothing else. Everything pointed to that venerable rock of British history, the respected and massive Public Record Office at Kew Gardens, London. All of the many RAF and Bomber Command records are filed there under Secret, Most Secret, and Ultra Secret categories.

Marlene Dietrich was part of Operation Eclipse.[18] She was to be the "Glenn Miller" of Radio Luxembourg, and was standing by as a USO entertainer – which of course she was. Her German was perfect and she had sworn to the side of the Allies. Both Niven and Marlene avoided mentioning Glenn in their respective post-war books, their omissions obvious in the overall cover-up.

It's amazing how the decades of lies and confusion and threats failed to disenchant the hard-working researchers for truth. But, naturally, in the Law of Totality, there has to be an exception.

Glenn Miller's loss gave one ex-British Liberator navigator an opportunity for publicity and perhaps cash. Forty years after the war Fred Shaw from South Africa claimed that he held a log which proved "Glenn Miller's plane had been hit by a 4,000 pound 'cookie' bomb, jettisoned from his own Lancaster bomber. He said, "On an aborted run scheduled for Siegen, Germany, it happened. We started, turned back, dropped our bombs in the Channel. I saw our 'cookie' hit a small plane flying near the surface below." Sure enough, the date of the personal log he had scribbled out—not the official one—matched the declared date of Glenn's "disappearance." He and two witnesses had seen the explosion a mile below in cloudy weather; he had self-penned it in his "log." Both British and American governments leaped on the gimmick as "conclusive."

The Glenn Miller Society of Britain sent a committee to South Africa to interview the crewman, Fred Shaw. His story was that from 6,000 feet height, required altitude for jettisoning, the explosion below was seen and that the pilot, Lt. Gregory, also knew about it. Pilot Gregory was interviewed by others (including Wilbur Wright) but had no remembrance of such an accident. Nor of a briefing to explain the aborting. The two witnesses to Shaw's story had meanwhile died but the British press grabbed onto the incident, determined it conclusive, and both governments "didn't disagree." With a massive bombing mission as the Siegen objective (108 Lancasters) a briefing would have been imperative. What results? What reports? What losses? Briefings detailed plane by plane tabulations. All shoulders were shrugged. What was the real story of that now-famous flight? Still secret, was the answer. "Why were million-dollar bombs jettisoned in the first place?" Shaw was asked. His limp rejoinder: Cookie bombs carried under the hull might scrape the tarmac upon landing back in England. "It didn't take long for researchers to poke holes in Shaw's theory, but the impact of the Glenn Miller sob-story movie was such that proof was ignored." Fred Shaw passed away in 1999 and his wife put up the personally-drawn "log" for auction. It fetched $35,000, sold to a collector, William Suitts from Boulder, Colorado.

This outlandish sum for an unofficial piece of paper caused 'The Screaming Eagles' of the 101st" to gather in protest. Not one pilot of the heroic dozens still alive today believes in either the "Twinwood" theory or the "Lancaster" theory. Consequently, some of the "Band of Brothers" who Stephen Spielberg put together for a TV drama joined our foray. There weren't many in E Company left but uncanny memories of the real tide of events back then gave Sid Robinson and me encouragement.

To Warrant Officer John Morgan, EC64 Norseman pilot, who has, perhaps, more honestly than any "disappeared," I say sorry...and sorry again to his niece who has never given up writing to find out where his body might be. Maybe he wrenched a twist to his steering apparatus, or saw angry waves and curls of fog in his face before drowning, or lay bloody and untended in a totaled EC64 wreckage found near Merville, France. Wherever he or his soul might rest, it's doubtful he could have imagined that his demise would fill sixty years of curiousity, analysis, contradiction and exaggeration as has occurred all over the world. It is high time to clear the air. Baessell, supposed a passenger of Morgan's, was not aboard, as is now proven. He was said by some to have died finally in East Africa, getting a U.S. pension.

To John Morgan's niece—your uncle was a casualty of the war. Like many.

My colleague Sid Robinson produced the man from Austin, Texas, a captain and distinguished retired colonel, who was an ace pilot in Morgan's unit, 2nd SAD. Harry Witt throws both governments' claim into a bladed fan and let's us watch the feces scatter. Captain Harry F. Witt was waiting at Villacoublais, France in the American wing of the French airport for his fellow flyer John "Pee Wee" Morgan to show up. Morgan had taken off from Wattisham in England, northeast of Bedford, to fly directly to France that morning of December 15, 1944. No passengers. Base Ops posted this data as required. It was a late morning take off, no stops planned. Twinwood was closed. The weather was atrocious. Morgan became due. One hour overdue. Two hours. No Morgan. Base Ops, according to Colonel Witt, announced the missing craft, asked him to fly a search—as was the custom. This, particularly, as Morgan was a pal. Witt took off, flying low, scanning both sides. Weather stopped him as he reached the Seine. He turned back. Next morning (16th) when the weather cleared, he flew all the way to Wattisham along the path authorized for 2nd SAD pilots to fly. Nothing. No wreckage. Morgan, solo, had either gone off course or plummeted in the waves.

Baessell was not aboard, else Witt would have known it from Base Ops. In no way could Glenn have been aboard.

Colonel Witt, one of the top pilots in Europe during World War Two had volunteered for the RAF in Battle of Britain days, had then transferred to the US Air Corps. This sums up his email messages to AACS News Letter readers, anxious for the key to the Glenn Miller Mystery. Witt's recollection and notes taped by our researcher, Sid Robinson:

"Harry Witt was a RAF pilot from 1939 to 1942. In 1942 he became a pilot in the US Army Air Corps. His tour of duty in the ETO was from 1939 throughout the duration of WWII. Witt was assigned to the 8th Air Force Service Command—2nd Strategic Air Depot. Lieutenant Col. Norman F. Baessell and Flight Officer John R. Morgan were also members of the 8th AFSC 2nd SAD. Witt was well-acquainted with Morgan and Baessell. On December 15, 1944 Witt was on duty at Villacoublay airfield near Paris. Villacoublay was the destination of pilot John R. Morgan on a flight from England. Morgan failed to arrive at Villacoublay at his (Morgan's) ETA (estimated time of arrival.) Witt was ordered to fly a "Look/See" search along the known path that Morgan would be flying which was from Beachy Head on the English coast to Fecamp on the French coast. At Fecamp Morgan would follow the Seine River up to Paris. Witt departed Villacoublay in search of Morgan's aircraft but the total overcast produced zero visibility all the way from Paris to Fecamp. Witt flew back to Villacoublay and made a second search at daylight 16 December, 1944. No trace was found."

THIS FROM HARRY WITT: "Comments to Sid and others regarding the UC-64 Noorduyn Norseman-—A very good bush operation type aircraft. Bush flying is not for the novice pilot, and this aircraft was no flying delight, it was not very forgiving of sins. Get a copy of the Pilots Notes for the aircraft. Look under the heading Carburetor Ice. In my days it was a redline item. You did not fly into known carburetor icing conditions except in an emergency. Winter time, 200 foot ceiling, fog and free air temperatures just above freezing invited carburetor ice. That meant engine quit and those great big undercarriage legs and wheels had to have an ideal piece of ground. A water landing would certainly put you on your back, tall grass, wheat/corn, hedgerows, probably. One sputter due to ice on takeoff would put you in trouble. Morgan breaking out of cloud to make a landing and takeoff when the field was closed due to weather? Remember, you can get carburetor ice out of clear air if temperature and humidity were right. The venture in the carb would induce it. On Morgan himself—Somebody sent me a copy of his service record. It stated that he did Elementary and Service Pilot Training in Canada. (That's when he would have gotten his RAF wings.) A year later his record stated that he attended a second Elementary and Service Flying Training Schools in England. Transfers of US citizens who were in the British/Allied Services began in the summer of 1942. By summer of 1943 almost all those eligible (and who wished to do so) had transferred. I transferred as a Flight Officer in January 1943. By the time I joined 2SAD I was a Captain. Morgan, wherever he had been, was still a Flight Officer! Curious! Morgan came from Nowhere and disappeared to Nowhere! Wilbur Wright writes of having known that a C-64 was dived on off the coast of France (by enemy aircraft). Ignore it... Why?" HARRY F. WITT.

Col Witt was certainly a bastion in clarifying puzzles. I was pleased that Witt gave credence to Joan Heath's snow at Versailles—"Could have been that day, gone tomorrow and snow again with rain and sleet the next day." On Stephen Early, architect, ipso facto, of the rigged disappearance of Glenn at Twinwood, Witt says: "An interesting thought on your part." He adds that Brigadier Elliot Roosevelt, Commander of the 8th Air Force, 325th Reconnaissance Wing, "could have had a hand in it, too." Witt points out that, "The President's son was FDR's back channel messenger to all levels of the British government, to Ike and the Supreme Command."

Perhaps his clearest point is answer to the most frequent question asked since Miller disappeared. Witt: "Morgan did not land and take off at Twinwood on December 15, 1944."

Next there comes a whole new ball game. Into that venerable castle of hush-hush with hands-on documents dating back to the ancient Battle of Hastings (1066)—we are invited into the sanctuary of Britain's PRO, Public Record Office, where facts cannot be made up: They are what they are.

CHAPTER **9**

Into the House of Secrets

The noble Institute which guards British truths, infamies, justice and secrets from time immemorial is called the Public Record Office (PRO). Given its sprawling mass of building at Kew Gardens, London, it claims, without much denial, that it can prove "1066... and all that." Especially the "all that."

Whatever its true scope, the PRO is said to hide the peculations of Edward VII, the wild parties of George IV at Brockett Hall with Lady Caroline Lamb climbing nude from a giant soup tureen, and perhaps even more recently, whatever happened to Princess Diana.

I'd been after them for years to let me at the SECRET files of RAF Stations and AIR 14, 24, 25 and 27. These would have included the notorious details of Bomber Harris's obliterating 1945 raid over Dresden which destroyed the whole city in a fire-tsunami—naturally a bit awkward and possibly embarrassing to be gotten into at this friendly stage with the Germans. Whatever, reluctance was the byword, even though "Bomber" Harris had nothing to do with that "Sunday-go-to-Meeting" flight which supposedly dropped a bomb on unsuspecting Glenn. PRO was always gentlemanly and courteous, but in the SECRET sector—"I beg your pardon."

Finally, considering which was more important to let go of: the name of the Cromwell spy who turned in Charles II to be executed, or the falsity of the Glenn Miller claims, after seven years they let me inside.

Getting to the nub of things, I felt like being tipped on the shoulder by Her Majesty's blade. I was walking with a lot of ghosts pushing me... Jack Taylor, Herb Miller, John Edwards, Clive Ward, Dennis Cottam, Wilbur Wright and dozens more Miller researchers, not to count those still alive: Dale Titler, Sid Robinson, Ed Polic, Richard Leive, etc., and Mr. Bowler.

Who was Mr. Bowler? The RAF Museum in Croydon, England records him as Air Traffic controller assigned to Twinwood Airfield. He was on duty that day of December 15, 1944.

Here in the files, Bowler verified that a closed airport meant exactly what it said. He named an aircraft engineer and two WAAFs "who would support his statement that no plane landed at Twinwood or took off that day." To do either demanded an open Control Tower, with VHF radio linked to a radio DF facility. No pilot would risk a landing there when a signals square (flag) outside the Tower was flown. Nor in low overcast (which Haynes would have encountered) could a pilot come down without radio assistance. Not to overkill the point – "Security in a closed airfield," Bowler is quoted, "means fire or rescue vehicles on standby that day. A pilot would never risk himself or his plane or his record unless of dire emergency."

To superkill any overkill, the Public Record Office went back to that day which it had well recorded, and pulled out its SECRET documents for Twinwood and Cranfield. Their records contained all other available and necessary data re: inspections, repairs, what planes were there, how many, what needed to be done, what was done. The information on Dec. 15, 1944 was clear enough—no flying today. Airfield closed. Twinwood and Cranfield Airfields closed.

It was inevitable, I suppose, with fact-digging on "declared dead in the Channel Glenn" that I would get warnings to stop, or else! It was never made clear what the "or else" was. Whatever, it frightened off John Edwards, Clive Ward and a couple of others but not Wilbur Wright- as reported by Wilbur's son David. Wilbur just thumbed his nose and kept going. My threat was claimed to be from Steven Miller, Glenn's son in the U.S. Two Royal engineers from British Telecom quickly proved otherwise. The Gloucestershire police were called in, (I lived near Prince Charles in Tetbury). The "or else" phone threat was investigated, but I was never told what the Police did except that they found the instigators and laid it on the line. If it happened again, the culprits would face jail. No more calls. But one of the "jokers" had a quirky idea. He framed a three-page letter and sent it to my press contacts in the US. It stated that I had been found dead in a body bag, tossed on the rear entrance to the German Embassy in London. My name was said to be Adolph Hitler's pseudonym and I had been an escaped Nazi finally caught up with. Pictures were offered to prove I was Hitler in disguise. I don't suppose my birth certificate from Baltimore, Maryland, younger than *Der Fuehrer*, would have supported their case.

These attempts to install fear fell a bit short. My "body in a bag assassins" should have looked at my war record in

Vietnam and the Big Two before they hung a death threat on my head. I had a real one in Nam for anti-Commie broadcasts to the North. That threat was intercepted by the MSU Police Mission with the U.S. Embassy, and then a USIS Library was blown apart next to my house in 1957. If I survived those, no Glenn Miller hatchet men were going to put me down.

My search in Kew PRO found documents not even the UK government was aware of.[36, 38, 39, 40, 41] Here I was, confronted with AIR 24, 25 and 27 sectors of paper I had tried for years to get to. They were piled high to the ceiling. I had to give my able guide Roger Barrington some idea of what, in this incredible mass of SECRETS, I was looking for.

This is what the Glenn Miller Society of England was saying at the time: "Shaw's bomber crew was part of a large squadron which aborted a mission to Siegen, Germany on December 15, 1944. On return to England, the squadron let loose their 4,000 pound bombs over the English Channel rather than land at airfields with them aboard. The bombs which were time-delayed exploded just above the surface of the water. Navigator Shaw in one of the bombers saw his Cookie bomb explode against a small aircraft flying below. The time differential from Twinwood airfield to the jettison point coincided with that of the bombing squadron's release of bombs in the Channel."

This story, born in the '70s, is still believed by the various Glenn Miller enterprises in Boulder, Colorado and at Glenn Miller's birthplace in Clarinda, Iowa. An "infinite" number of facts weigh against this, most importantly perhaps is that the Fred Shaw's "log" was self-manufactured and has nothing to do with official details of the flight itself. But Navigator Fred Shaw had magic words and an even more vivid imagination. This is what he said:

"I remember seeing a small plane spiraling out of control toward the water. Around it I could see the sea bubbling and blistering with the exploding bombs. As each bomb burst I could see the blast wave from it radiating outward, it was obvious to me that airplane below was in trouble. Eventually I saw it disappear into the English Channel."

The only proof Shaw could muster for these words was that the incident occurred on December 15th and was near the time of the alleged Twinwood departure. He said such a claim would settle the Glenn Miller mystery forever. It didn't and it doesn't. It is necessary in 2008 to compile our observations and our documents which prove otherwise. Here is the case from evidence at PRO and other files as indicated:

FROM MINISTRY OF DEFENCE, UK (to Fred Shaw): "There is no record of the existence of a Southern jettison Zone. It would be a waste of time to search for something that did not exist."

FROM THEODORE V. CARLSON, 65TH AACS group: In the 1990's decade, I started a project with Bob Cloer, editor of the Army Air Corps News Letter, to get American pilots' opinions on jettisoning unused bombs on return, and where and when it was allowed. Bob sent me this comment from Theodore Carlson, decorated American pilot, with a near maximum count of bombing sorties to his credit. It was printed in the AACS News Letter and appeared to be a majority opinion. "It is true that returning bombers would sometimes come off a raid with un-dropped bombs and dump them in the sea before reaching England. However, I was usually briefed up to drop them in the North Sea and not into the Channel. Perhaps someone did jettison bombs over the Channel, but the odds of hitting a small aircraft would seem to be quite small."

FROM THE ASSOCIATED PRESS (July 2001) – "The English Channel was full of Allied ships at all times. The military could not possibly have established exclusion zones for the safe dropping of armed bombs."

FROM RAF BOMBER COMMAND RECORDS: "Standard procedure was that Allied bombers brought back all bombs not dropped on enemy targets. On a mission the group had primary, secondary and alternative other targets. Jettisoning of bombs was allowed only if the aircraft was damaged to such degree that its return home was questionable, or if severely wounded men were aboard."

FROM DON HANSON, RICHFIELD, MN: He was one of the American airmen flying parts from England to France to repair and reconditions downed aircraft, the same general job as John Morgan. The single-engine Norseman was the favorite transporting plane. Thus Hanson's opinion has singular significance. His comment was also printed in the AACS News Letter. "The people I knew in France who flew Norseman airplanes were of the opinion that Morgan tried to fly under the 'soup', got his undercarriage down too low, and crashed into the Channel. I haven't seen any evidence that could change that theory."

FROM RICHARD LEIVE, LUCASVILLE, OHIO: "I believe the Joe Dobson story is credible. If so, then Miller was alive and well on the 17th. His co-pilot Glen Ellerman told the same story before he died several years ago. George Ferguson, who was stationed in Brussels and had been a pilot for Baessell earlier, said he heard radio traffic about Morgan's overdue status on the 15th. Don Hanson, who was at SAD5 in Merville, said his CO informed his group on the 16th that Morgan was missing in flight. If radio traffic about the status of Morgan was heavy on the 15th and 16th, then why did Don Haynes say he was not aware that Miller was missing until he and the band arrived at Orly on the 18th?"

FROM ED POLIC, MILPITAS, CA: Ed Polic's two-volume, privately published Encyclopedia of Glenn Miller has been mentioned at times in this book. It can be bought by contacting the publisher of this book. Ed gave these comments on Shaw's jettisoning story to Sid Robinson who passed them to me: "Several points in Fred Shaw's story are highly improbable. I find it hard to believe that he could identify the airplane that he claimed he saw as a US64 because of the large difference in altitudes, as he claimed, between the two airplanes, and because of the way he would have had to position himself to view almost straight down in the airplane that he was in, and because of the extremely short time he would have had, even if the weather had been perfect."

FROM SID ROBINSON, DEQUINCY, LA: Of all U.S. Glenn Miller researchers, my colleague Sid Robinson was the only one who took time, trouble and expense to get a copy of Fred Shaw's contentious report of the jettisoning. Here he describes the self-written observation of it in a letter to me, (we corresponded once or twice a week for several years): "The entry in the Shaw log reads:

15 12 44 1200 Lancaster 970 f/o Gregory navigator (remarks)

Date hour aircraft type /number pilot duty (remarks)

The remarks read: Ops. Siegen. Canceled. Jettison Southern area.

The above log makes no mention of sighting a Norseman below. During World War Two all crewmen of all bombers kept diaries, no two of which were alike, even among members of the same crews. The official records were kept by Bomber Group Command. Shaw's was not the official record. I have seen the log Bill Suitts paid $35,000 for. It's the best example of the Emperor's New Clothes. Shaw's letter was written in 1989."

FROM WILBUR WRIGHT, SOUTHAMPTON: "The Lancaster Bombs theory enjoyed an ephemeral popularity for a year or so, but the factual evidence was always against it, in reference to flight times, routes, airspeeds, restricted areas and the like. Crew members I contacted, including the pilot, Flt. Lt. Gregory, had seen nothing and Shaw did not make a formal report on returning to base, as he was obliged to do by regulations."

Obviously, these truths lay in the records of Bomber Command I was now investigating. These were long-languid secrets. They were dusty enough to prove their age. Since "Bomber" Harris's devastating raid on Dresden in 1945, leveling half of the city and its civilian population, files were unavailable. Then, just as Kew PRO was starting to relax its classifications, a statue went up in England celebrating the hero, "Bomber" Harris himself. German newspapers cried out. Old wounds were opened. Eventually, though, everybody relaxed. Finally, I got the invitation long cherished.

So the long awaited look-see at the real Siegen bombing raid of December 15, 1944 could be examined. I don't know why I was surprised but I was. The Siegen bombing raid of December 15th never took place. That was our first big shock.

True, there was a December 16th raid on Siegen which actually took place. The briefing reports showed this clearly, who was in the raid and who was not. Gregory's Lancaster, meaning Shaw, was not in the Siegen raid and never was. So Shaw lied. And the raid was successful. It was not aborted but was on a <u>different date</u>.

The real Siegen raid is indicated in Operations Record

Book (Form 540) which details every raid planned in December. Day by day Bomber Command's inexorable print flows, giving plane-by-plane results: enemy action, bombs on target or not, weather, altitude, count and types of bombs, jettison if any, pilot comments, losses, etc.[38, 41]

Here is the record[24]—13 Dec. No operations—14 Dec. (night 14/15 Dec)—10 aircraft for mining operations—15 Dec. No operations—16 Dec. Target—Siegen. (With all details as above listed.) Mission successful. All drops over target. No jettisoning. No Lt. Gregory. Gregory's bomber, meaning Shaw, was not among the 108 Lancasters dispatched to bomb Siegen. And all of the squadrons returned without jettisoning.

The strike on enemy railyards at Siegen (near Bonn) was scheduled for 16 December, the date of Hitler's breakthrough. It was a vast armada of 108 Lancasters. The drop was aimed at disrupting SS reinforcements coming from the Eastern Front. It was a long flight, there and back. It was successful. It was not aborted. There was no jettisoning in the English Channel or anywhere as claimed by Shaw. In fact, Shaw and the Gregory crew were not present. The unarguable records of PRO Kew prove the fact and I'm allowed to show you here in this book in your hands. To put an end to the clamor, Bomber Command estimated its Siegen run (in a very real briefing) as "a very successful G.H. operation." So much for the flight which Shaw bamboozled. Next, a fair question—what happened to the flight Shaw was really on? Did he get mixed up? If he did, it was purposeful. His flight (Lt. Gregory commanding) went to Trier. It flew four days later, December 19. 1944. Shaw couldn't lay claim to the Trier flight. It wouldn't match Twinwood.

The bomb described by Shaw as "the Cookie" is not aboard the plane. The mission's entire cargo of bombs went on target over Trier, Gregory's report shows. There was no jettisoning in the English Channel for any of the airships in either the Siegen run or the Trier run.[34, 41] Whew!!!

PRO came up with another discovery, a shock that went to the top. This totally respectable "secret storehouse" of British history is not without its own stealthy burglar who tries to steer history. My able guide in the paper maze puzzled over an error never before noticed up to my visit. Roger Barrington lived close to Kew in Twickenham, Middlesex. A genial, most engaging chap of moderate years, he was at home in this bewildering ocean of paper. I felt that if he by accident got lost, he could find his way outside just by following his nose, smelling the paper. But the Glenn Miller Search for Truth caught him up short.

"There is something amiss here," he said, frowning. He held up a clutch of documents. Each sheet detailed various squadrons participating in the Siegen raid, and a lot of squadrons made up the 108 bombers in that successful raid. Shaw's bomber (Flight Lt. Gregory) was one of those listed for Siegen with Gregory's name at the bottom. But how could that be when his plane was not on that mission? All details were present for all the other planes: type of bombs dropped, weight, casualties, time run, damage effect—all of this. But on a torn piece of paper: names were there, and Gregory's. No details. Somebody had tampered. The details which might have proved Gregory's participation in Siegen were absent, as if someone had carelessly torn away the Trier text. There were uneven edges on the tear. Could we find the matching piece of paper where the torn piece would fit? That then would provide Gregory's flight details.

"Ahhhh...." said Barrington, shaking one of the ledger pages, the one showing the number of planes in Squadron 149. All other squadrons were intact with full information.

Only Gregory's flight with names on a torn piece of paper had no details. We added up the total of planes... 108; exactly as targeted. 108 WITHOUT the Gregory/Shaw's craft, which would add up to 109—Wrong! Could those extra names have been slipped in to verify Shaw's presence on the Siegen raid, thus "prove" his Glenn Miller story? There could be no other explanation. If we could only find the rest of that raggedly-torn piece of paper where details would be fully informational....

"Who would dare come in here and alter the records?" Barrington said angrily. "That's treacherous. That's a crime!"

"How about the government?" I offered the question as more of a statement, and I wasn't being sarcastic. He didn't say anything. The frown returned with a knit of eyebrows. "So he was not on the Siegen raid. He must have been on another raid, and got his stories wrong."

He went scurrying and the dust, which a weekly vacuuming wouldn't phase, covered the wrinkles on his forehead. "Here it is.... Shaw was never on the Siegen run. He was on Trier, a run three days later. Here it is, Gregory's name at the bottom, just like the torn off page in Siegen, and this is torn off exactly the same. Look at the tear.... It fits." He scrambled the files in his hand. "See? A perfect joining. So the details belong to Trier, not Siegen. Trier was also a successful run. Three days later. Bombs on target, none jettisoned. None aborted. The rips across the page put together make one page. There's even the Trier destination printed on the detailed part of the page."[38] Look now at the full page from the Trier Mission (matched to page 1's tear-off). 'Trier' is clearly marked and so is Gregory's name as the last plane in the squadron. Those flights were separated by three days. (December 16-December 19.)[39, 40, 41]

Now, what was that about a bomb hitting Glenn on December 15?

So the first and second theories of Glenn Miller's vanishing have been 100% wiped out. The proof exists that he was on a secret mission, an integral mission in SHAEF's effort to win the war early.

In a previous chapter we left off Glenn planning for Paris in his quarters at London Mount Royal hotel. Officialdom, crooking a finger, told everybody he was in Bedford with the band. Highly unlikely that he would drive to some off-beat location near Bedford, through potholes and V-missile damage in a dense fog, to say goodbye to a band he would be seeing shortly in Paris.

The shuttle out of Bovington to Paris had two destinations: Orly or Villacoublais, the latter for anyone wanting Versailles. There was limited demand for Ike's Headquarters to which entrance was severely restricted. Possibly Glenn's shuttle was to Orly (main Paris destination), to be in his room at the Raphael when called. It's probable at that desperate moment: no-one knew of Hitler's quadrupling of forces, not even Bradley or Intelligence. The attack was expected as Little Slam, not Grand Slam.

Now we shift to Paris during the early afternoon of December 16th—time for the Armistice's broadcaster to gather up his tapes, don combat uniform and stand by for orders. Bradley is on his way to Paris from his Headquarters at the Alpha Hotel in Luxembourg City. Urgent is his planned after-lunch meeting with Eisenhower. It would take a day or two to confirm if Von Rundstedt's SS Armies had been pushed forward as "promised." Unlike most accounts that he didn't learn of it until that afternoon (16th), Bradley knew of the initial early morning strike before he left Spa for Paris. If David Niven in Spa had learned it, if General

Higgins in London at the Savoy Hotel had learned of it; with tanks rumbling across the Our River—it's dead certain Bradley knew. And for sure, Glenn standing by at his hotel knew. Patton was already on the move to close the "gap" in the Ardennes. Even Paul Josef Goebbels in Berlin knew enough to pinpoint where the three-plus German armies had encountered opposition. He indicated the areas by townships in his secret, unpublished diaries in German (University of Trier Library) reported by Nana Wendt, assigned translator.

All in all, enough evidence is at hand to put Major Miller at Versailles by early evening for last-minute conferences and instructions. After the about-midnight takeoff at Buc Field, Glenn had been cleared as far as Krefeld with a go-ahead to Berlin. On paper it looks good—to be met by the freedom loving Gisevius and the valiant Braun firemen. And on to *Deutschlandsender* to announce an end to three million casualties. Then that most vital of messages, to be delivered to the mysterious General Dornberger in Peenemuende from General George Marshall in Washington, a message on which hung the future of space conquest.

Who flew him? To me, there is no doubt but it was that duo of flyers Joan Heath described: Tony Bartley and Tony Pulitzer. No other pair equalled the flying trust Eisenhower placed in them.

There are no German or U.S. records to substantiate how Odin 7/13 (GM) fared at Krefeld. He was nicked, for sure. Skorzeny, who liked the Miller music programs, could have been there at Krefeld (as Schellenberg and Bormann conspired), put him in a JU-88, which Skorzeny could fly, and pretend that they had to be on the way to Berlin to beat the surrender. GM may have been told that the underground was waiting to hide him until the 101st paradrop. The other airborne (US-British) units were to secure the headquarters of *Der Fuehrer* and Paul Josef Goebbels.

The shock when Glenn landed at *Outstation Olga*, home of the F.W. Stahl's KG-200—with ready-to-fly B-24s and Forts manned by US-dressed crewmen speaking "American"—must have been stupendous. Paradroppers (*Fallschirmjaegern*) were also standing by at *Outstation Olga*. They were there with gliders which could be easily dismantled on landing, burned or buried with absolutely no trace.

Hitler's Autumn Mist approached Zero Hour. Glenn, we have to presume, was in a rigged B-24 destined for Villacoublais. The gliders would be headed for the Meuse River over U.S. front lines to wreak as much confusion and damage as possible. They would be airborne just before dawn. Glenn's B-24 with its selected and ruthless killers had priority. Passing front lines, the renovated bombers were attuned to German codes beamed to command points. They would pass uncontested. Capt. Stahl, head of the *Olga* operation, explained to me, with some pride, that there was a password to get every German plane safely over into Allied territory.

The US checkers at the combat zones could be nonchalant. The B-24 silhouette was commonly known. English would be spoken in case of inquiry. Stahl admitted that his spy-craft had landed at every airport in Western Europe without challenge, and had even visited England. In his book <u>Geheim Geschwader: KG200</u> (1995), Captain P.W. Stahl told how Skorzeny and Schellenberg, his bosses, had sent a Stalin assassination team to within fifteen miles of Moscow. A last minute slip caused failure. He also let me know that he had been in Iran to organize an attempt on the young Mohammad-Reza "Shah-in-Shah" Pahlavi (the self-pronounced King of Kings). That's when I was there.

Was Otto Skorzeny on that B-24 with Glenn aboard? I say no. Others say he was in close touch by coded radio. I think he took another plane by himself to land at Orly not Villacoublais. (The original plan was for Ike assassins to meet in Pigalle near the *Café de la Paix*.) Yes, I think he flew by another plane for two reasons: Skorzeny had to get back, Hitler had made him promise. The others in Brigade 150 were expendable; they would have no way back. This is speculative. I have no proof. The one survivor of *Greif* we talked to in 1998 wouldn't have known. That was in 1998, an ex-Soldat hiding from a religious search of his soul who telephoned me of his guilt. Skorzeny was a qualified pilot. He could have flown or ridden up front with someone else flying the B-24 or a Nazi-renovated Flying Fort. I expect he took along a pilot, and slept, landing it only. Of all in the *Greif* operation, he alone had to get back. Hitler's orders.

Dirty work obviously was done on the hostage plane during flight. Glenn would have to be unconscious and on a stretcher for the American-appearing "boys" to get him through at Villacoublais. No problem in checking out jeeps or ambulance from Quartermaster in the active US sector of the airfield. Where to park so as to avoid notice? It was easy for KG 200; just go to a non-tended side of the field. "Emergency" would have been the word, "to get this officer to the hospital, wounded in early stages of the breakthrough." Let me repeat: these little details are what is suggested as likely, considering the weight of surrounding fact. Once in Paris, the MPs were lords of *les rues*. On the virtually deserted streets of Paris, U.S. army vehicles were "in." No one would challenge any US-marked transport, even at high speed.

Nothing is documented between the shocking discovery

of the German equipped B-24 at Villacoublais by French General Juin who alerted Ike, and days later when MPs patrolling Pigalle, found Glenn Miller's body. Ex-Luftwaffe Captain F.W. Stahl refused to be drawn into involvement or knowledge of this part of the story, and I can't say I blame him. His job—and he made it consistently clear—was to furnish Nazi-camouflaged U.S. transport and see that it got across enemy lines. *"Ich selbst war eigentlich kaum mehr als ein 'Transporteur',"* he wrote me in German. "I was actually nothing more than a transporter." It's not to be expected that anyone today would come forward to say that he participated in or witnessed what was dished out to Glenn in the Sphinx. I am sure we spoke, Cathe Baker and I, to the last survivor of that obnoxious operation, Dr. Butron, and he didn't want to talk, much less think about it. Obviously, GM refused to lead the U.S. uniformed Nazi killers to Ike at St. Germain en Laye or to Versailles. Skorzeny's mafia knew exactly where they wanted to go, but they needed that familiar figure to get past guards to complete the kill. This "patented" Skorzeny trick had gotten him close to Stalin, to Tito, to Horthy, and to Mussolini (to free him). Glenn may have tried to escape as he was being tortured, was clouted hard, for sure—too hard.

A conclusive section to my hobby—duty—pastime—career (choose one, perhaps all) is essential. The questions here are not necessarily asked per se, but who needs to know the answers? (1) those historians wanting to be right. (2) the military compatriots in all sections of government who know something and would like to spill the beans. (3) those great Miller music fans whose dedication through the years has made this book possible.

Q: "Who was the "Early bird" who dangled that worm which we fish bit on? Was it Stephen Early, the President's

Press Secretary, or that elusive colonel, James F. Early, said to have been in charge of the Special Services organization up where the band lived?"

UPDATE—Man about the globe Stephen Early was involved in virtually every aspect of SHAEF Public Relations. He was a quick fix to problems perplexing FDR as well as DDE. He has to be the author of that 'telegram to Ike' being buried purposefully for forty years. I carried on an extensive correspondence with the FDR Library at Hyde Park, New York re: those December '44 weeks. Director and personnel were most courteous, but in the end I was told flatly: "Material found classified during the set-up of the Library was handed over to the War Department, now Department of Defense."

The Pentagon, unlike the National Personal Records Center at St. Louis, has shown itself singularly uncooperative in answering my inquiries re: Stephen Early and Colonel James F. Early. Wilbur Wright had the same rejoinder tossed back at him as he, Wright, recorded in his <u>The Glenn Miller Burial File</u> (1988). Wright tried to find the "James F." colonel in Milton Earnest, in Bedford, in London. If he existed, the bird colonel was never around. At 8th AAC Service Command in High Wycombe, England, near where I lived, there is no evidence of his presence except the current full page blow-up on Internet where all the references are to Air Force and not AAC Service Command, the nomenclature in usage when Col. Early is said to have been there. Was he sent to take Roosevelt's Steve Early off the hook? Mmmm. He got a star on his shoulder shortly thereafter. So it comes as no surprise to anyone—it was Stephen. An officer would never address a telegram to the Supreme Commander, even a lesser commander, <u>without including his rank</u>.

Q: "Has more evidences of threats come to light over

your and others' poking questions into the Miller files? You mentioned that it seemed to be an occupational hazard to be shadowed and possibly frightened off."

UPDATE—Virtually every serious researcher has been subject to this sort of harassment. There is one which I just learned of that took place a good while ago. It needs to be reported and I do so now. James E. Norwood is a retired Air Force serviceman. He was assigned to U.S. Intelligence Services when he got interested in Miller, enough to look into the secret files, definitely counter to CIA rules. He caught hell. This is what Norwood writes: "Officially, I disappeared from the radar screen. I underwent a forced change of identity. My wife, Mary Catherine, got the same treatment from the CIA. I mean that everything was blotted out about both of us, as though we had never existed at all." What had Norwood done? He explained further: "I knew something about the 'crash' that Glenn was alleged to have died in. There was no crash. The entire incident was staged by the intelligence services to cover something up. The Miller disappearance is related to something much larger."

Q: "I am, like you, a fan of General Omar Bradley. He was a great strategist and in time history will award him more credit for our Allied victory. You seem to have been a confidant of his. Why, in his book A Soldier's Story (1978), does he not go into details on Operation Eclipse, or as we know now the 'generals' deal' to end the war in 1944?"

UPDATE—You are correct. I was a confidant of Bradley during the two years we maneuvered in Louisiana and at Florida's Camp Gordon Johnson. I enjoyed being in a car pool with him, and his wife and mine were fast friends. We met in Washington post-war. Operation Eclipse was highly classified, even after the war, and Brad was ever mindful of

Ike's caution not to tell about the Bulge. We corresponded occasionally, and following his unfortunate early death, I was close to his wife Kitty, providing her with quips and anecdotes I remembered from our field conditions. Brad was a hard soldier himself. He was always first through the obstacle course, and more than any other general he camped with minimum luxury. Of course, he was in favor of getting the war over early and thought Eclipse could work. This is how Joseph Persico depicts Bradley's role in Piercing the Reich (1979) "Dulles sent a representative to General Omar Bradley and to Allied officials in London to ask them to consider using captured German generals as conduits to their brother officers. The effort won Bradley's blessing." Three months later, Von Rundstedt double-crossed Bradley. Bradley confirmed this to me post-war and said, "This was the first indication that the SS fanatics had taken over the traditionally honorable Junkers. Our mistake was to trust the 'gentlemen Junkers.'"

Q: "Can you explain more about the diaries Don Haynes kept for the band and why they are considered today to be false and misleading?"

From Ed Polic who is considered by the world-wide Glenn Miller Organization (Birthplace, Society, Archives) to be the Number One Miller historian:

"Don Haynes did not tell the truth, the whole truth and nothing but the truth, and that (certainly) he promoted himself and was self-serving. Neither the two Don Haynes Diaries that exist—the red book at the Library of Congress, nor the manuscript "Minus One"—are original and there are discrepancies between those two. Don did keep daily diaries throughout his life … and I am also sure that he destroyed the original diaries for that period for personal reasons. Don was a womanizer and I have several photographs of him with his lady friend in Europe in 1945. Of course, Don had a wife in the USA. I am positive that Don did not want his wife to see the real 1944 and 1945 diaries. I am not moralizing, just stating facts."

Q: "Is there any real proof as to what happened to Morgan's plane, the lost Norseman?"

UPDATE-- Richard H. Leive of Lucasville, Ohio has made Miller and his music a lifetime hobby. He owns a phenomenal collection of every known Miller recording. Leive has corresponded with me, with Dale Titler and Sid Robinson. His efforts have known no bounds: He wrote me: "I have corresponded with Robert Noorduyn, the son of the Norseman builder, who now lives at Columbus, Ohio. Bob has records on all Norsemen built by his father's company and he informed me that—I repeat—no Norsemen were lost on December 15, 1944. Have you heard the story about 44-70285 (Morgan's craft) having been found abandoned in a farmer's field in Normandy, France in January, 1945? According to the story, it was taken, probably flown, to SAD5 at Merville where it remained operational until it was involved in a crash on takeoff early in 1947 when an insecure load shifted. An eyewitness to the crash said the aircraft was completely wiped out. Then there is the company report of it being salvaged in New Jersey in 1947 as scrap. The plane's disappearance is as eerie as Morgan's himself."[2]

Q: "You have indicated publicly that the Internet has been a tremendous help in clearing some of the hidden corners of the Miller tragedy. The one you speak of is the deal General Marshall effected with German rocket scientists in which Glenn Miller's trip to Berlin was in part to reach General Dornberger. Once that had been done (and it was by other means), how did Dornberger and Von Braun ever manage to lead a group of hundreds, a contingent of professors, women and children across half of Europe from the far northern Baltic Sea down to Austria where they could surrender to the Americans?"

UPDATE —"You are referring to one of the most spectacular movement of peoples with a purpose of freedom in World War Two. It was January 1945 when the offer reached Dornberger and Von Braun, but by now that the Army had lost control of the scientists to the SS, they were under constant surveillance. Moving in a block would not be easy and plans were mulled, waiting for better weather. In which direction would they strike to encounter the former enemy, now offering sanctity? Not easy. Dornberger reckoned if they could eavesdrop on *Wehrmacht* troops to find where General Patton's army was headed, that might be the quickest way to get to surrender. They would have to guess two months or so ahead. The trip would take that long and it would probably be Bavaria or Austria. Von Braun came up with a typical brilliant plan. After setting a date to "disappear," a date to go, they should make plans to settle first in seven different villages, direction Berlin. Then seven more and seven more, all splitting up. By the time the Nazis caught up with the scheme, they could have a good start along the way. Everything depended on lip-buttoning and the general frenzy among the country people, fleeing from bombing, seeking relatives, soldiers, milling aimlessly. The group made it work. By the time the Nazis found them gone, they were in their second "seven villages" looking ahead to seven more nearer Berlin. Outside Berlin, they had luck. They stole a train, loaded everybody on, headed south. In the Harz Mountains, they were able to bury documents, designs and equipment vital to ballistic missile invention. Near *Fuerth bei Nuremberg* the train was caught. Kammler, the Nazi chief came on them now with a vengeance. They were marched toward Oberammergau and their fate would be decided there. Dornberger did his best to locate the approaching American armies. He sent the younger men at night to hide near retreating German troops, and pick up intelligence. Near Oberammergau there was a showdown. To meet the Americans, the group had to change course, move into the Tyrol. By now it was spring 1945 and by then no German believed in a Hitler victory. Dornberger stood has ground against Kammler. The RSHA Headquarters was a shambles. Kammler gave up, ordered his Adjutant to execute him. The group was finally free of bondage. They virtually ran to a village in the Tyrol, Schattwald, where fighter jets were screaming, and the sound of gunfire diminishing. Gen. Dornberger called up the young brother of Wernher Von Braun, "Magnus," he said, "Go find the nearest American soldier and surrender us." Young Magnus was cautious. He came upon a soldier all by himself eating a tin of rations. "We surrender," he said in good English and told PFC Fred Schneikert of the 324th Regimental Anti-Tank Company who they were. Schneikert from Sheboygan, Wisconsin, shook his head in disbelief. "Okay," he said, "You're probably nuts, but we'll investigate. Just stand by." End of the line—and the beginning of a space career for many of these who escaped the Nazis. It was May 2, 1945.

Q: "You have spoken several times about meeting Otto Skorzeny in Madrid during the '70s when you lived there. You accidentally encountered him at lunch. What did you learn from this offhand meeting?"

UPDATE— "My wife Chelito and I lived in Madrid during the '70s and we occasionally visited a little restaurant near Independenzia Plaza for lunch. It was called *Horcher's* from

a far more famed 3-starrer in Berlin when Hitler ruled the
roost. It was no surprise to learn that Madrid's Papa Horcher
was also the elite chef of that Berlin restaurant catering to
Marshal and Mrs. Goering, and other top Nazis with a taste
for French cuisine. Here he was in Madrid—Papa Horcher
himself—as wise in politics as he was in cookbooks. He had
vanished, as so many in the Third Reich, only to surface in
Spain where he lived with his family in culinary glory. His
food was fabulous, especially at lunch, when Papa himself
supervised. He dressed in a square apron with square hands,
slapping them often to wake tardy Spanish waitresses. In
fact, Horchers' entire interior was square—tables, somber
paintings, napkins, trays, windows. Only Papa's cherubic
face and the dishes were round. His son held sway in the
evening where meals were not half so delectably cooked,
or as well served or seasoned as the old man could do
them. German and Spanish were spoken at lunch and Papa
eventually accepted without reservation a pair of outsider
Americans, me—ex-enemy and my Philippino wife,
Chelito.

"That's Otto Skorzeny," he whispered one day in broken
English, nodding to a corner of well-dressed business men.
He expected me to know who Skorzeny was. I did. The ex-
colonel had been on television a few times, had won a few
civic awards and was now part of Madrilena's hoi-polloi. I
knew this much at least: He had gotten off at Nuremberg,
although the Russians wanted to execute him. Hired by
the CIA, he turned up next in Egypt to fight Nasser, had
gone then to assist Peron in Argentina, wound up as lover
to Evita, and had now retired to invest his loot in Spanish
businesses. He wasn't much like the picture I remember
seeing—a stiff, formidable soldier for Hitler in books of my
library. A huge man in height with scarred face, he had let

the bulges break through here and there, and there was not much hair left. His hands were enormous and wiry as he lifted forkfuls with his left hand, eating the European way. I excused myself from Chelito and ventured over.

What I knew about him at that time (1973) was black and white. in the SS files I saw in Berlin his name was noted near Glenn Miller's, but that proved nothing in particular. I knew he was a Nuremberg baddie. He was supposed to have led German soldiers dressed as Americans into our back lines and was stingingly rebuffed. He also had Eisenhower in his sights (as per Harry Butcher's page-long diary, page 616, of his "Three Years" book. To Ike, Skorzeny was the "most dangerous man in Europe," an epithet Otto quoted on Spanish TV, "as being proud of." I had no idea when we talked that he was the killer of my hero Glenn. His fame rested purely on the feat of rescuing Mussolini from the Gran Sasso mountain prison, and delivering him to a grateful *Fuehrer*. What we had in common at that luncheon was from his written recollection (1957) that he had set up a group of Iranian insurgents to assassinate the young Shah, and they had failed because he wasn't there to lead them. They had been hanged, I knew. I was present personally when one was executed in a public Teheran square.

From Skorzeny's Special Memoirs (1957)—he had parachuted into Northwest Iran in the summer of 1943 to lead armed nomads to get rid of the young Shah Reza Mohammed Pahlevi. The Nazis wanted to kill off the supply of armaments Americans and Brits were delivering across the Persian desert and mountains to the Russians. But more personally, there was animosity toward the Allies among tribes who preferred the bounties of the Old Shah, Mohammad's father, now dead. Skorzeny's "uprising" had failed, and I was interested because that was my territory from 1943 to 1945. And I was involved in stopping an assassination attempt.

There was no extra chair to sit down at the table, so I stood. They were all men and the lingua franca was German. I went with the language, introduced myself and said I only wanted to know about his Iranian tribal coup as I had been there when it failed. I told him it was on the day we broadcast by shortwave radio the "One Millionth Ton of Supplies for the Russians"—a remote broadcast from the MRS Railyards of Teheran to NBC America, via Basra and London transmitters. One of our Persian workers had picked up a rumored plot against the Shah to take place when he stepped up to speak aside the steam-puffing train. (The National Farm and Home Hour—NBC.) At the gleaned threat, which I passed on to the Shah, the VIPs attending decided not to risk the rail yards. They spoke from a safer location, but a trap was set, and the assassins were caught.

Skorzeny seemed delighted at the conversation. A chair was drawn up, Chelito invited over. He changed to English in which he was fluent. Yes, he had trained a number of insurgents near Azerbaijan's border with Iran, and parachuted them close to Teheran. He checkmated a rumor that he had tried for Stalin, Churchill, and Roosevelt when they attended the Teheran Conference. Not true. Skorzeny absolved himself. "We wouldn't have known about it in time to make it work."

His manner was now open, gregarious. His companions merely listened. I told him I had seen his name in the Document Center's files in Berlin, postwar. That really caught his attention. He was most interested. "The entry was connected to Major Glenn Miller's radio program as harming to the *Wehrmacht*." I asked if he knew anything about his disappearance.

Skorzeny turned his head slightly. There was no reaction from the others. "I only know of his broadcasts in German. His music was good. I still enjoy it. Now, I have some business to attend to," he said in German and immediately translated for me in English. The conversation cooled. I got up, excused myself in German, bowed the compulsory bow, and said, "Lucky we didn't meet in Teheran."

"Ich wuerde Sie auch gern geschnappt," he said. "I would have grabbed you up, too," was the meaning. Not long after that, Otto Skorzeny died. Since then, and with all I know now about his hunt for Eisenhower and brazen kidnapping of Glenn to reach his target, I have thought again and again over the expression he used.... *Geschnappt* means to grab. *Gern* is a peculiar word which has a special meaning of strength and joy...he would have gotten me happily...is what he meant, but that word *auch* said it all. *Auch* is very significant in German. It means 'also' or 'too', but it can take over the sentence. If Skorzeny had been there in the Teheran rail yards himself, with his craftiness, guile and determination to grab or kill the Shah, he would have gotten me, too? Also!! *Auch*. For what purpose? I may have been the guy he would have grabbed to get him past guards to bring his killers, undoubtedly dressed as guests, to the speakers' stand. Nobody would have stopped my bringing in late arrivals. *"Gern geschnappt...."*I would have grabbed you up... ALSO!" Well, maybe I was thinking too much.

That's why since that lunch in 1973 I have worked so hard on the Miller Mystery. Thank God it didn't go the way Skorzeny could have planned it. Would I have had the same courage as Major Glenn?

SKORZENY'S PERSONAL TARGETS:

"Operation Fritz" – Shah of Iran; "Operation Oak" –

Mussolini; "Operation Sosselsprung" - Tito; "Operation
Panzerfaust" - Petain; "Operation Mouse" - Admiral
Horthy's son; "Operation Zeppelin" - Stalin; "Operation
Greif" - Eisenhower.

THE FINAL CHINK OF PROOF—A PHONE CALL FROM
BERLIN. Southampton resident Cathe Baker had a break
from her postal service and agreed to be my secretary in
logging material from Wilbur Wright's 4,000 documents.
Also, she embarked on a ceaseless chase after any survivor
of *Operation Greif* or *Brigade 150* or any German
Fallschirmjaeger, or *Luftwaffe* soldier stationed at Krefeld
airfield who might have known about Odin 7/13. We
already had sufficient verification as to Glenn's welcoming
committee at *Tempelhof* in Berlin, which of course
was affirmed by Nazi telegrams. The Internet for Cathe
spewed papers for weeks without luck. We advertised for
information in Berlin newspapers. Cathe concentrated hard
on the parachute warriors, most of whom stemmed from
the *Brandenburg Division* headquartered in Berlin. A Dr.
Butron called. He was following up our inquiries in the
newspaper for anyone familiar with Glenn Miller's death.
Immediately I got on the extension. Cathe and I both heard
his reluctant story and made notes. Let Cathe tell it:

"He spoke very good English, but there was the accent.
We checked later and the call was from Berlin. He wanted
to speak with Wilbur Wright but I told him Mr. Wright
had passed on. I gave Mr. Downs the phone and we both
listened. He gave his name and spelled it out. A medical
doctor, Butron, from Spandau. He had some information on
the Glenn Miller tragedy and wanted the lovers of Glenn
Miller to know there were still millions of fans in Germany.
He was truly sorry that so many of his countrymen had
been led astray by Hitler.

"Mainly, he wanted us to know that there was brave resistance in Berlin but the Allies didn't follow up. Finally he got to the point. He wanted to get this off his chest to right the shame he felt for destroying Glenn Miller. He was an *Unteroffizier* with the *Greif Gruppe*. He had witnessed the torture of the hapless major who refused to bring Skorzeny to Eisenhower, but he himself (Butron) could not interfere. He had lived with this shame silently all these years and now, with cancer...his voice broke. We tried to retrieve him but the line had gone dead. The following week he called for the second time. Mr. Downs tried to get his address, his phone number, but he would not answer. He wanted to know if we had gotten his message when he called before. We told him that we had. There was a blank again and there was nothing wrong with the telephone service. We rang back to get the number he called from. British Telecom could do that, but apparently he called from a public phone. We never heard again."

(Signed) Cathe Baker

Dr. Butron certainly existed and his confession from his own lips must be counted as true. No one could describe the horrific details of torture to a man he called by name unless he had been there, and could identify place, date and circumstances. An unidentified survivor to *Brigade 150* telephoned from Brussels, admitted his presence at the bordello when Glenn was prisoner but failed to confirm an appointment to meet. Cathe's contacts with the Berlin Brandenburg "alumni" could not locate a Butron among lists of wartime *Fallschirmjaegern*, nor could they identify any present Brussels resident as a former parachutist. We found that there was no roll-call of Skorzeny deadly assassins in extant records. Or if there was one, it had long gone the way of Nazi ashes.

To report what passes for history is exacting for any journalist. In my own search, I have gone by four rules which I discovered while studying classic Greek. Thucydides (Thu-cy-did-ese—with accent on the "cy") was a famed historian circa time of the great Herodotus, who was called the Father of History (Fourth Century BC). Thucydides, author of the "History of the Peloponnesian War," was a general, and was called "the first scientific historian, critical and skeptical" ever in the world. "His was mankind's first attempt at accurate chronology. He was first to provide dramatic skill in narrative and first to underline the political and social realism of the time." (A Guide to the Humanities (1971) a scholarly analysis of this remarkable original history, as researched by Meyer Reinhold of Brooklyn College.)

Professor Reinhold takes pain to analyze Thucydides's strictures of writing. These were the four sources he depended upon in drawing his verbal conclusions. "They were (1) Keen personal observation, (2) Official documents, (3) Literary sources, critically appraised, (4) Trustworthy oral sources."

I have tried as much as I could to follow these precepts. So, in saying Good Luck, *Bonne Chance, Buena Suerte* and *Viel Glueck*, I believe I have brought you the rightful answers to the puzzle surrounding Glenn Miller.

Index

A

AACS 16, 117, 141, 144, 149, 161, 168, 169
Algiers 26, 27
ALSOS 60
Amana 15
Joe Angelico 11
Army Air Corps 141, 145, 161, 168
Autumn Mist 13, 57, 66, 72, 104, 109, 116, 127, 138, 177

B

Captain Robert Baker 40
Baron DeLannoy 47
Tony Bartley 41, 176
Battle of the Bulge 4, 10, 13, 24, 55, 73, 77, 85, 87, 110
BBC 5, 7, 22, 26, 28, 29, 40, 41, 57, 89, 91, 92, 145
BBC Bush House 40
Bedfordshire 57, 59, 87
Tex Beneke 32, 135
Johnny Best 10
Bletchley Park 11, 14, 39, 104, 106, 135, 136, 152
Boulder, Colorado 16, 159, 167
General Omar N. Bradley 45, 48
Bronze Star 25, 78, 117

C

Captain Gregory 3
Alan Cass 33
Mattie Lou Cavander 15
Channel 2, 3, 24, 32, 42, 57, 77, 83, 91, 93, 96, 98, 132, 137, 148, 149, 151,
         158, 166, 167, 168, 169, 172, 173
Chesterfield 17, 18
CIA 5, 6, 7, 19, 48, 62, 76, 87, 91, 93, 100, 140, 147, 181, 186
Clarinda, Iowa 15, 33, 167
Miles Copeland 7, 62
Brod Crawford 6, 9, 41, 128, 129

D

Baron DeLannoy 47
Johnny Desmond 30, 31, 43
Marlene Dietrich 59, 122, 157
General "Wild Bill" Donovan 19
Dornberger 22, 61, 62, 63, 64, 65, 153, 172, 179, 180, 181
Dorsey, Tommy and Jimmy 16
Allen Dulles 40, 46, 50, 52, 53, 70, 74, 112, 140, 147

E

Dwight D. Eisenhower 1, 15, 22
English Channel 2, 3, 42, 77, 83, 91, 137, 148, 149, 167, 168, 169, 172,
        173

F

FDR 12, 19, 52, 55, 61, 73, 96, 117, 163, 180

G

Hans Bernd Gisevius 52
Josef Goebbels 5, 51, 176, 177
Samuel Goudsmit 55, 59, 61, 144
Grand Slam 58, 75, 77, 106, 108, 109, 175

H

Lt. Don Haynes 31, 32, 36, 44, 59, 87
Joan Heath 10, 62, 126, 127, 131, 135, 136, 155, 162, 176
Werner Heisenberg 56
Heinrich Himmler 42, 78, 81, 82, 101, 122
Alger Hiss 12, 55
Adolf Hitler 44, 55, 58, 82, 100, 107, 124
Hitler 5, 9, 11, 13, 19, 20, 26, 27, 38, 40, 42, 45, 46, 48, 51, 52, 53, 54, 56,
        58, 60, 66, 68, 71, 72, 75, 76, 82, 84, 85, 92, 97, 98, 101, 102, 103,
        104, 105, 106, 108, 109, 110, 111, 112, 113, 114, 118, 123, 127, 145,
        156, 157, 166, 172, 175, 177, 178, 185, 186, 187, 191

I

Internet 23, 64, 96, 180, 183, 190

K

Helmut Kohl 17, 38
Krefeld 14, 46, 52, 58, 62, 71, 83, 112, 114, 117, 128, 137, 143, 176, 190

L

Library of Congress 33, 34, 182
Richard H. Lieve 43
Little Slam 58, 75, 77, 106, 108, 110, 145, 175

M

General George C. Marshall 8, 62, 44, 172
Alton Glenn Miller 1, 25
Glenn Miller 1, 2, 3, 4, 5, 7, 8, 9, 10, 11, 12, 13, 14, 15, 16, 17, 18, 20, 24,
         25, 26, 29, 30, 31, 32, 33, 34, 35, 36, 37, 38, 39, 42, 47, 58, 61, 62,
         63, 65, 66, 69, 71, 75, 77, 78, 83, 84, 85, 87, 88, 89, 90, 91, 92, 93,
         95, 96, 98, 102, 110, 112, 113, 114, 115, 116, 117, 120, 121, 122,
         124, 125, 126, 127, 131, 132, 135, 136, 137, 141, 145, 146, 147, 148,
         149, 150, 151, 153, 155, 156, 157, 158, 159, 161, 165, 167, 168, 170,
         173, 174, 175, 179, 180, 182, 183, 187, 189, 190, 191, 192
Helen Miller 33
Herbert Miller 91, 145
W.O. John Morgan 57, 142
Morgenthau Plan 49, 50
Mt. Royal Hotel 31

N

Col. David Niven 42, 66

O

Odin 7/13 20, 58, 59, 75, 106, 114, 117, 137, 140, 176, 190
Operation Eclipse 12, 46, 47, 54, 55, 58, 59, 62, 65, 68, 69, 71, 74, 75, 78,
         117, 149, 157, 181
Orchestra Wives 9, 17
OSS 7, 19, 20, 45, 46, 51, 70, 71, 75, 87, 91, 117, 156
OWI (Office of War Information) 19

P

General Patton 45, 73, 184
Peenemuende 62, 63, 64, 65, 68, 172
Joseph Persico 54, 74, 182
Kim Philby 12, 55
Vic Porter 10, 13, 128, 136
Tony Pulitzer 41, 176

R

Red Army 55, 63, 79, 80
Gen. Von Rundstedt 62
Sid Robinson 32, 34, 61, 135, 141, 142, 144, 149, 151, 159, 160, 161, 165, 170, 183
Franklin D. Roosevelt 95

S

General David Sarnoff 21, 27
Walter Schellenberg 8, 98, 101, 102, 106
Secret Broadcasts 19
SHAEF 1, 2, 4, 8, 9, 10, 11, 12, 13, 37, 44, 45, 49, 57, 66, 69, 85, 87, 88, 91, 95, 96, 97, 105, 106, 117, 126, 129, 133, 135, 136, 145, 148, 149, 175, 180
Fred Shaw 3, 4, 158, 159, 167, 168, 170
Otto Skorzeny 8, 69, 75, 84, 85, 98, 100, 107, 110, 117, 143, 178, 185, 186, 189
General Speidel 46, 52, 70
Stalin 12, 55, 73, 101, 106, 112, 177, 179, 188, 190
Sun Valley Serenade 9, 17

T

Teheran, Iran 26
Tempelhof 190
Dale Titler 34, 88, 148, 165, 183
Trianon Palace 8, 11, 13, 49, 60, 83, 127, 130, 131, 133, 138
Twinwood 2, 6, 14, 31, 34, 57, 87, 89, 90, 117, 141, 143, 151, 152, 159, 160, 163, 165, 166, 167, 168, 172

V

Von Braun 62, 63, 64, 65, 179, 180, 181
Gen. Von Rundstedt 62

Glossary

AAC or AACSC - Army Air Corps Service Command. The air arm was part of the U.S. Army during most of the war. In 1945 it became the U.S. Air Force.

Abwehr - German word referring to Defense.

AFN - American Forces Network. U.S. Servicemen radio stations in Europe.

Ahnenerbe - Heinrich Himmler's established "Kultur" department of the Nazi movement.

Ardennes - Thicketed mountain area embracing border country of Germany, Luxembourg and Holland. It was the path of Hitler's 1940 invasion of Western Europe; also his surprise attack of 1944 which led to the Battle of the Bulge.

BBC - British Broadcasting Corporation. Provided studio services for American broadcasters.

Black Orchestra - Common name for the underground movement gaining sway in Berlin after the failed assassination of Hitler, July 20, 1944.

Bletchley Park - Most Secret location north of London where German codes were intercepted, translated and furnished U.S., UK and Canadian commanders.

Bridge Too Far - Common expression describing Allied operation devised by Montgomery to reach the Rhine River into Germany during 1944. It failed in crossing over several bridges as the last one was "too far."

CIC - Counter Intelligence Corps. The CIC preceded its noteworthy successor, CIA, as did the OSS, Office of Strategic Services, psywar arm of the American Forces battling in Europe.

DDE - Initials of Dwight D Eisenhower, Allied Commander.

Deutschlandsender - German National Radio headquartered in Berlin. Controlled all radio in Third Reich with exception of Radio Luxembourg, captured by the Allies in August, 1944.

DFC - Distinguished Flying Cross. An award for a singular act of heroism while on air duty.

Deuxiéme Bureau - Secret Service of the French government, the "second bureau".

DOD - Department of Defense.

Document Center - Innocent, neutralizing title applied by U.S. authorities in Berlin (1951) to a treasure trove of Nazi-hidden documents found underground and containing most of the papers of Himmler's death organizations (SS, Gestapo, SD, concentration camps). Discovery was concealed until turned over to new Federal Republic of Germany.

Dornberger, General Walter - German officer of WWI and WWII of good repute who led space scientists in their discoveries of ballistic missiles, and who engineered escape of the group with Wernher von Braun from Nazi territory and Russians in 1945.

Erlass - German word meaning Decree. Generally associated with Hitler Decree (*Fuehrer Erlass*).

ETO - European Theatre of Operations.

Generals Rommel, Stulpnagel and Von Rundstedt - The three most powerful among German generals planning the coup to end the war early.

Goebbels - Nazi propaganda chief under Hitler, cunning and powerful.

Goering - WWOne flying ace, appointed by Hitler head of the German Air Force, the *Luftwaffe*.

Group B Armies - German Designation for total army strength facing Allies on the Western Front, prior to the Battle of the Bulge.

Irrefuehrung – meaning Dirty Tricks, assigned by Hitler in 1944 to be led by Col. Walter Schellenberg and Col. Otto Skorzeny. This was the Nazi element which captured and killed Major Glenn Miller.

KZ – German initialing for Konzentration Zentrum, meaning concentration camp.

Lancaster – British bomber used almost exclusively in mass raids by the British on German facilities.

Magnetophon – instrument for recording by tape, a German invention, more practical than wire or wax.

Musee de l'Erotique – a five-storey museum established in Paris Pigalle, devoted to the erotic in French culture.

Musik fuer die Wehrmacht – Psychological warfare radio program broadcast by the Allies into Germany, aimed especially at German troops (*Wehrmacht*). Glenn Miller, speaking German, was host presenting his famous Miller music.

Northolt Airfield – called the King and Queen's airfield. Just outside London, it served VIPs.

NSDAP – Official designation of the Nazi Party: National Socialist German Workers Party.

OCS – Officer Candidate School.

OKW – In the German military set-up, means: *Oberkommando der Wehrmacht* or Highest Command of Troops.

Operation Eclipse – An operation held ultra-secret, conjoined by generals of both sides, to end the war by tricking SS units loyal to Hitler into an inescapable vise, then arresting the dictator. It failed largely due to leaky intelligence.

OSS – Office of Strategic Services. World War Two-born U.S. agency to coordinate secret and psychological warfare. Became the CIA under President Truman, post war.

OWI – Office of War Information, U.S. agency for coordinating programs in the U.S. to further and support the war effort. Glenn Miller and his service orchestra contributed to this agency before their assignments overseas.

POW – Prisoner of War.

Pigalle – Sometimes called "Pig Alley," this sector of Paris which was and is the most popular tourist hot-spot for "Paris by night," an area combining the exotic, erotic and classical.

PRO – Public Record Office of Great Britain, located at Kew Gardens, England.

Radio Calais – Allied propaganda radio station, established on the French coast after the invasion.

RAF – Royal Air Force.

Reichbanner – The insurgency wave against Hitler centered in Berlin. It promised massive help to an Allied paradrop over the city, and was central to Operation Eclipse. However, its principles went against Allied agreement with the USSR which demanded Unconditional Surrender by the Germans.

RSHA – Short term for a long word in German meaning the head office of top security for the entire Third Reich. Schellenberg and Skorzeny commanded this Nazi element for Himmler toward war's end.

SHAEF – Supreme Headquarters Allied Expeditionary Forces. Under Supreme Commander Eisenhower, headquarters were in London, Versailles and Frankfurt respectively.

SIS Phantoms – British commando group operating raids and secret activities in Nazi-held Europe. Col. David Niven, Major Miller's superior, was a key member of the Phantoms.

SOE – Special Operations Executive, a British organization which penetrated the Nazi organization in Belgium, Holland and France to establish footholds.

St. Germain en Laye – a French township near Versailles, overlooking the Seine River, where Eisenhower had residence.

Tiflis, Georgia – Major city in the USSR state of Georgia (Tbilisi) where U.S. bombers held rights to land and refuel in their round-the-clock attacks on the Ploesti Oil Fields of Rumania.

Twinwood – The controversial RAF airfield near Bedford said by both U.S. and UK governments to be where Major Glenn Miller was picked up for a plane lift to France, then vanished. The airfield was proven closed on the particular date, December 15, 1944.

Thucydides - Greek historian, more critical and scientific-minded than his predecessor Herodotus, said by author Downs to have been his model in reporting this piece of war history.

Unter den Linden - A major boulevard in central Berlin leading to the Brandenburg Gate. The linden tree was considered Berlin's glory.

USAREUR - Postwar tag for U.S. Army Europe.

USSR - The Soviet Republics with Josef Stalin as leader.

VIP - Very Important Person.

Wehrmacht - German word for Armed Forces.

ZI - Zone of the Interior. A war term which meant going home for GIs.

Bibliography

Works Cited

Ambrose, Stephen E. *The Supreme Commander the War Years of General Dwight D. Eisenhower.* Jackson: University P of Mississippi, 1999.

Bailey, George. *The Germans*, New York. Discuss 1974

Bartley, Anthony. *Smoke Trails in the Sky*. London, 1984. *Royal Air Force.*

Belew, Leland F., *Skylab, Our First Space Flight Center,* Marshall Flight Center, Huntsville, AL. 1977

Bormann, Martin, Gerda Bormann, and H. R. Trevor-Roper. *The Bormann Letters.* New York: AMSP, 1981.

Boudard, Alphonse. *La Fermature*. Paris, France: Robert Laffont, 1996. *La Fin Des Maisons Closes.*

Bradley, Omar Nelson. *A Soldier's Story.* Chicago: Rand McNally, 1978. *George C. Marshall, Organizer of Victory* (with Forrest C.Pogue) New York Viking 1999.

Brassai, M. De. *Paris: Secrete Des Annees 30s.* Paris: Gallimard, 1966. *Paris: Secret of the 1930 Years.*

Browder, George C. *Hitler's Enforcers the Gestapo and the SS Security Service in the Nazi Revolution*. New York: Oxford UP, 1996.

Brown, Anthony Cave. *The Last Hero Wild Bill Donovan: the Biography and Political Experience of Major General William J. Donovan, Founder of the OSS and "Father" of the CIA, From His Personal and Secret Papers and the Diaries of Ruth Donovan*. 1st Vintage Books Ed. ed. New York: Vintage Books, 1984.

Bullock, Alan. *Hitler, a Study in Tyranny*. Completely Rev. Ed. ed. Harmondsworth, Eng: Penguin Books, 1962.

Butcher, Harry C. *My Three Years with Eisenhower*. New York: Simon and Schuster, 1946.

Byg, Barton. *Leni-the Life and Work of Leni Riefenstahl*. New York: Alfred A. Knopf, 2007.

Calvocoressi, Peter. *Top Secret Ultra*. London: Cassell, 1980.

Casey, William J. *The Secret War Against Hitler*. New York, NY: Distributed to the Trade by Kampmann, 1988.

Chevalier, Louis. *Montmartre Du Plaisir Et Du Crime*. Paris, France, 1980. Montmartre—Pleasures and Crimes.

Churchill, Winston. *Never Give in, the Best of Winston Churchill Speeches*. London: Hyperion, 2004.

Cocteau, Jean, La Voie Humaine, Edition de la Sirene Paris 1947.

Cookridge, E. H. *Gehlen; Spy of the Century*. 1st American Ed. ed. New York: Random House, 1972. *Inside Story of SOE (Special Operations Executive)*. :London: Thomas Crowell, 1966.

Cray, Ed. *General of the Army* (Marshall) New York, WW Norton, 1990.

D'este, Carlo. *Patton a Genius for War.* 1st Ed. ed. New York: Harper-Collins, 1995.

Davrey, Felician. *The French Bordellos- Les Maisons Closes.* Paris: Pygmalion, 1980.

Dornberger, *Walter. Bantam War Book Series.* New York: Bantam, 1954. *Paperback Editions on Space Rocketry.* 27 Feb. 2008. *Peenemuende: History of the V-Weapons.* New York and Berlin: Private: U.S. and German, 1981. *Die Geschichte Der V-Waffen.* 2008.

Downs, Hunton. *Murder in the Mood.* Southampton, England: Wright Books, 1998.

Dulles, Allen Welsh. *The Craft of Intelligence.* 1st Ed. ed. New York: Harper & Row, 1963.

Eisenhower, David. *Eisenhower At War, 1943-1945.* 1st Ed. ed. New York: Random House, 1986.

Eisenhower, Dwight D. *Crusade in Europe.* 1st Ed. ed. Garden City, N.Y.: Doubleday, 1948.

Enever, Ted. *Bletchley's Best Kept Secret.* London: Enever, 1994.

Fest, Joachim C. *Plotting Hitler's Death the Story of the German Resistance.* 1st American Ed. ed. New York: Metropolitan Books., 1996. *The Face of the Third Reich.* London: Weidenfeld & Nicolson, 1970. *Hitler.* New York. Harcourt 2002.

Foot, M. R. D. *European Resistance to Naziism.* London: SOE Executive, 1976. *Special Operations in France-SOE.* London: Executive P, 1966.

Gelb, Norman. *Ike and Monte: Generals At War.* London: UK, 1994.

Genrikh, Borovik. *The Philby Files.* Moscow: USSR Printing (English), 1974.

Gisevius, Hans Bernd. *Hitler: Versuch Einer Deutung.* Berlin,Germany: Gisevius, 1963. *My Search for the Meaning of Hitler.*

Goebbels, Josef. *Goebbels Diaries.* 1942-1043 New York: Doubleday, 1948. *Edited, Transated by Lous P. Lochner, AP Bureau Chief in Berlin, Diaries* 1944 Translation (Classified) Downs/Wendt Univ. Trier, Germany 1997.

Goudsmit, Samuel Abraham. *Alsos.* Los Angeles, CA: Tomash, 1983.

Griehl, Manfred. *Junkers JU88: Star of the Luftwaffe.* Berlin: Germany Only, 1990.

Grose, Peter. *Gentleman Spy: The Life of Allen Dulles.* Boston: Houghton Mifflin, 1994.

Hitler, Adolf. *Hitler: Table Talk, Letters, Speeches.* Berlin, Koblenz, Aachen, Freiburg: Bundesarchiven, Germany, 1955. *Tischegespraeche, Briefe, Notizen, Reden.*

Hohne, Heinz. *Order of the Death's Head: the Story of Hitler's SS.* New York: Penguin Books, 1971.

Husted, Stewart W. *George C. Marshall, The Rubrics of Leadership.* Paradoxical P. 2007.

Irving, David John Cawdell. *The War Between the Generals.* 1st Ed. ed. New York: Distributed by St. Martin&Apos;S P, 1981.

Jenkins, Roy. *Churchill a Biography.* 1st Ed. ed. New York: Farrar, Straus and Giroux, 2001.

Jones, R. V. *Most Secret War.* Alexandria, Va: Time-Life, 1991.

Knightly, Philip. *Philby: Life and Views of the KGB.*
London, 1989.

Lasly, Clare(nce). *Project Paperclip.* Held classified by
Dept. State pending Truman, Churchill, Stalin postwar
meeting Potsdam. Only public reference at meeting:
"The space scientists covered their designs with such
secrecy that it bedevilled the President" (Truman).
Washington, D.C. 1947.

Lemestre, Marthe (Martoune). *Madame Sphinx Vous Parle.*
Paris, France: Euredif, 2 Bis, Rue De La Baume. *Le Paris:
Secrete Des Annees 30s.* Paris: Gallimard, 1976. *Paris:
Secret of the 1930 Years.*

Lewin, Ronald. *Ultra Goes to War the Secret Story.*
London: Hutchinson, 1978.

Liddel-Hart, B. H. *The German Generals Talk.* New York:
Hawthorne, 1971. 1st Edition: 1948.

Lowden, John L. *Silent Wings At War Combat Gliders in
World War II.* Washington: Smithsonian Institution P,
1992.

Lucas, James Sidney. *Hitler's Enforcers Leaders of the
German War Machine, 1939-1945.* London: Cassell,
2000.

Macdonald, Charles B. *The Battle of the Bulge.* New York:
Bantam, 1984.

Manvell & Fraenkel, Roger And Heinrich. *Dr. Goebbels.*
London: Roger Fraenkel Private, 1960.

Marshall, George C. *The George C. Marshall Papers
1932-1960* Lexington VA Foundation Washington
DC 1981. George C. Marshall, Robert Lester, and
Blair Hydrick. Foundation provides overview of 213

separate and individual collections (papers, letters, diary notes) identified by contact name. Range is wide extending from private to Secretariats to Presidents FDR and Truman. *The Papers of George C. Marshall Selected World War II Correspondence.* Bethesda, MD: University Publications of America, 1992.

McGovern, James. *Martin Bormann.* London: Barker, 1968.

Mendelssohn, Peter. *The Nuremberg Documents.* London: G. Allen & Unwin Ltd, 1946.

Neufeld, Michael J. *The Rocket and the Reich.* New York: Free P., 1995. *Peenemuende: Arrival of the Ballistic Missile Era.*

Niven, David. *The Moon's A Balloon* (1971) and *Bring on the Empty Horses* (1975)

Nobâecourt, Jacques. *Hitler's Last Gamble.* New York: Schocken Books, 1967.

Patton, George S., Paul D. Harkins, and Beatrice Banning Ayer Patton. *War as I Knew It.* Boston: Houghton Mifflin Co., 1947.

Payne, Robert. *The Life and Death of Adolf Hitler.* New York: Praeger, 1973. *The Marshall Story.* New York Prentice Hall, 1951.

Perry, Mark *Partners in Command George Marshall & Dwight Eisenhower.* New York Penguin 2007.

Persico, Joseph E. *Piercing the Reich the Penetration of Nazi Germany by American Secret Agents During World War II.* New York: Viking P, 1979.

Philby, Kim. *My Silent War: Autobiography of a Spy.* London. *Forward: Graham Greene.*

Pogue, Forrest C. *George C. Marshall*. New York: Viking P, 1963. *George C. Marshall, Organizer of Victory* (with Omar N. Bradley) New York Viking 1999.

Polic, Ed. His Encyclopedia is privately printed. Found no sales reference, no price or availability other than it is a two volume edition with personal data, band movements, etc. covering Glenn's U.S. career. 702 Glenn Court, Milpitas, CA, 95035-3330.

Pyle, Ernie. *Brave Men*. New York: H. Holt and Company, 1944.

Riefenstahl, Leni. *Leni Riefenstahl a Memoir*. New York: St. Martins P, 1995.

Reinhold, Meyer. *Guide to the Humanities*. Barron's Essentials. New York, June 1971.

Saunders, Alan. *George C. Marshall a General for Peace*. New York: Facts on File, 1996.

Schaeper, Thomas J. *Crisis and Renewal in 20th Century France*. Highlights in career Philippe Leclerc of Free French Forces, *Marachal de France*. New York: Duke Univ. P. Berghahn, 2001.

Schellenberg, Walter. *Schellenberg Memoirs Ed: Louis Hagen*. London, 1956.

Schlabrendorff, Fabian Von. *The Secret War Against Hitler*. London: Hodder & Stoughton, 1966.

Seale, Patrick, and Maureen McConville. *Philby: the Long Road to Moscow*. London: Hamilton, 1973.

Shirer, William L. *The Rise and Fall of the Third Reich a History of Nazi Germany*. 1st. One-Vol. Touchstone Ed. ed. New York: Simon and Schuster, 1981.

Simon, George Thomas. *Glenn Miller and His Orchestra.* New York: T. Y. Crowell Co, 1974.

Sixsmith, E. K. G. *Eisenhower as Military Commander.* New York: Stein and Day, 1973.

Skorzeny, Otto. *Special Memoirs.* London, 1957.

Speer, Albert. *Inside the Third Reich.* New York: Macmillan, 1970.

Speidel, Hans. *Major General German Wehrmacht, Memoirs, Invasion 1944.* Translated. London. Regnery 1950.

Stahl, P.W. *Geheim Geschwader: KG 200.* Stuttgart: Motorbuch Verlag, 1995. *The Secret Luftwaffe After 40 Years.*

Stevenson, William. *A Man Called Intrepid: the Secret War.* London: Sphere, 1988.

Stoler, Mark A. *George C. Marshall Soldier Statesman.* New York: Simon & Schuster, 1989.

Strawson, John. *The Battle for the Ardennes.* London: Batsford, 1972.

Stulinger, Ernst. *Crusader for Space.* Comb. ed. Krieger Pub Co. English, 1996.

Thucydides. *Greek. History of the Peloponnisian War.* Translated: Richard Crawley. 431 B.C.

Troy, Thomas F. *Donovan and the CIA.* New York: University Publications of America, 1981. *History of Establishment of CIA.*

Ulfkotte, Udo. *Secret Files of the BND.* Berlin, Germany, 1996. *Bundesnachrichtendienst.*

Viereck, Peter. *Metapolitics: Roots of the Nazi Mind*. New York: Capricorn, 1961.

Von Braun, Wernher. *Space Frontier*. 1st Ed. ed. New York: Holt, Rinehart and Winston, 1967. *Mein Leben fuer die Raumfahrt*. My Life for Space Flight. HB Burda Verlag. Offenberg, Germany, lst German ed. 1969.

Ward, Bob. *Dr. Space: the Life of Wernher Von Braun*. Washington, D.C.: Smithsonian Institute P, 2004.

Whiting, Charles. *Ardennes the Secret War*. New York: Stein and Day, 1985. *The Last Assault the Battle of the Bulge Reassessed*. London: Leo Cooper, 1994. *The Other Battle of the Bulge Operation Northwind*. 1st American Ed. ed. Chelsea, MI: Scarborough House, 1990. *Battle for the German Frontier*. Moreton-in-Marsh UK Windrush. *The Spymasters*. New York Dutton & Co 1976.

Winterbotham, F. W. *The Ultra Secret*. London: Futura Publications, 1975. *The Ultra Spy*. London: Macmillan, 1989.

Wright, David. *Millergate the Final Solution*. Southampton, England: Wrightway, 1998.

Wright, Wilbur. *Millergate*. Southampton, England: Wrightway, 1990. *The Glenn Miller Burial File*. Southampton, England: Wrightway, 1993.

Ziemke, Earl. *Battle for Berlin: End of the Third Reich*. New York: Ballantine, 1968.

Documents

The numbers refer to the footnotes used throughout the text. Each footnote has a document location and sometimes a brief explanation of the document. The actual document image is found by using a lettering system. The alphabetically lettered documents section follows the numbered footnote section.

1 **A**—English Channel radar questioned the secret flight of 7/13 Odin (heading into enemy territory), the flight bearing Major Miller on his "Mission for Ike." Miller's move to Krefeld, German General Von Rundstedt's Headquarters, was a preliminary step in the thought-to-be-pending Armistice. These messages, top classified and priority, were provided Hunton Downs from the Croydon RAF base files.

2 **B**—The single-engine "Norseman," alleged in the government's claim of Miller's disappearance to have been unaccountably lost, had Miller listed as a passenger. W.O. John Morgan, the pilot, was never found, but a falsification of the required MACR, Missing Air Crew Report, eventually indicated there were no passengers aboard and that the French destination had been altered.

3   **C**—Broderick Crawford, Glenn's closest friend at Yale.

4   **D**—David Niven's Operational Records of the Royal Air Force.

5   **E**—Portions of the real and false MACR documents (Missing Air Crew Report) a required filing. Note: the different typewriter spacings to add the names of Miller and Baessell to the original. The signature of Cramer, the original preparer, was judged forged. A Scotland Yard agent, Ansell, reviewed the file and confirmed inaccuracies in the Ansell Report. The original, hidden away for 40-plus years, was discovered accidentally when President Reagan ordered a shift of Miller-related papers released to the public (1987).

6   **F**—More than one typewriter used to fake A-42 destination.

7   **G**—RAF Flight Officer (Ret.) Wilbur Wright was the foremost Glenn Miller researcher of the 1990s, authoring two books on the subject. This is the answer Wright received from the State of New Jersey when he inquired as to the date of Alton Glenn Miller's death. Miller was a New Jersey resident. Several days later, this letter was denied in another letter to Wright when the office learned that Alton Glenn was in fact the real Glenn Miller.

8   **H**—Colonel DuPuy, head of SHAEF Public Relations in December 1944 had the job of telling the American public Glenn Miller had vanished without trace. Here is part of the intricate staff work involved in releasing the news. DuPuy, no stranger to regulations, was not about to be caught up in language which could embarrass him later. Military assignments sometimes

prove ironical. At American Forces Network in Frank-furt/Heidelberg in 1953, Col. DuPuy became my boss. I was warned by his Sgt. Major, "Don't ask about Glenn Miller." One day, the subject just landed on the table between us. He heard about my off-duty interest and without my even posing a question said, "There's nothing I can tell you. An unfortunate loss, to be sure, but Glenn Miller was just one of the officers lost in the Battle of the Bulge. Too bad. He was a fine musician."

9   **I**—The official (classified) report of Major Miller's disappearance dated December 22, 1944, two days after the Early Report to Eisenhower. Note: a rather unusual formatting of sender and receiver: -- directed to an unnamed Commanding General of the European Theatre of Operation from (unnamed) Supreme Commander, SHAEF.

10   **J**—Sid Robinson's note.

11   **K**—None of the 1946-56 Miller researchers were able to put a finger on Col. James F. Early, rumored to be in charge of the Miller disappearance follow-up. He was presumed to be in either England or France, but could be found in neither. Decades later the Air Force confirmed his presence there in a full-page picture on the Internet. The more logical candidate for signing this brisk telegram (no mention of military rank) is Steven Early, FDR's pressman, a VIP of rank who announced the tragedy of Pearl Harbor on national radio and the President's death in April, 1945. Col. Early would have had to indicate his rank in such a message to his Commander-in-Chief.

12   **L**—Major Miller post-war was to receive a Bronze Star medal with eulogies for same and a marker at the

Arlington Memorial site. But to win a Bronze Star requires combat and this notification of SHAEF to the War Department specifies "non-battle."

13   **M**—This request by Glenn's brother, Herbert, to the Mountain View Cemetery, Altadena, CA, was on behalf of Wilbur Wright who wanted to visit the site and obtain information as to who was buried in the Miller family plot. According to Wright's son David (Wilbur died in 1994), no satisfactory answer was ever received, only a family rebuff to Herbcrt, reported in Wright's <u>The Glenn Miller Burial File</u>. No approval granted. No visit made.

14   **N**—(top) Evidence of Glenn Miller's psywar program in German, *"Musik fuer die Wehrmacht."* Albums and tapes are currently on sale, but only music of the Miller band. None of Glenn's pleas for the *Wehrmacht* to surrender and Germany's fighting men to revolt against Hitler are included.

15   **O**—Photos of Walter Schellenberg, Martin Bormann, Otto Skorzeny and Hitler.

16   **P**—Photo of General Eisenhower at Paris 1945 leaving one of his rare press conferences scheduled at the Hotel Scribe in Paris, near the Opera. Holding the car door is his assigned driver, Kay Summesby.

17   **Q**—Images of General Eisenhower's hideaway.

18   **R**—(left to right) Two of the respected Junker generals in the German OKW, Von Rundstedt and Rommel... Screenstar Marlene Dietrich, German, had sided with the Allies. She was a voice on captured Radio Luxemburg... Alfonse Boudard, native French writer, authored the history of French bordellos, <u>La Fermature</u> (1946)

meaning The Closing... Wilbur Wright, author of <u>Miller-gate</u> (1990) and <u>The Glenn Miller Burial File</u> (1993).

19 **S**—Dr. Udo Ulfkotte finds evidence and writes about Glenn Miller.

20 **T**—Hitler's concept of success in his plan to thwart Operation Eclipse and gain a winter advantage over the Allies. Map indicates his goals: crossing the Meuse River, splitting the 12th and 21st Army Groups (Montgomery's and Bradley's) and reaching Antwerp, Belgium, major port for Allied war supplies.

21 **U**—Nazi documents.

22 **V**—Trianon Palace where WWI's Peace Treaty was signed used for SHAEF (Supreme Headquarters Allied Expeditionary Forces).

23 **W**—Villa and bunker of Eisenhower residence showing attempted break-in point.

24 **X**—Operations record.

25 **Y**—Site where Glenn Miller's body was found.

26 **Z**—(top) Books of two enemies—face to face in the end—Skorzeny and Miller.

(bottom) Postcard with information verifying Operation Eclipse from Charles Whiting to Hunton Downs. Whiting in books alone published on the Battle of the Bulge leads other writers.

27 **AA**— Portion of Miller Questionnaire (1938) for Bluebird Records. Answers handwritten by Glenn.

28 **AB**—The falsified MACR (Missing Air Crew Report) as revealed in contrast with the true MACR, discovered in 1994. The Ansell Report by a Scotland Yard agent

traces the purposeful wrong answers designed to mislead, confuse, or both. (CONTINUED ON **AC**)

30 **AD**—A Scotland Yard investigator, Michael Ansell, prepared this report utilizing scientific comparisons and measurements for both true and false records.

31 **AE**—The obvious disclaimer to any belief that Twinwood RAF Air Base was open for traffic on December 15, 1944.

32 **AF**—A typical *Chefsache* order from Hitler to Captain F.W. Stahl's KG-200 flight of American captured planes to go full speed on a mission, usually involving the crossing of borders and Allied front lines. The B-17 and Liberator B-24 silhouettes got the enemy planes past observation points without challenge. *Chef* was a German word meaning Chief, and referred to Hitler himself. *Sache* was understood to mean thing, or concern, or more to the point, an order.

33 **AG**—A Nazi-produced document proving the 7/13 GM Odin movement to Krefeld and Berlin, as preface to a declared Armistice and arrest of Hitler (Operation Eclipse). The 7/13, alphabetically G and M, was accepted as referring to Glenn Miller on board. The signature of Bergmann was traced with writer Joachim Fest's help to Martin Bormann. Bergmann was his sobriquet. *Oberst* means Highest. Bormann in rank was next to Hitler.

34 **AH**—A Nazi-produced document proving the 7/13 GM Odin movement to Krefeld and Berlin, as preface to a declared Armistice and arrest of Hitler (Operation Eclipse). The 7/13, alphabetically G and M, was accepted as referring to Glenn Miller on board. The signature

of Walter Schellenberg was traced at the German *Archivenzentrum* in Freiburg, where the Nazi files still in German hands are catalogued.

35 **AI**—Britain's Bomber Command (1998) puts to rest any claim of a mass raid on the German city of Siegen (near Bonn) on December 15, 1944. There were no operations that day. A Siegen raid was scheduled for December 16, the orders for which went out to ATS bombing groups in southeast England the day before. Lt. Gregory's bomber with navigator Fred Shaw aboard did NOT accompany that raid, or any other that day Gregory's first raid in which he piloted came December 19th to Trier, Germany.

36 **AJ**—The Bomber Command order for a Siegen, Germany bombing on December 16, 1944. The order, dated the 15th, preceded the mass movement of planes by one day (page 1).

37 **AK**—The Bomber Command order (page 2).

38 **AL**—Part of the Siegen file.

39 **AM**—Part of the Siegen file.

40 **AN**—The Trier raid of December 19.

41 **AO**—Trier Run briefing in Siegen file and proof of Shaw fakery.

42 **AP**—Memo from Sid Robinson, Army Air Corps veteran from WWII.

43 **AQ**—GCHQ is the term for British Intelligence Agencies, located in Cheltenham, GLOS., northwest of London. The secret of Glenn Miller's Odin 7/13 flight was there, held in papers said transferred by Walter Schellenberg to guarantee his safety after his surrender. I

was after those papers and finally got them (AG and AH), and that started bids on my book. <u>Murder in the Mood</u> for TV. To prevent this, CCHQ clamped down on the Royal Post and forbad shipment of the books to the film producer, Daniel O'Toole.

That's when I interceded. As I held residence in Tetbury, a tiny town where Prince Charles lived on his estate Highgrove, I often met him and Diana while shopping. I called him and asked him if delivery is guaranteed by the Royal Post. "Of course it is," he replied with some indignity. I told him then of the held-up shipment. He was shocked, promised to fix it. And he did. One box of books was lost but another arrived spic and span. This was the headline in the Cheltenham, Glos newspaper, the *Echo*, a full columned front page. Courtesy of *Gloucestershire Echo*.

44 **AR**—Telegram with sparse details advising Miller's demise.

45 **AS**—Magnus von Braun, two U.S. soldiers, Walter Dornberger, Herbert Axter, Wernher von Braun, Hans Lindenberg, and Bernhard Tessmann after surrendering to the Allies in 1945.

46 **AT**—Joe Dobson image and note. Captain Joe Dobson, pilot for the 101st Division's Commanding General Maxwell Tayler, was a decorated hero (DFC) of Normandy and the 101st backup defense perimeter at Bastogne. He attained the rank of Colonel and never retreated from or denied his oft-told story of meeting Glenn Miller by happenstance at Northolt Airport in London well after the SHAEF declaration that he was missing.

47 **AU**—To win a "Bronze Star" medal requires a situation of combat verified. It is thus stated in Army Regulations.

48 **AV**—A casualty of friendly fire in one's own territory does not qualify. Eisenhower's staff hid the citation well.

49 **AW**—Newspaper article in 1976 reported Glenn Miller was murdered and there was a cover-up.

A

MESSAGE SENT
DAY BEFORE
BATTLE OF THE BULGE

MESSAGE SENT
NIGHT OF
BATTLE OF THE BULGE

IMPERIAL WAR
MUSEUM

B

"NORSEMAN" MANUFACTURER SAYS HE GOT 'GLENN'S PLANE' BACK - #44-70285

ROBERT NOORDUYN ON AIRCRAFT ACCOUNTABILITY

Robert Noorduyn is the grandson of the Norseman Aircraft Builder that was based in Canada during the war. He now resides in Columbus, Ohio. Noorduyn stated that when an aircraft is assigned to a certain entity it is recorded on that entities property records as a 'gain'. If the aircraft is transferred to another entity, it is recorded as a 'loss' on the property records of the assigning entity and a 'gain' on the property records of the receiving entity. If an aircraft is lost for some reason, it is deleted and recorded as a 'loss' on the property records to which it was originally assigned. With this in mind, and since Norseman #44-70285 was assigned to Abbots Ripton, it would have been the responsibility of Abbots Ripton to have recorded it as a 'loss' and to have deleted aircraft from its records. Rather, Norseman #44-70285 was assigned Adjusted Loss Salvage at Merville, SAD5 on 6May47. This would indicate that, at some point in time, the aircraft was transferred from Abbots Ripton, SAD2, to Merville, SAD5 and that the aircraft remained operational until it was salvaged in May, 1947. Noorduyn has kept very close records on all Norsemen involved in WWII. He says that there were no Norsemen lost on 15Dec44.

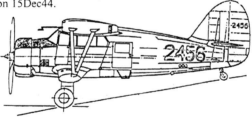

NOORDUYN UC64A NORSEMAN

Manufactured by Noorduyn Aviation Ltd.
Montreal, Canada.

Specifications and Performance

Rate of Climb	600 fpm
Wingspan	51ft. 6in.
Length	31ft. 8in.
Wing Area	325 sq.ft.
Power Loading	11.73 lb/hp
Empty Weight	3,753 lb.
Useful Load	2,692 lb.
Maximum Speed	170 mph
Stall Speed	55 mph
Range,Still Air	600 miles

C

BRODERICK CRAWFORD
(Paris -- 1944-45 -Note Medals
and Crossed Pistols (Mil.Police)
Crawford was Glenn's closest friend
at Yale, in London and Paris.He
kept the secret until 1978 when he
told me the TRUE STORY.

D

PUBLIC
RECORD
OFFICE
The National Archives

Operational Records of the Royal Air Force

Military Records Information 70

GLENN MILLER: 'MISSING PRESUMED MURDERED?'

Meanwhile, controversy still rages about Baesell, and even Lieutenant-Colonel David Niven's possible involvement in Miller's disappearance. On 15 December the British film star was in Spa, Belgium visiting Army friends, having arrived in France from England one month before. Little has been written about David Niven's mysterious wartime career and details are notable by their absence in his autobiography, *The Moon's a Balloon*. In fact Niven, who could speak fluent German, served in F Squadron GHQ Reconnaissance Regiment (Phantom), a highly secret, fully mobile

* *The Special Air Service* Philip Warner (Kimber)

organization developed during the threat of German invasion of Britain. Phantom did excellent work behind the enemy lines with the SAS after the invasion of Normandy, severely hindering the German effort and pinpointing targets for RAF bombers.*

Dennis Cottam recalls: 'Several people contacted Niven about his association with Miller. He just wrote back to them and said 'Sorry old boy, only met the man twice.' Yet, of the hundreds of documents I received from Washington every order, every movement, is countersigned by David Niven. Also, Miller used to have regular meetings at SHAEF HQ and obviously met Niven time and time again.'

The David Niven identification posted in the RAF Museum of Croydon, England is part of the Public Record Office, the National Archives. The notation is found at Croydon under the heading Military Records Information 70-that is, if one has credentials to view classified material of a British nature. Niven is officially described as having served in F Squadron of General Headquarters Reconnaissance Regiment, known as the "Phantoms," with the dry comment "excellent work behind enemy lines" provided herein by RAF researcher Philip Warner. 1950s' Miller investigator Dennis Cottam also got into the Croydon file. Niven's photo he was told, was added at Niven's personal request together with the biting sub-head, "Glenn Miller Missing, Presumed Murdered." There is no other material there on Niven or Miller.

E

GOVERNMENT FORGED MILLER PLANE RECORD
TRUE ORIGINAL WAS "BURIED' FOR 44 YEARS
MORGAN FLEW ALONE. NO TWINWOOD STOP

CONFIDENTIAL

CLASSIFICATION ALTERED

The False

WAR DEPARTMENT
HEADQUARTERS ARMY AIR FORCES
WASHINGTON

MISSING AIR CREW REPORT

Classification changed
to UNCLASSIFIED
by A. A. EZACURAS, Lt. Col., AC
by F. M. WEDGE, Capt., AC
Date, Jun 18 1946

11. xxxxxxNon Battle Casualty

11. NUMBER OF PERSONS ABOARD AIRCRAFT: Crew 1 ; Passengers 2 ; Total 3
     (Starting with Pilot, furnish the following particulars; If more than 11
     persons were aboard aircraft, list similar particulars on separate sheet
     and attach original to this form.)

Crew Position	Name in Full (Last Name First)	Rank	Serial Number	Current Status
1. Pilot	Morgan, John R.S.	F/O	T-190776	Missing ,AC
2. Passenger	Baessell, Norman F.	Lt Col	O-905387	Missing ,AC
3. Passenger	Miller, Alton G.	Major	O-505273	Missing ,AC
4.				

TWO NAMES ADDED DIFFERENT SPACING

For the Commanding Officer:

Date of Report 23 December 1944

(Signature of Preparing Officer)

FORGED SIGNATURE

17. REMARKS OR EYEWITNESS STATEMENTS: None

The Real

SCOTLAND YARD TICKS OFF GLARING TYPOS
ORIGINAL MATCHES COL. WITT'S ACCOUNT

For The Commanding Officer:

Date of Report_____ 23 December 1944.

(Signature of Preparing Officer)

RALPH S. CRAMER
Capt-AC
Adjutant

REMARKS:

CRAMER WOULDN'T SIGN!

ORIGINAL

F

MORE THAN ONE TYPEWRITER USED TO FAKE A-42 DESTINATION PROVED TO BE VERSAILLES AIR FORCE SENT US "ORIGINAL" BY MISTAKE

From *Millergate* by Wilbur Wright (1990): reproduced courtesy of Imperial War Museum, London:

"We were the first to note the typeface anomalies and we commissioned a New Scotland Yard expert Michael Ansell to examine the document and prepare a report on its authenticity (the Fake). Our first clue came when we saw that a capital 'B' in 'Bordeaux' was slightly depressed, whereas the 'B' in 'Baessell ' was not. Second, the figure '2' in 'A-42' was twisted slightly clockwise, whereas that in Miller's serial number was not. Third, misaligments in the crew list suggested that the names of Baessell and Miller had been inserted at a different time to that of John Morgan. Further, we noted that a capital 'B' in 'Bradunas' in the Declassification Certificate exhibited a characteristic depression similar to that in 'Bordeaux,' from which we and Mr. Ansell concluded that one of the machines used to type the MACR (supposedly compiled in 1944) had been used to complete the Declassification Certificate in 1946 (when the Fake was issued, presumably 'found.')

"And now we see the personal dilemma of Captain Ralph S. Cramer, the Adjutant at Abbots Ripton, the plane's home base. He had been ordered to delay compilation of the MACR, but Cramer by then had known his Norseman was missing since Saturday when Air Traffic Control notified (the network of the missing craft.). We have no doubt that Cramer conducted his own local inquiry as per regulations, including the impounding of the aircraft documents."

What he omitted from the MACR, unquestionably on orders from SHAEF, were (1) weather (2) engine number (3) take-off witness, and for his own legally-shaky hide, (4) his signature.

Attached: Fake Report   Original Report   Ansell Report

from
Hunton Downs

G

(EVIDENCE GATHERED BY WILBUR
WRIGHT CONCERNING GLENN
MILLER DISPOSITION-----
            Courtesy:
            Imperial War
            Museum, London

State of New Jersey

DEPARTMENT OF HEALTH

CN 360, TRENTON, N.J. 08625-0360

MOLLY JOEL COYE, M.D., M.P.H.
COMMISSIONER

April 10, 1987

Name: Alton G. Miller
Dod: 12/44
Pod: Ohio

Wilbur Wright
The Shrubs Allington Lane
Southampton S03 3HP
England

Dear Mr. Wright:

The death of Alton G. Miller occurred in the State
of Ohio. You should write to:

            Division of Vital Statistics
            Ohio Department of Health
            G-20 Ohio Departments Building
            65 South Front St.
            Columbus, OH 43215

Enclosed is a refund statement for $4.00.

                        Very truly yours,

                        Charles A. Karkut
                        State Registrar

SK:bp

H

PUBLIC RELATIONS DIVISION

S H A E F

_____

_____24 Dec._____ 1944

Memo to: __Capt Wade_____
Information Room

Here is the release on Glenn Miller, with the
embargo of 1800 hours tonight.

Colonel Dupuy merely wants a factual announcement
that he is missing. However, he also wants a statment
added to the effect that "no members of his band
were with him." Or something very much like that.

Capt. Cosgrove.

THIS CORRESPONDENCE MUST BE RETURNED. COLONEL DUPUY
DOES NOT HAVE TO SEE THE RELEASE BEFORE IT GOES OUT.

Done.

1150
Signature _____
24 Dec 44
P.VW1

8   1159

I

AG 201-AGF-Miller, Alton Glenn (Off)   PARIS, APO 757
                                                     22 December 1944

SUBJECT: Report of Missing Personnel.

TO   : Commanding General, European Theater of Operations, U. S. Army,
           APO 887.

1. It is reported that on 15 December 1944 Major Alton Glenn
Miller, O-505273, AC, Army Air Force Band (Special), Headquarters
Command, Supreme Headquarters AEF, departed from an airport in
England enroute to Paris, France, in an Eighth Air Force Service
Command airplane (C-64) piloted by a Flight Officer Morgan. There
was one (1) additional passenger on this plane - a Lieutenant Colonel
Baessel of the Eighth Air Force. Major Miller was taken to the air
field by an officer of the Army Air Force Band who witnessed the takeoff. No trace of this plane can be found and this headquarters has been
advised by the Eighth Air Force Service Command that this airplane is
considered missing. Likewise, Major Miller is considered to be missing.

2. It is requested that an immediate radio casualty report be
rendered to the War Department on Major Miller, and the War Department
be advised that in view of the circumstances set forth in paragraph 4
below, it is considered highly desirable that this information be released to the press here at 1800A hours, 24 December, and that the War
Department should confirm to your headquarters the next of kin has been
notified prior to that time.

3. The next of kin of Major Miller is Mrs. Helen D. Miller (wife),
Cotswold Apartments, Byrne Lane, Tenafly, New Jersey, telephone, Englewood
3-7311.

4. A Christmas Day broadcast has been scheduled which will be released to the United States. Major Miller was to have participated in this
program. It is thought considerable publicity has been given to this
broadcast in the United States.

"For the Supreme Commander"

                                          T. J. DAVIS,
                                          Brigadier General,
                                          Adjutant General.

                                          DECLASSIFIED
                                          DOD Dir. 5200.9/Sept. 27, 1958
                                          NMW by _____ date 8/28/10

CONFIDENTIAL

J

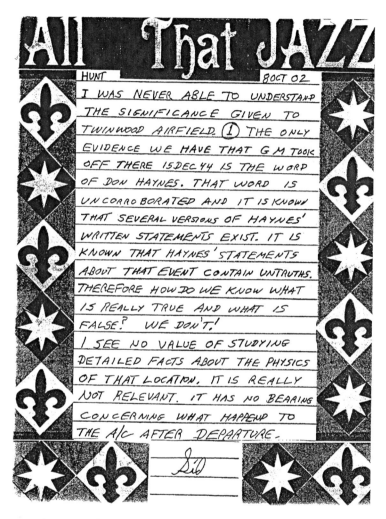

HUNT 8 OCT 02

I WAS NEVER ABLE TO UNDERSTAND
THE SIGNIFICANCE GIVEN TO
TWINWOOD AIRFIELD. (1) THE ONLY
EVIDENCE WE HAVE THAT G M TOOK
OFF THERE 15 DEC 44 IS THE WORD
OF DON HAYNES. THAT WORD IS
UNCORROBORATED AND IT IS KNOWN
THAT SEVERAL VERSIONS OF HAYNES'
WRITTEN STATEMENTS EXIST. IT IS
KNOWN THAT HAYNES' STATEMENTS
ABOUT THAT EVENT CONTAIN UNTRUTHS.
THEREFORE HOW DO WE KNOW WHAT
IS REALLY TRUE AND WHAT IS
FALSE? WE DON'T!
I SEE NO VALUE OF STUDYING
DETAILED FACTS ABOUT THE PHYSICS
OF THAT LOCATION. IT IS REALLY
NOT RELEVANT. IT HAS NO BEARING
CONCERNING WHAT HAPPEND TO
THE A/C AFTER DEPARTURE.

Sid

"Sid" is Sid Robinson, Army Air Corps veteran from
WWII. Brother-in-law of Tex Beneke, Miller's famous singer
and leader of the post-war band. Sid followed up on Tex's
disbelief of the government's claims and he began a search
for evidence among AAC pilots and crew members which
led to a huge library of "Beneke-Robinson Archives" of
which he is now intendant or director.

K

ANKORAGE

IN REPLY CITE : 8AFSC-D-832-G-27 A   DEC 20   INTERNAL ADDRESS :
FROM : HQ EIGHTH AFSC   TO : G-1 SECTION, SHAEF
                                                (MAIN) ATTN : GEN.
                                                BARKER

TO :   SHAEF (MAIN)

INFO : SHAEF (REAR)   SGD : EARLY
       HQ, USSTAFF

Confirming verbal information to G-1 SHAEF Rear C-64 airplane
number 44-70285 missing and unreported since departure Twinwood
Field 1355 hours 15 December for France pilot Flight Officer Morgan
2 passengers including Major Glenn Miller

USSTAFF MAIN DISTRIBUTION

     : H/OPS
       AG RECORDS

USSTAF MAIN IN 7055

Steve Early, FDR's PR Expert   *Col James Early, VIII AAF SC*

L

WAR DEPARTMENT
CLASSIFIED MESSAGE CENTER
INCOMING CLASSIFIED MESSAGE

Casualty Form Made
358007

SPECIAL

PRIORITY

ETO

From: Headquarters Communications Zone, European Theater of
Operations, US Army, **Paris**, France

To: War Department

Nr. E 77699   22 December 1944

SPXPC signed Eisenhower E 77699 AG Cas Div casualty
message 3028. Nonbattle.

Miller, Alton Glenn 0505273 Major AC Army Air Force
Band (special) Hq Command, Supreme Hq AEF is reported
missing since 15 December '44 enroute by Air from
England to Paris, France. Major Miller was taken to
the airfield by an officer of the Army Air Force Band
who witnessed the takeoff. No trace of this airplane
can be found and airplane is considered missing.

Request acknowledgement and that immediate information
be furnished by priority cable when next of kin has
been notified in order that suitable release may be
made to the press here at 1800A hours 24 December
as Major Miller was to have participated in Christmas
Day broadcast concerning which considerable publicity
has been given in the United States.

End

ACTION: TAG

INFO : CG AAF
        BPR

CM-IN-22031 (23 Dec 44) 03567 mcs

ACTION: CAS BRANCH

First Washington knowledge
of Glenn Miller's "missing."
Telegram Ike to WD, 22 Dec.
Note emphasis: Nonbattle

COPY NO.

M

The Adminstrator   46 Woodwarde Rd
Mountain View Cemetery   Dulwich Village
Altadena   London SE
Cal. U.S.A.   England

                                            15 January 1987

Dear Sir -

   This letter will introduce Mr.Wilbur Wright from Southampton in England, who is researching with my permission
and approval the resting places of various members of my
family.

   I refer particularly to my deceased sister-in-law, Mrs.
Helen Miller, who is buried in Grave No. 5, Lot 2584, and
her family.

   I would be deeply grateful if you would afford Mr.Wright
your full cooperation during his visit to Mountain View
Cemetery.

                              Yours sincerely

                              John Herbert Miller

                              JOHN HERBERT MILLER

(EVIDENCE GATHERED BY WILBUR
WRIGHT CONCERNING GLENN MILLER
DISPOSITION---Courtesy:
                Imperial War Museum
                London, UK

N

GLENN MILLER RECORDINGS

LE SPHINX

The battered old brothel-hotel known as Le Sphinx got a face lift and new occupancy in 2000. Karolina Krauss found records to prove Nazi ownership.

O

Martin Bormann, code
name "Bergmann," helped
plot Glenn Miller's
kidnapping while at
Hitler's side.

Walter Schellenberg was the
top Nazi spook. He founded
the Dirty Tricks sector of
Intellegence--Irrefuehrung.

Noses for treachery. Col.Otto Skorzeny
gets Hitler congratulations for freeing
Mussolini, and is entrusted with another
job--GET EISENHOWER.

P

Gen. Eisenhower
exiting SCRIBE HOTEL
Paris after Press
Conference,Jan.1945
Holding door with
cocked hat and salute
is his driver, Kay
Summersby.

Typical of Eisenhower
stringent press conditions
prevailed. No newsreels.
Private photographer (this
side of car). Pool photogs
beside MP motorcycle, only
two allowed. This sneak
shot from roof by AFP.

. . And back to his office at TRIANON PALACE (held Secret)

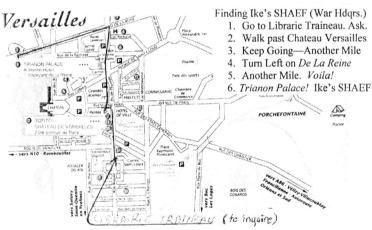

Finding Ike's SHAEF (War Hdqrs.)
1. Go to Librarie Traineau. Ask.
2. Walk past Chateau Versailles
3. Keep Going—Another Mile
4. Turn Left on *De La Reine*
5. Another Mile. *Voila!*
6. *Trianon Palace!* Ike's SHAEF

Q

32 RUE ALEXANDRE DUMAS (Corner AVENUE VICTOR HUGO) was
the secret hideaway address for General Eisenhower, as
it was for German Commander-in-Chief Von Rundstedt who
Occupied the residence for four years prior to Ike.
While Skorzeny's "German G.I.s" were after him, he
commuted to nearby Versailles by tank.

R

SOME PRINCIPALS IN GLENN MILLER'S "MISSION FOR IKE"
AND SOME WHO HELPED UNRAVEL THE 50-YEAR MYSTERY"

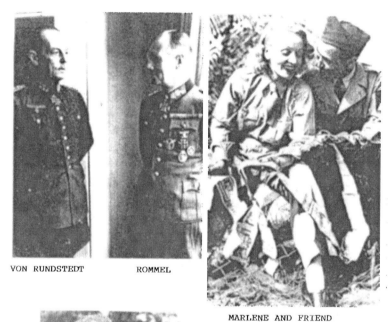

VON RUNDSTEDT   ROMMEL

MARLENE AND FRIEND

ALPHONSE BOUDARD

WILBUR WRIGHT

S

Frankfurter Allgemeine Zeitung

The Frankfurter Allgemeine Zeitung (English Frankfurt General Newspaper), also known as FAZ, is a national German newspaper, founded in 1949. It is published daily in Frankfurt am Main. The Sunday edition is the Frankfurter Allgemeine Sonntagszeitung. FAZ has a circulation of over 400,000.

Dr. Udo Ulfkotte

In winter of 1997, Dr. Udo Ulfkotte, a journalist with the prestigious Frankfurter Allgemeine Zeitung, was at home working on a book about a German Spy Service for which he had been commissioned when suddenly a blurb interrupted his Internet communication with BND, the secret agency in Berlin. His computer screen, monitoring old Washington-Berlin messages, popped up the name GLENN MILLER. (Top Secret) He read on, downloaded and hastened to FAZ, his newspaper, to write up the strange story of how history can vomit up its secrets. It was published and read all over the world.

S

Original text in German

Andere Tatsachen sind irgendwann einmal aus vermeintlicher Not heraus mit dem Schleier der Desinformation versehen worden und haben heute längst als angebliche „Wahrheiten" Eingang in die Geschichtsbücher gefunden: so fehlt in wohl keinem Lexikon der Hinweis, der amerikanische Band-Leader Glenn Miller sei wenige Tage vor Weihnachten 1944 bei einem Flugzeugabsturz über dem Ärmelkanal ums Leben gekommen. Die wahre Todesursache, laut Geheimdienst-Archiven ein Herzinfarkt beim Bordellbesuch, war in der stimmungsvollen Vorweihnachtszeit wohl eher unpassend, und so wurde der Geheimdienst beauftragt, eine stilvolle Legende um das Ableben des allseits beliebten Musikers zu stricken. Natürlich lagern in den Tresoren der Geheimdienste unzählige weitaus brisantere Erkenntnisse.

English Translation

(In the story about Glenn's fate)… Other facts were supplied which were undoubtedly thought needed or necessary to establish a veil of disinformation over what history has up to today well-recorded in a lexicon of references, the fate of the band leader GLENN MILLER. To be believed—that several days before Christmas of 1944, he lost his life in a plane accident over the English Channel. The true cause of death, according to the secret archives was a heart attack in a bordello, that in the precipitous days before Christmas (beginning of the Bulge) went unnoticed, and thus the Secret Service was obligated to knit up a unique legend over the loss of this on-all-sides beloved musician. For sure, there lies in the treasure of this Secret Service (U.S.), numerous further flappable bits of knowledge.

T

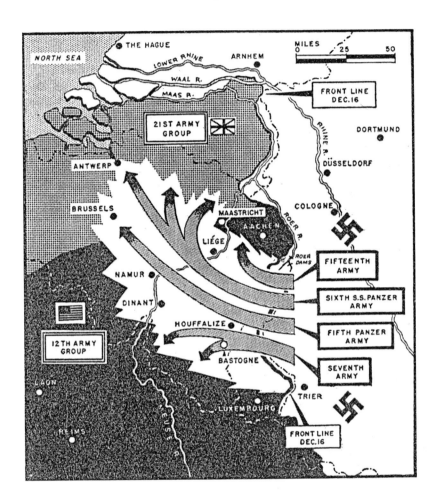

U

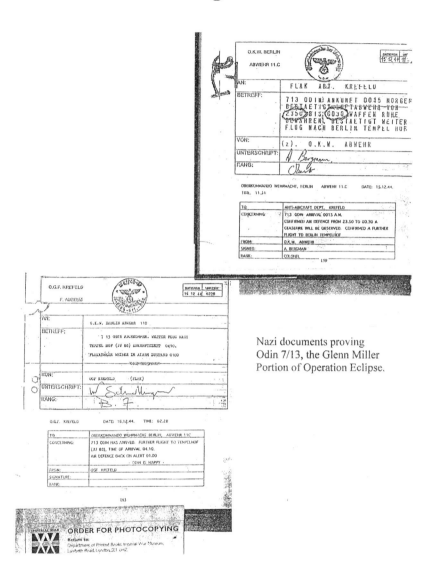

Nazi documents proving
Odin 7/13, the Glenn Miller
Portion of Operation Eclipse.

V

Trianon Palace, where World War One's Peace Treaty was signed, was chosen by Ike to be SHAEF, Supreme Headquarters Allied Expeditionary Forces. Location was Secret, no Press allowed. Eisenhower did rare public appearances at the Scribe Hotel in Paris.

W

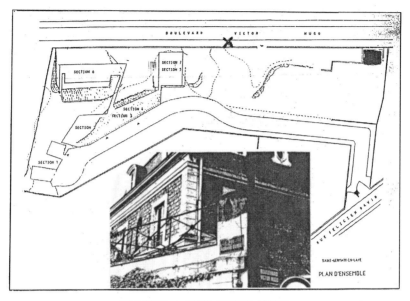

IKE'S VILLA & SEVEN SECTION BUNKER

(The black SQUARE is the villa. The
CROSSMARK on Blvd. Victor Hugo
where a forced entry point by dynamite
failed (to meet a tunnel connection
to the house.)

X

SR 1/12A

Date: ₁ ₁₄/₁₂₀₀

December 15, 1944. "No
Operations Today"—"No
Flying Today."

PUBLIC
RECORD
OFFICE

The National Archives

OPERATIONS RECORD BOOK   Pₑ

of (Unit or Formation) CRANFIELD AND TWINWOOD.   No. of pages used for

Date	Time	Summary of Events	SECRET.
14.12.44.		Seven hours flying by day only. Beaufighter Mk. 1. R.2151 - Repairs Completed - Ex Cat "EJ" taken on Unit charge and removed from No. 43 Group D/A. Mosquito Mk.11.DZ.746 - Repairs Completed - EX Cat "AC" - taken on Unit charge and removed from No. 43 Group D/A. 82 aircraft serviceable, 43 unserviceable. In addition 1 serviceable Beaufighter Mk.1. detached to Odiham. 1 serviceable Wellington Mk. 18 detached to Church Fenton. 1 serviceable Hurricane Mk. 11C detached to Church Fenton. 2 unserviceable Wellington Mk. 18 detached to Weybridge, 3 serviceable Mosquito Mk.11, 3 unserviceable Mosquito Mk.11, 3 serviceable Mosquito Mk.111, 1 unserviceable Mosquito 111, 5 serviceable Martinet, 3 unserviceable Martinet, also 1 serviceable Master Mk.11, and 1 unserviceable Master Mk.11, all detached to Middle Wallop. Mr. S.J. Schofield of Oxford again spoke in the S.H.Q. Lecture Room to-night on "Full Employment" and Sir William Beveridge's plan for keeping unemployment below 3%.	
15.12.44. ✓		There was no flying to-day. Beaufort 1. Dual N.1077 - Repairs Completed - Ex Cat "AC" - taken on Unit charge and removed from No. 43 Group D/A. 83 aircraft serviceable, 40 unserviceable. In addition 1 serviceable Beaufighter Mk. 1. detached to Odiham. 1 serviceable Wellington Mk. 18 detached to Church Fenton. 1 serviceable Hurricane Mk. 11C detached to Church Fenton, 2 unserviceable Wellington Mk. 18 detached to Weybridge. 5 serviceable Mosquito Mk.11. 4 unserviceable Mosquito Mk.11. 3 serviceable Mosquito Mk.111, 1 unserviceable Mosquito 111, 7 serviceable Martinet, 1 unserviceable Martinet, also 1 serviceable Master Mk.11, and 1 unserviceable Master Mk.11, all detached to Middle Wallop.	

Date		Summary	
13 Dec.		No operations.	B.
14 Dec.		(Night 14/15 Dec). 10 aircraft carried out mining operations, all were	B.
		successful, and were successfully diverted to Lossiemouth on return.	O.
15 Dec. ✓		No operations.	B.
16 Dec.		Target - Siegen. Detailed - 108, Cancelled - nil, Abortive - 16, Missing - 1.	B.
		The large number of abortives were due to bad weather. Iceing cloud existed	O.
		over base and as far as 0600E up to 20,000 feet.	
		At the fighter rendezvous point, when the cloud began to break up,	
		leaders found that they were up to 15 mins early, so they orbited, and the	
		Group formed into a very good formation, going on to carry out a very	

Y

Fifty years tracking down a G.I. rumor leads investigator Hunton Downs to site in Paris where Miller's body was found.

Z

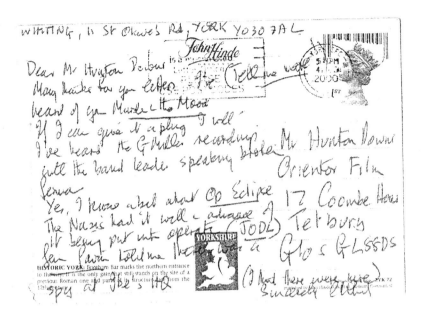

"...Yes, I know a bit about <u>Op Eclipse</u>.
The Nazis had it well in advance of it
being put into operation (JODL). Gen.
Gavin told me there was a spy at Ike's
HQ. I think there were more.
                    Sincerely Charles (whiting)
                    Foremost Bulge Historian

AA

PART 1 - REFERENCE INFORMATION

NAME, AS USED IN RECORDING AND OTHER PROFESSIONAL WORK:

Glenn Miller

TYPE OF PROFESSIONAL WORK:

Orchestra Leader

FULL NAME IN PRIVATE LIFE:

Alton Glenn Miller

ADDRESS: *3760 88th St*   PHONE NUMBER: *Havemeyer*
        Jackson Heights L.I. N.Y.   *6-0671*

YOUR INSTRUMENT, IF ANY; OR IF VOCAL, WHAT VOICE:

Trombone + Arranger

HOW LONG HAVE YOU BEEN A VICTOR OR BLUEBIRD RECORDING ARTIST:

1 Month

NAME OF YOUR PERSONAL MANAGER, IF ANY:

Cy Shribman

HIS ADDRESS: .   HIS PHONE NUMBER:

Little Building, Boston, Mass.   *Hancock 8125*

NAME OF PRIVATE PRESS AGENT, IF ANY:

Howard Richmond

HIS ADDRESS: HIS PHONE NUMBER:

799 7th Ave
N.Y.C.

AA

MONTH, DAY AND YEAR OF BIRTH:
March 1st 1908

CITY AND STATE, (OR COUNTRY) OF BIRTH:
Clarinda, Iowa

FATHER'S NAME: FATHER'S OCCUPATION:
Lewis Elmer Miller   _Building Contractor_

MOTHER'S NAME (BEFORE MARRIAGE):
Matty Lou Cavender

ARE YOU MARRIED?   IF SO, TO WHOM?
Yes   _To Mrs Miller_

WHEN WERE YOU MARRIED?

WHERE DID YOU MEET YOUR } HUSBAND?
                         } WIFE? _In College_

NAMES AND AGES OF CHILDREN, IF ANY:
None

WHAT WAS YOUR CHILDHOOD AMBITION?
Professional BaseBall Player

WHO WAS YOUR CHILDHOOD HERO (A) IN FICTION?
Horatio Alger

(B) IN REAL LIFE?
Teddy Roosevelt

AA

WHAT IS YOUR FAVORITE COLOR? *Blue*

WHAT IS YOUR CHIEF REASON FOR LIKING IT? *Restful*

TO WHAT COLOR DO YOU FEEL AN AVERSION? *ORANGE*

TO WHAT TYPE OF INDIVIDUAL OF EITHER SEX ARE YOU MOST ATTRACTED?
A Natural Person

WHAT WAS YOUR NICKNAME WHILE IN SCHOOL?
"Mill"

WHAT IS YOUR NICKNAME NOW?
"Mill"

WILL YOU TELL US FIVE THINGS YOU'RE FOND OF IN LIFE AND OF WHICH YOU'D NEVER HAD ENOUGH?
— Trout Fishing
Baseball Playing
Sleep
Good Music
Money

DO YOUR CORRESPONDENTS EVER MISSPELL YOUR NAME? *Yes*

IF SO, WHAT HAVE BEEN SOME AMUSING VARIATIONS?
Glen Mueller
Glen(n) Milner
Clem Mueller

HAVE ANY OF YOUR CORRESPONDENTS EVER TRIED TO IDENTIFY YOU AS A LONG-LOST RELATIVE?
No

AA

WHAT DO YOU CONSIDER THE THREE GREATEST BOOKS EVER WRITTEN?

The Bible

DO YOU LIKE POETRY? *No*

WHO ARE YOUR FAVORITE POETS? _____

AND WHAT ARE YOUR FAVORITE QUOTATIONS?

It Dont Mean A Thing If It Aint Got That Swing

WHAT ONE PERSON HAS PARTICULARLY AIDED YOU IN YOUR WORK?

Tommy Dorsey

WHAT WAS THE FIRST JOB OF ANY KIND YOU EVER HELD AND WHAT, IF YOU DON'T MIND TELLING, WAS THE SALARY?

Milking A Cow Salary $1.00 per week

WHOM DO YOU CONSIDER THE FIVE GREATEST CHARACTERS IN HISTORY?

Abe Lincoln
Thomas Jefferson

ARE YOU EVEN-TEMPERED? OR DO YOU RUN TO EXTREMES OF DEPRESSION AND ELATION?

Yes Fairly Even Tempered

DO YOU ENVY PEOPLE WHO POSSESS TEMPERAMENTS OPPOSITE TO YOUR OWN? IF SO, WHY?

I envy perfectly controlled Tempers

HAVE YOU CONFIDENCE IN YOUR OWN ABILITY AND JUDGMENT?

Yes

AA

IN ADDITION TO OR OUTSIDE OF YOUR MUSICAL CAREER, TRACE BRIEFLY WHAT OTHER WORK YOU HAVE DONE.

"Soda Jerk" while Going To High School
Worked in a Sugar Factory while going to
High School

DID YOU EVER HAVE "MIKE FRIGHT"?

Yes

DO YOU STILL HAVE IT?

Yes At Times

IF SO, PLEASE DESCRIBE.

Drying of the Mouth
Shaking of the Knees
Blankness of the Mind

IF YOU HAVE OVERCOME IT DID IT DROP AWAY NATURALLY AS YOU BECAME EXPERIENCED OR DID YOU ADOPT SOME SPECIFIC DEVICE TO GET RID OF IT? IF THE LATTER, PLEASE DESCRIBE THE DEVICE.

I have practically overcome it by developing
Confidence in Myself And my band.
Deep Abdominal Breathing Is Helpful

WHAT DO YOU CONSIDER THE TURNING POINT IN YOUR CAREER?

Forming Of My Own Band

HAVE YOU APPEARED IN THE MOVIES, IN MOVIE SHORTS, IN VAUDEVILLE, IN PLAYS OR IN MUSICAL SHOWS? PLEASE TRACE THE HIGH SPOTS:

No

Continuation on file

AB

WAR DEPARTMENT
HEADQUARTERS ARMY AIR FORCES
WASHINGTON

MISSING AIR CREW REPORT

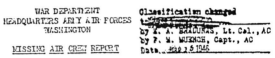
Classification changed
t̶o̶ ̶R̶E̶S̶T̶R̶I̶C̶T̶E̶D̶
by E. A. BRADUNAS, Lt. Col., AC
by P. M. WUENCH, Capt., AC
Date...Sep 2 5 1946

IMPORTANT: This Report will be compiled in triplicate by each Army Air
Forces organization within 48 hours of the time an air crew
member is officially reported missing.

Ripton
1. ORGANIZATION: Location, by Name Abbotts ; Command or Air ForceVIII Air Force SvC
   Group 35th ADG ; Squadron Repair ; Detachment 2d Strategic Air Depot
2. SPECIFY: Place of DepartureAbbotts Ripton Course Bordeaux Via A-42
   Target or Intended DestinationBordeaux; A-42 Type of Mission A
3. WEATHER CONDITIONS AND VISIBILITY AT TIME OF CRASH OR WHEN LAST REPORTED:
   Unknown
4. GIVE: (a) Day 15 MonthDec Year 44 ; Time1355 ; and Location Twinwood
   of last known whereabouts of missing aircraft.
   (b) Specify whether aircraft was last sighted ( ); last XXXXXXXXXXXXXXX
   XXXXXXXXXXXXXXXXXXXXXXXXXXXXXXXXXXXXXXXX Information not Available ( )
5. AIRCRAFT WAS LOST, OR IS BELIEVED TO HAVE BEEN LOST, AS A RESULT OF: (Check
   only one) Enemy Aircraft ( ); Enemy Anti-Aircraft ( ); Other Circumstances
   as Follows: Unknown
6. AIRCRAFT: Type, Model and SeriesUC-64A ; AAF Serial Number 44-70285
7. NICKNAME OF AIRCRAFT, If Any Norseman
8. ENGINES: Type, Model and Series Radial - 1340 P&W ; AAF Serial
   Number (a)Unknown ; (b) ; (c) ; (d)
9. INSTALLED WEAPONS (Furnish below Make, Type and Serial Number); None
   (a) ; (b) ; (c) ; (d) ;
   (e) ; (f) ; (g) ; (h) ;
   (i) ; (j) ; (k) ; (l) ;
   (m) ; (n) ; (o) ; (p) ;
10. THE PERSONS LISTED BELOW WERE REPORTED AS: XXXXXXXXXXXXXXXXX
    XXXXXXXXXNon Battle Casualty
11. NUMBER OF PERSONS ABOARD AIRCRAFT: Crew 1 ; Passengers 2 ; Total 3
    (Starting with Pilot, furnish the following particulars: If more than 11
    persons were aboard aircraft, list similar particulars on separate sheet
    and attach original to this form.)

Crew Position	Name in Full (Last Name First)	Rank	Serial Number	Current Status
1. Pilot	Morgan, John R.S.	F/O	T-190776	Missing ,AC
2. Passenger	Baessell, Norman F.	Lt Col	0-905387	Missing ,AC
3. Passenger	Miller, Alton G.	Major	0-505273	Missing ,AC
4.				
5.				
6.				
7.				
8.				
9.				
10.				
11.				

12. IDENTIFY BELOW THOSE PERSONS WHO ARE BELIEVED TO HAVE LAST KNOWLEDGE OF AIR-
    CRAFT, AND CHECK APPROPRIATE COLUMN TO INDICATE BASIS FOR SAME:-

Check Only One Column,

Name in Full (Last Name First)	Rank	Serial Number	Contacted by Radio	Last Sighted	Saw Crash	Saw Forced Landing
1. Unknown						
2.						
3.						

CONFIDENTIAL

AC

CONFIDENTIAL

13. IF PERSONNEL ARE BELIEVED TO HAVE SURVIVED, ANSWER YES TO ONE OF THE FOLLOWING STATEMENTS: (a) Parachutes were used ___; (b) Persons were seen walking away from scene of crash ___; or (c) Any other reason (Specify) ___Unknown___

14. ATTACH AERIAL PHOTOGRAPH, MAP, CHART, OR SKETCH, SHOWING APPROXIMATE LOCATION WHERE AIRCRAFT WAS LAST SEEN OR HEARD FROM.

15. ATTACH EYEWITNESS DESCRIPTION OF CRASH, FORCED LANDING, OR OTHER CIRCUM-STANCES PERTAINING TO MISSING AIRCRAFT.

16. GIVE NAME, RANK AND SERIAL NUMBER OF OFFICER IN CHARGE OF SEARCH, IF ANY, INCLUDING DESCRIPTION AND EXTENT ___None___

For the Commanding Officer:

Date of Report ___23 December 1944___

(Signature of Preparing Officer)

17. REMARKS OR EYEWITNESS STATEMENTS: None

JAN 22 1945

RECEIVED

AD

REPORT OF MICHAEL ANSELL MA
No. 861205
in the matter of
MISSING AIRCREW REPORT
15 January 1987

Introduction

I hold the degrees of B.A. and M.A. at the University of Oxford, and I am experienced in the scientific examination of documents and handwriting, having retired from the post of Deputy Head of Documents Section of the Metropolitan Police Forensic Laboratory in October 1983. During my 14 years exclusive experience I have examined tens of thousands of documents on behalf of the Police, Government Departments, Banks, Building Societies and other companies, as well as for private individuals. During part of my time at the MPFL I was the British representative on the Interpol Committee for identification of typescript.

On 4th December 1986 I received by post from Wilbur Wright of Southampton a number of photocopy items as listed below.

1. Missing Aircrew Report – 2 pages.
2. Fig. 33 (later renumbered 17) Blow-Up of Item 1.
3. Fig. 31 (later renumbered 18) Classification Change.
4. Fig. 12 Record Card of Flight Officer Morgan.
5. App. 13 Non-Battle Casualty Report (Glenn Miller).

I have examined these.

Assumptions

I have taken these items to be true copes of their originals except where they have been reasonably edited or enlarged in order to illustrate certain points in the text of the book.

Instructions

I have been asked to express an opinion as to:-

(a) Whether the route details were typed by a similar model but different machine to that used in the rest of the Report.
(b) Whether, if (a) be correct, the same other machine was used to type the Classification Change Certificate.
(c) Whether either of these machines was used on both first and second pages of the Report, such that a falsified first page could have been attached to a genuine signed second page.

Observations

There are two restrictions to my examination. Firstly, the examination of photocopies is never as good as the examination of originals for a number of reasons, and secondly because the type of machine(s) used here, as is often the case with Government machines, particularly of that period, were of poor quality having a number of loose characters.

The first limitation means, for example, the colour of ink and depth of impression cannot be seen. The second means that, for example, the same machine can easily type a raised 'B' on one occasion and a lowered 'B' on a different occasion. This means that two apparently-different, in regard to defects, entries may in fact be by the same typewriter and vice versa.

However, the impression is given here that the Missing Aircrew Report was printed or duplicated in some way, albeit from a possibly-typed original which incorporated the word 'pilot' as part of the original document. The particulars 'Morgan. John R.S., F/O, T-190776' and 'Missing' appear to have been typed by one machine which I designate 'A'. The particulars 'Passenger' against 2 and 3 appear to have been made by a different machine which I designate 'B'. The remaining particulars for the two passengers and the three entries ',AC' including that against Pilot appear to have been typed by machine B but on a different occasion.

I also notice that the number of passengers '2' and total '3' have a peculiar 'thick' appearance as if they may have been typed more than once. I also note that the 'B' is consistently lowered in 'Bordeaux' in the route details. This also occurs in the words 'Norseman' and 'Morgan' but not 'Norman' or 'Major' against Passenger details.

Conclusions

It is difficult to reach any firm conclusions because of the combination of the photocopying process and variable and poor quality of the typescript. It is not possible to tell, for example, how many of the details at the top right were typed, and how many stamped. However, I am able to comment that the following are likely to have taken place:

A. The Pilot's particulars (Para. 11-1) except ',AC' were typed by machine 'A'.
B. The words 'Passenger' (Paras. 11-2 and 11-3) were typed by machine 'B'.
C. All other passenger details including the three words ',AC' were typed by machine 'B' but on a different occasion.

I am unable to account for the peculiar appearance of the figures '2' and '3' for the number of passengers and total. The words 'unknown' on each sheet all appear to have been typed by the same machine, therefore I think it unlikely that the first sheet was a complete substitution unless it was by a different person with access to the same machine. However, I do think it possible that the whole Report was prepared for Pilot only and the number of passengers and their details added later, for whatever reason.

M. Ansell M.A. 15th January 1987

AE

OPERATIONS RECORD BOOK

of (Unit or Formation) CRANFIELD AND TWINWOOD.

No. of pages used for

Pa

m in K.R. and A.C.I.,
ll. chapter XX. and

Date	Time	Summary of Events
14.12.44.		Seven hours flying by day only. Beaufighter Mk. 1. P.2151 - Repairs Completed - Ex Cat "AC" taken on Unit charge and removed from No. 43 Group D/A. Mosquito Mk.11. DZ.746 - Repairs Completed - EX Cat "AC" - taken on Unit charge and removed from No. 43 Group D/A. 82 aircraft serviceable, 43 unserviceable. In addition 1 serviceable Beaufighter Mk.1v detached to Odiham. 1 serviceable Wellington Mk. 18 detached to Church Fenton. 1 serviceable Hurricane Mk. 11C detached to Church Fenton. 2 unserviceable Wellington Mk. 18 detached to Weybridge, 3 serviceable Mosquito Mk.11, 3 unserviceable Mosquito Mk.11, 1 unserviceable Mosquito Mk.111, 5 serviceable Mosquito Mk.111, 1 serviceable Master Mk.11, and 1 unserviceable Master Mk.11, all detached to Middle Wallop. Mr. S.J. Schofield of Oxford again spoke in the S.H.Q. Lecture Room to-night on "Full Employment" and Sir William Beveridge's plan for keeping unemployment below 3%.
15.12.44.		There was no flying to-day. Beaufort 1. Dual N.1077 - Repairs Completed - Ex Cat "AC" - taken on Unit charge and removed from No. 43 Group D/A. 83 aircraft serviceable, 40 unserviceable. In addition 1 serviceable Beaufighter Mk.1 detached to Odiham. 1 serviceable Wellington Mk. 18 detached to Church Fenton. 1 serviceable Hurricane Mk. 11C detached to Church Fenton. 2 unserviceable Wellington Mk. 18 detached to Weybridge. 5 serviceable Mosquito Mk.11, 4 unserviceable Mosquito Mk.11, 3 serviceable Mosquito Mk.111, 1 unserviceable Mosquito Mk.111, 7 serviceable Martinet, 1 unserviceable Martinet, also 1 serviceable Master Mk.11, and 1 unserviceable Master Mk.11, all detached to Middle Wallop.
16.12.44.		No night flying but 17 hours by day. Beaufighter Mk.1 X.7872 - Repairs Completed Ex Cat "AC" - taken on Unit charge and removed from No. 43 Group D/A. 84 aircraft serviceable 40 unserviceabl

AF

Chef-Sache!
Geheim

Geheime Kommandosache

+ SSD ROBINSON 07219 19. 10. (2200) -

AN LFL KDO 6

GLTD: AN KG 200 - LFL KDO 6 - VO LW B CHEF BENST D H -
LW FUEST ROEM EINS C KURFUERST -
ADJ REICHSMARSCHALL NACHRICHTLICH
- GEHEIME KOMMANDOSACHE CHEFSACHE NUR DURCH OFFIZIER -
BEZUG: LFL KDO 6 ROEM EINS C NR 2412/44 GKDOS CHEFSACHE
VOM 17. 10. - 1.) MIT DURCHFUEHRUNG VERBINDUNGSAUFNAHME
UND VERSORGUNGSFLUEGE FUER DEUTSCHE KAMPFGRUPPE RAUM
BERESINO WIRD KG 200 BEAUFTRAGT, DAS ENG ZUSAMMENARBEIT
MIT LFL 6 UND HEERESGRUPPE MITTE. FLUGZEUGE UND
BETRIEBSSTOFF STELLT KG 200. SONDERZUWEISUNG ERFOLGT NICHT.
2.) ZUNAECHST BESTEHEN KAMPFGRUPPE FESTSTELLEN UND
ERKUNDUNG LANDEPLAETZE DURCHFUEHREN. RUECKKEHR
ERKUNDUNGSOFFIZIERS ERFORDERLICH, DA FUNKSPRUECHE NICHT
ALS AUSREICHEND SICHERE MELDUNG ANZUSEHEN.
3.) ABSICHTEN SIND VOR DURCHFUEHRUNG ZU MELDEN.
V GEZ: K R E I P E, OKL FUEST (ROBINSON) NR 10303/44
CHEFSACHE ++
+ 2300UHR EINE CHEFSACHE OKL FUEST (ROBINSON) NR 10303/44
GKDOS CHEFS. ERHALTEN WOCH OBLT LJKO+

AG

O.K.W. BERLIN		DATIEREN	UHRZEIT
ABWEHR 11.C		15' 12 44	11 34

AN:	F L A K A B T . K R E F E L D
BETREFF:	713 ODIN! ANKUNFT 0015 MORGEN BESTAETIGT LUFTABWEHR VON 2350 BIS 0030 WAFFEN RUHE BEWAHREN! BESTAETIGT WEITER FLUG NACH BERLIN TEMPELHOF
VON:	(z). O.K.W. ABWEHR
UNTERSCHRIFT:	A. Bergmann,
RANG:	Oberst

OBERKOMMANDO WEHRMACHT, BERLIN   ABWEHR 11.C   DATE: 15.12.44.
TIME: 11.34

TO:	ANTI-AIRCRAFT DEPT. KREFELD
CONCERNING:	713 ODIN ARRIVAL 0015 A.M. CONFIRMED AIR DEFENCE FROM 23.50 TO 00.30 A CEASEFIRE WILL BE OBSERVED. CONFIRMED A FURTHER FLIGHT TO BERLIN TEMPELHOF
FROM:	O.K.W. ABWEHR
SIGNED:	A. BERGMAN
RANK:	COLONEL

159

AH

DOCUMENT TRANSMITTED POST-WAR (FILE)
to MI-5, UK, BEING AN ESSENTIAL KEY
TO "OPERATION 7-13 ODIN" -- (7 FOR G,
13 FOR M), SHAEF'S SECRET PLAN TO END
THE WAR. (SIGNED: WALTER SCHELLENBERG)

O.G.F. KREFELD		DATIEREN	UHRZEIT
F. ADLBUM		16 12 44	0228

AN:	O.K.W. BERLIN ABWEHR 11C
BETREFF:	7 13 ODIN ANGEKOMMEN. WEITER FLUG NACH TEMPEL HOF (JU 88) ANKUNFTSZEIT 0410. FLAKABWEHR WEIDER IM ALARM ZUSTAND 0100 ~~ODIN HOSPNONS~~
VON:	OGF KREFELD (FLAK)
UNTERSCHRIFT:	
RANG:	B. 7.

O.G.F. KREFELD   DATE: 16.12.44.   TIME: 02.28

TO:	OBERKOMMANDO WEHRMACHT BERLIN, ABWEHR 11C
CONCERNING:	713 ODIN HAS ARRIVED. FURTHER FLIGHT TO TEMPELHOF (JU 88), TIME OF ARRIVAL 04.10. AIR DEFENCE BACK ON ALERT 01.00 - ODIN IS HAPPY -
FROM:	OGF KREFELD
SIGNATURE:	
RANK:	

163

AI

Page No. 4

Place	Date	Time	Summary of Events	References to Appendices
EXNING	12 Dec.		7 miles behind. The escorting fighters were looking after the larger bunch, but had the foresight to send one squadron ahead to cover it, if only thinly. A large force of enemy fighters had been waiting for us over the Ruhr, and broke up the smaller bunch of bombers ahead of the main concentration, but did not attack the larger force. Therefore, although the bombs were at first scattered, the bombing of the main bunch was very concentrated (for seeing the combats ahead, they closed up to form the tightest formation ever!) Flak varied from moderate predicted at first, to slight barrage in the latter stages of the attack.	B.394.
			G.H. was good, 40 bombing on their equipment out of the 46 planned.	
			At least 3 of the missing aircraft have either landed in France or have successfully "ditched".	
			This was the heaviest enemy daylight fighter interception carried out on Bomber Command aircraft since June, when the new series of B.C. daylight attacks started. We claim 4 enemy aircraft shot down and the escort claims at least 6 destroyed.	
	13 Dec.		No operations.	
	14 Dec.		(Night 14/15 Dec). 10 aircraft carried out mining operations, all were successful, and were successfully diverted to Lossiemouth on return.	B.395. 0.430.
	15 Dec.		No operations.	
	16 Dec.		Target - Siegen. Detailed - 108. Cancelled - nil. Abortive - 16. Missing - 1. The large number of abortives were due to bad weather. Icing cloud existed over base and as far as 0600E up to 20,000 feet. At the fighter rendezvous point, when the cloud began to break up, leaders found that they were up to 15 mins early, so they orbited, and the Group formed into a very good formation, going on to carry out a very	B.396/7. B.398/9. 0.431/432.

AJ

SECRET   IMMEDIATE.

From: Headquarters, No. 3 Group.

To : 31,32,33 Bases and sub-stations (except Newmarket,
      Shepherds Grove) R.A.F.Station,Methwold, (R) H.Q.,
      Bomber Command, 11 and 100 Group.

A. Form B. 726.   B. 15th December,   E. Day 16th December,
                        1944.   1944.

C. Other Groups   Sorties   Target

                    N I L

F.   GZ. 2973. - A.P.
 31 Base   29 (including 12GH.)   049H 047V on
                                         Illustration 48/2
 32 Base   34 (including 18 GH)   -do-

 33 Base   60 (including 15 GH)   -do-

 Methwold   14 (including 6 GH)   -do-

K & L ROUTES.

BASE - BURY ST.EDMUNDS - BISHOPS STORTFORD - GRAVESEND -
BEACHY HEAD - 50.00N 02.00E - 50.00N 04.00E - 0.33N 07.36E -
TARGET - 50.57N 07.53E - 50.29N 06.54E - 50.10 05.00E -
THE NAZE - BASE.

M. TIMING.   "H" - 14,00 Hours.

1st Wave - T.O.T. H to H + 3 (60 L. of 33 Base.
                             (8 L. of Methwold.
2nd Wave. T.O.T. H + 3 to
                 H + 6   29 L. of 31 Base
                             34 L. of 32 Base
                              6 L. of Methwold.

BOMB LOADS.   70% of aircraft - PLUM DUFF
                30% of aircraft - SEAR USUAL.
NOTE: G.H.aircraft are to take "PLUM DUFF" modified to include
      One flare RED with GREEN Stars on the first position of
      the preselector, fused No.6 Or U/12 Capsule.
      Distributor Settings:- Plum Duff 0.5 secs.
N.SPECIAL INSTRUCTIONS.   Sear Usual 0.1 secs.

1.   Forming up and Tactics as laid down in Appendix "A"
      Revised to this Headquarters Letter 3G/S.2274/Ops,dated
      28th Oct.1944. Formations to be flown in Vics of three
      or Boxes of four.
2.   Bases are to make their own arrangements for forming up.
3.   Group Rendezvous Point - BISHOPS STORTFORD at a height and
      time to be passed later.
4.   Bombing Heights - 16,000 to 18,000 feet.

5.   AIRSPEEDS- Cruising to 04.00E on Outward journey - 165 R.A.S.
                Climbing from 04.00E to 15,000 feet. - 155 R.A.S.
                 "   " 15,000 feet to bombing
                                          height - 150 R.A.S.
                Cruising at bombing height to Target - 160 R.A.S.
                After H + 6 cruise at bombing height
                to 06.00E on return   - 170 R.A.S.
                After 06.00E and losing height to
                cross Belgian Coast not below 8000 ft - 190 R.A.S.

AK

-2-

6. Heading for aircraft bombing on the flares will be passed later.

7. The importance of aircraft maintaining as close a formation as possible over enemy territory is to be stressed to all crews in view of the depth of the penetration, so that Fighters may give adequate cover.

8. Radar and W/T silence is to be maintained to 05.30E on route out.

9. Aircraft are to keep as low as possible below 8,000 feet to 04.00E on outward journey to prevent the enemy from obtaining early warning. This height will be confirmed or altered if necessary in the light of later Met.information.

10. A bombing wind will be broadcast at 13.30 hours.

11. 8 Squadrons of Mustangs of 11 Group will rendezvous at 04.00E on track.

12. Window is to be dropped at Rate "D" from 06.00E on outward journey to 06.00E on return journey.

13. I.F.F. - Refer to 3G/S.2000/1/Ops dated 5th Oct.1944.

14. All aircraft are to carry Cameras.

15. One aircraft of 33 Base and one of Methwold to report if Target attacked.

Air Commodore,
Senior Air Staff Officer,
No. 3 Group.

P. 1832 A
1830

AL

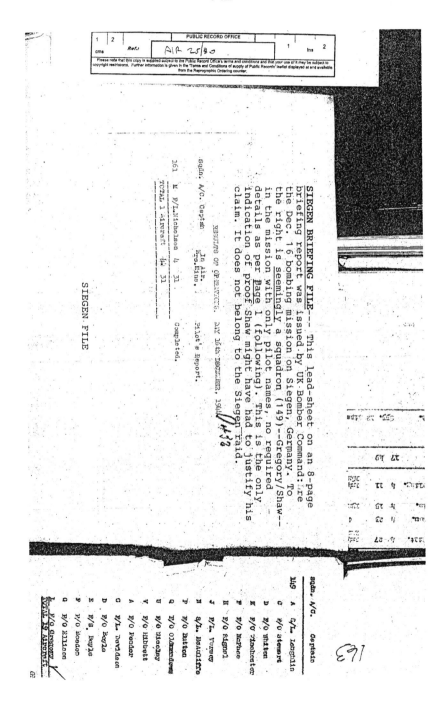

SIEGEN BRIEFING FILE--- This lead-sheet on an 8-page briefing report was issued by UK Bomber Command: re the Dec. 16 bombing mission on Siegen, Germany. To the right is seemingly a squadron (149)--Gregory/Shaw-- in the mission with only pilot names, no required details as per Page 1 (following). This is the only indication of proof Shaw might have had to justify his claim. It does not belong to the Siegen raid.

SIEGEN FILE

AM

PAGE 1 OF SIEGEN BRIEFING.--Note requirements for every Plane: Air Time; Weight Bombs Carried; Weight Bombs Dropped; Height of Attack; Pilot's Report. Pages 2 to 7 are similar in requirement for all squadrons in the mission. There is no mention or details of the Gregory/Shaw 149. All listed planes added up to 108, (total) without Gregory/Shaw. There is no record of this squadron in the Siegen Mission. No off-target jettison. Mission on Siegen successful.

Page 1.

RESULTS OF OPERATIONS. DAY 16th DECEMBER, 1944. Pilot's Report.

A/C.	Captain.	Time in Air. Hrs. Min.	Wt. bombs carried lbs.	Wt. bombs Dropped lbs.	Ht. of Attack	Pilot's Report.
D	F/S. Giles	5.37	1x4000 150G24		17,000	Bombed on K/15. Cookies seen exploding in built-up area.
A	F/S. McHardy	5.37	-do-	10,600	17,800	Bombed on KD aircraft. Bombing concentrated.
B	F/O. Jennings	5.35	-do-	10,300	17,500	Bombed on G.H. Bombing appeared well together.
G	F/O. Sellwood	5.32	1x12,000	12,000	17,300	Bombed on leader J. B/A. Cookies seen to burst.
J	F/O. H. Cuthbert	5.44	1x4000 150G24	10,600	18,000	Bombed on G.H./149/0. Bombing well concentrated.
K	F/O. Slaughter	5.46	150G24 -do-	10,600	17,000	Bombed on G.H. Leader looked good concentrated attack.
L	F/S. Gray	5.35	-do-	-do-	17,300	Bombed on G.H. Leader. Bombs seen to burst on built-up area.
M	F/O. Marriott	5.46	-do-	10,600	18,500	Bombed on G.H. Bombing concentrated.
V	F/O. Lewis	5.37	1x12000	12,000	18,000	Bombed on G.H. Leader. Saw bombs burst in Railway Yards.
W	F/S. Bithell	5.51	-do-	12,000	17,500	Bombed on G.H. Leader. No results seen.
X	F/S. Williams	4.32	1x4000 150G24	Nil.	N/A.	Mission abandoned. All bombs jett. 521SH 0315E. Could not find formation and icing.
Y	F/O. Cavillor	5.48	1x4000 150G24	10,600	17,000	Bombed on G.H. Bombing looked concentrated.
D	F/O. McDowall	3.17	1x4000 5x500	Nil.	N/A.	Mission abandoned due to icing. 5x1000 jett. 501SH 0015E. Rest brought back.
J	F/O. Flaxman	4.32	-do-	11,500	17,500	Bombed with G.H. Leader. Good concentration.
M	F/S. Stills	3.42	-do-	Nil.	N/A.	Returned early - lost stream. 2x500 jett. 585GH 0020E. Remainder brought back.
H	F/O. Curling	5.31	1x8000 1x1000	11,500	18,000	Bombed where other aircraft where bombing. Concentrated attack.
b	F/S. Carvill	5.35	5x500	11,500		on G.H. Leader. Bombing seemed concentrated

AN

THE TRIER RAID OF DECEMBER 19---Sqdn 149 is first noted in a totally diferent raid. Diffrent target; different squadrons. There is noereturn-area jettisoning--a completely different packet of details. Note! Gregory/Shaw 149 at bottom. This was first raid of record for Fred Shaw. All bombs on target. E-excl.

DAY 19th DECEMBER 1944.

Sqdn. N/C.	Captain		In Air.	Bombs Carried.	Time of.	Height.	Pilot's Report.
149	A	S/L. Laughlin	4	22	102500	N/A	Abortive over target owing to G.H. Falure, All bombs jett.5206.N.
	C	F/O Stewart	4	97	10,000	17,500	Bombed on G.H. Nothing seen.
	D	F/O Whiten	4	52	10,000	17,500	Bombed on G.H. Bombs bursting on S. side of Town.
	E	F/O Winchester	3	51	N/A	N/A	Bombs hung up over target and all brought back.
	F	F/O McPhee	4	59	10,000	17,000	Bombed on leader. Bombs going down on N side of river.
	H	F/O Signal	4	14	10,000	18,000	Bombed on G.H. Most bombs were bursting on East end of town.
	J	F/L. Vracey	5	12	N/A	N/A	Abortive over target due to leaders G.H. failure.
	K	S/L. McAuliffe	4	13	10,000	17,500	Bombed on G.H. No results seen.
	P	F/O Button	4	51	10,000	18,000	Bombed on G.H. Good concentration of bombs.
	Q	F/O Oldmeadows	3	48	10,000	17,000	Bombed visually and by G.H. aircraft. Big explosion just after we
	R	F/O Hinckley	4	06	10,000	17,900	Bombed on leader. Saw large column of smoke just after we bombed.
	V	F/O Mabbott	4	09	10,000	18,000	Bombed on G.H. Bombs seen to burst well inside target area.
	A	F/O Pender	4	66	10,000	17,000	Bombed on G.H. No results seen.
	C	F/L. Davidson	4	03	10,000	18,000	Bombed on leaders. Bombs were going down on West side of town.
	D	F/O Boyle	4	05	10,000	17,900	Bombed on G.H. Bombs were dropping on East side of town.
	E	F/S. Boyle	4	04	10,000	17,500	Bombed on leader. Bombs bursting in centre of town East of river.
	F	F/O Mondan	3	59	10,000	17,200	Bombed on G.H. Several sticks seen bursting in town on N. side of
	G	F/O Ellison	4	11	10,000	18,000	Bombed on G.H. No results seen.
	L	F/O Gregory		12	10,000	17,700	Bombed on G.H. leader. No results seen.
	TOTAL 19 AIRCRAFT		16	21	190,000		

GRAND TOTAL 32 aircraft 243 hours 25 mins. 281,750 lbs.

A match the ends - cover up

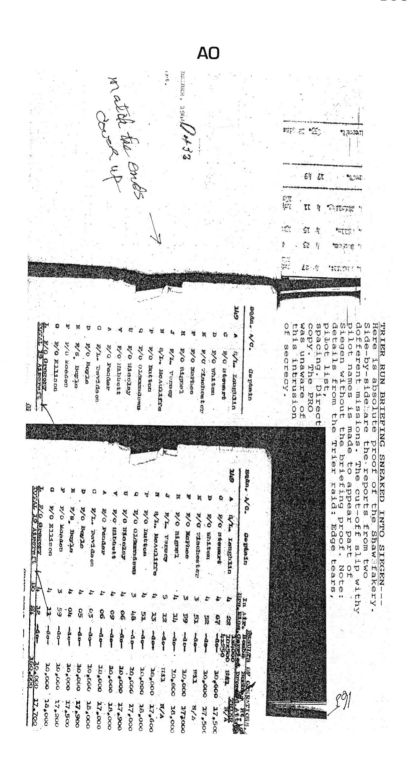

AO

TRIER RUN BRIEFING SNEAKED INTO SIEGEN---
Here is absolute proof of the Shaw fakery.
Side-by-side are the reports from two
different missions. The cut-off slip with
pilot names is made to appear part of
Siegen without the briefing proof. Note:
details from the Trier raid; Edge tears,
pilot list, Direct
spacing. The PRO
copy. The PRO
was unaware of
this intrusion
of secrecy.

match the ends
cover up

AP

HUNT   Memo   Memo 000724

JOE WAS STAYING AT THE REGENT PALACE
HOTEL IN LONDON. GENERAL HIGGINS AND
HIS STAFF STAYED AT A LUXURY HOTEL
ACROSS THE STREET FROM THE REGENT
PALACE, JOE SAID IT WAS THE SAVOY.
JOE NEVER KNEW THE OFFICER WITH MILLER
BY NAME, THE NAME BAESSELL WAS NOT
MENTIONED.
THE OFFICE SAID HE WAS A COMMAND PILOT
JOE SAW THE TWO MEN CLIMB ABOARD SMALL PLANE.
JOE SAW PLANE TAXI DOWN RUNWAY AND DISAPPEAR.
I TOOK THIS TO MEAN THAT THE AIRPLANE EVENTUALLY
TOOK OFF FROM NORTHOLT. IF THEY WENT ON TO
BOVINGDON THAT DAY THEY WOULD HAVE HAD TO
TAKE OFF AT NORTHOLT AND FLY TO BOVINGDON.
JOE WAS NOT AWARE OF A THIRD PERSON IN PARTY.

Sid

"Sid" is Sid Robinson, Army Air Corps veteran from
WWII.

AQ

10.75
CAT FM
Price 30p

GLOUCESTERSHIRE

ECHO
Cotswolds edition

JOB
SEARCH
Dozens of jobs, p 4

Tel: 01242-271900   Tomorrow's weather: cloudy with showers   Tuesday, September 29th, 1998

Spies fiddled with my post

Glenn Miller tale is too hot for GCHQ

Film producer Daniel O'Toole says GCHQ is involved in trying to sabotage his film about big band leader Glenn Miller.

Mr O'Toole has given up posting his scripts about Murder In The Mood to Hollywood because he believes his mail is being intercepted.

"I've had to change the way I send material because so much of it just vanishes. This could become a major problem once the filming starts," said Mr O'Toole from Cirencester.

"It crossed my mind that it could be something to do with GCHQ because of its close proximity to us."

The fact-based Murder In The Mood claims the legendary band leader did not die in a plane crash over the English Channel in 1944 as is popularly believed.

In the film, Miller flies to Germany where he is captured by the SS, who try to force him to be a decoy in an attempt to assassinate Dwight Eisenhower, commander of the US forces in Europe. Miller refuses and is left dying outside the Sphinx brothel in Paris.

Mr O'Toole, whose father Stanley produced The Boys From Brazil and Enemy Mine, said: "It's a very scary situation. I believe security forces on both sides of the Atlantic are trying to stop the facts from coming out."

The scriptwriter, Hunton Downs, of Tetbury, has experienced similar problems. David Wright, the researcher on whose work the film is based, believes his mail has been opened by the security services.

Mr Downs, 78, has worked on more than 60 films, including Francis Ford Coppola's Apocalypse Now and Escape to Athena.

He said: "Around £2,000 worth of our material has gone missing in the post.

"There are a lot of people who have let the facts be kept quiet for this long and they're not happy about them coming out now."

Mr O'Toole hopes to shoot some of the film turn to page 2

Band leader: Glenn Miller

B I
S H

Parking
... eye s

From the m(
Beechwood'
keeping a w
We have the

Great .

Courtesy of Gloucestershire Echo.

AR

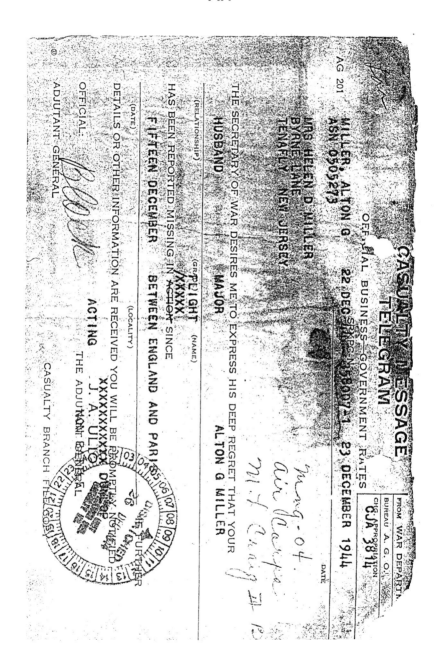

AS

Magnus von Braun, two U.S. soldiers, Walter Dornberger, Herbert Axter, Wernher von Braun, Hans Lindenberg, and Bernhard Tessmann after surrendering to the Allies in 1945.

AT

129

At 7 A M on the ~~17~~ 16th of December General Higgins received a message
from General McAuliffe ordering the group back to Rheims immediately.

I went out to Northolt Airfield arriving at about 9 A M on the ~~17~~ 16th
of December and was out there until about 4 P M. Weather conditions
were so bad that it was unsafe to fly.

It was upon this day (16th of December 1944) that I encountered a
LT. Colonel and Glenn Miller under the control tower of Northolt
airfield.

To the best of my knowledge the time was *a.m. of 16th*

To the best of my knowledge they took off at *JD saw them taxiing off. does n. remember precise time*

I went back to the Northolt Airfield control tower on ~~17~~ 16 December 1944
and at about 10 00 A M the weather cleared and I called General Higgins
to come on out for takeoff.

We departed Northolt at about
on the morning of December ~~18~~th 1944 and returned to Rheims.

JOE DOBSON (AACS)---deceased 2003

REIMS IS CORRECT SPELLING
NOT RHEIMS

ALL MARGINAL NOTES ARE
MADE BY PEGGY DOBSON
FOR JOE DOBSON AND IN
PRESENCE OF JOE DOBSON

JD = JOE DOBSON

AU

BATTLE

(GENERAL ORDERS No. 65 cont'd)

Not remaining idle, he took active part in the liberation of Clermont-Ferrand after which he collected information on the Gestapo and the French Milice of the region. His outstanding service reflects high credit upon himself and the allied forces.

Sous-Lieutenant Daniel Pomeranz, French Army, for meritorious achievement in connection with military operations from 1 June 1944 to 25 August 1944. Sous-Lieutenant Pomeranz was parachuted in civilian clothes into the region of the Loire Valley with a team-mate, and for the next two and three quarters months, operated as the radio-operator of an intelligence team in Vincennes (Seine). Due to the loss of his radio sets, he was not able to establish wireless contact with London until receiving new equipment. During the last thirteen days of the mission, he transmitted no fewer than forty-nine messages covering enemy movements and depots in the Paris area. The outstanding services rendered by Sous-Lieutenant Pomeranz reflect high credit upon himself and the allied forces.

Sous-Lieutenant Henri Tosy, French Army, for meritorious achievement in connection with military operations from 7 June 1944 to 1 September 1944. Sous-Lieutenant Tosy was parachuted in civilian clothes into the Department of the Marne, where he gathered intelligence on the Coulommier and Coubron airfields, on enemy movements, and on gasoline and ammunition depots. As radio operator of the team, he suffered from the fact that his principal radio set was seriously damaged upon being parachuted and was not repaired until 15 July 1944. However, he and his team-mate organized their network efficiently, and, until they had established radio communication with London, passed their intelligence to a resistance group working in the Paris area. The outstanding manner in which he carried out his mission reflects high credit upon himself and the allied forces.

Sous-Lieutenant Michel Walon, French Army, for meritorious service in connection with military operations from 18 August 1944 to 12 September 1944. Sous-Lieutenant Walon, as a secret intelligence agent and radio operator, was parachuted into the region of Allier. Received on the ground by a Maquis, he moved with them to the region of the Creuse, where he was assigned to work. Unfortunately all of his radio equipment was destroyed on landing; through the failure of its parachute to open. He was able to contact London only through the set of another mission which he found at Aubusson (Creuse). Just as new equipment was about to be dropped to him, it was learned that Roanne had been liberated. By entering enemy territory as a secret agent in civilian clothes; and succeeding in passing information of tactical value, through the Maquis, he contributed in a large measure to the success of the allied forces.

2. By direction of the President, under the provisions of AR 600-45, 22 September 1943, as amended, the Bronze Star Medal is awarded, for meritorious service in connection with military operations during the respective periods indicated, to:

Lieutenant Colonel R. Newell Lusby (Army Serial No 0368640), General Staff Corps, United States Army — 1 March 1944 to 10 October 1944.

Technician Fourth Grade Fred A. McRae (Army Serial No 34198040), Infantry, United States Army — February, 1943, to May, 1943.

Major Alton Glenn Miller (Army Serial No 0505273), Air Corps, United States Army — 9 July 1944 to 15 December 1944.

By command of General EISENHOWER:

R. B. LORD,
Major General, GSC, Deputy Chief of Staff

OFFICIAL:

R. B. Lovett

R. B. LOVETT,
Brigadier General, USA, Adjutant General.

DISTRIBUTION: E

— 2 —

AV

NON BATTLE

WAR DEPARTMENT
Ｃ SSIFIED MESSAGE CENᴛᴇR
INCOMING CLASSIFIED MESSAGE

358007

SPECIAL

From: Headquarters Communications Zone, European Theater of
         Operations, US Army, Paris, France

To: War Department

Nr.   E 77699   22 December 1944

          SPXPC signed Eisenhower E 77699 AG Cas Div casualty
message 3028. Nonbattle.

Miller, Alton Glenn 0505273 Major AC Army Air Force
Band (special) Hq Command, Supreme Hq AEF is reported
missing since 15 December 144 enroute by Air from
England to Paris, France. Major Miller was taken to
the airfield by an officer of the Army Air Force Band
who witnessed the takeoff. No trace of this airplane
can be found and airplane is considered missing.

Request acknowledgement and that immediate information
be furnished by priority cable when next of kin has
been notified in order that suitable release may be
made to the press here at 1800A hours 24 December
as Major Miller was to have participated in Christmas
Day broadcast concerning which considerable publicity
has been given in the United States.

                                                    End

ACTION: TAG

INFO   CG AAF
         BPR

OM-1N-22031 (23

                              180

THE MAKING OF AN EXACT COPY OF THIS MESSAGE IS FORBIDDEN

AW

JOHN EDWARDS

REVEILLE, April 30, 1976

GLENN MILLER 'WAS MURDERED'

by FRANK DURHAM

A MAN who has spent more than £7,000 and devoted 12 years to solving the mystery of American bandleader Glenn Miller's death has come up with a startling new theory.

Thirty - five - year - old John Edwards says that Miller was not aboard the plane in which most people believe he died when it crashed into the Channel.

He claims he has evidence that the bandleader was murdered in Paris three days AFTER the plane plunged into the sea.

Mr. Edwards believes that Miller, who was a bit of a lad with the ladies, died of a fractured skull somewhere in the city's red light district of Pigalle.

Cover-up

And he suggests that the fact that the Norseman plane he was supposed to have been aboard crashed was seized on by the authorities and became a convenient cover-up for Miller's death.

Among the evidence that Mr. Edwards has collected to support the theory that Miller was not aboard the fatal flight in 1944 is the eye-witness account of a man who says he saw Miller board a Dakota plane at RAF Bovingdon, Herts, the day of the crash.

This, claims Mr. Edwards, is the plane that Miller actually flew to France in.

The original journey began when the ill-fated Norseman aircraft

Continued on Page 21

Continued from Page 1
took off from Twinwoods airfield, near Bedford.

According to Mr. Edwards's research the Norseman later landed at Bovingdon where Miller left the plane before it took off again for Paris.

Then Miller joined the Dakota and made the cross-Channel trip.

The new facts came to light because Mr. Edwards actually set out to disprove earlier suggestions that Miller was not aboard the Norseman when it crashed.

"Now I have to admit that I was probably wrong. It looks as if it is true that he was *not* on the plane."

Now Mr. Edwards wants to put an end to speculation by raising the crashed plane from the sea bed.

He believes he has found the spot where the plane plunged into the sea and hopes to raise the £15,000 needed to salvage the wreck.

"I have the military numbers of all three men who took off in the plane —Miller's is one of them. Their metal identity tags should still be intact. "But the way the evi-

Did he die in Paris?

dence is piling up I don't expect to find Glenn's body in that aircraft," said Mr. Edwards.

Mr. Edwards backs his theory of an official cover-up of the real circumstances of Miller's death with the fact that there was never a proper official inquiry.

The "missing aircrew report" of the incident is vague, says Mr. Edwards.

"Even the weather conditions were listed as unknown. But more than 30 years later I have been able to discover the most detailed meteorological reports for the day in question."

Mr. Edwards added: "I have met with difficulty when trying to solve the mystery. Records have been reported burned and other information — such as the missing aircrew report—is unaccountably vague.

"A firm which had shown interest in backing my project to raise the aircraft from the Channel was advised not

Glenn Miller: New facts

to do so by the Glenn Miller estate."

Why does he believe that Glenn Miller was murdered?

Mr. Edwards, a former RAF officer and now a sales export manager, says: "Pieces of information that I have collected over the years have all suddenly fallen into place.

"I have evidence that an American military doctor in Paris signed Glenn Miller's death certificate.

"And retired U.S. Air Force Lieutenant-Colonel Thomas F. Corrigan, recalls that a member of the Provost Marshal's police office in Paris had told him of Miller's murder.

"I now have in my possession a list, which includes the name of the provost officer who dealt with the case, together with other names of the Provost Marshal's staff. All can confirm this account.

"I also have the name of a man who played in the band with Miller, who states that it was common knowledge that those close to him knew very well he was murdered in Paris."